Grey Area

Grey Area

Regulating Amsterdam's Coffeeshops

Scott Jacques

UCLPRESS

First published in 2019 by
UCL Press
University College London
Gower Street
London WC1E 6BT

Available to download free: www.ucl.ac.uk/ucl-press

A CIP catalogue record for this book is available from The British Library.

ISBN: 978–1-78735–590-3 (Hbk.)
ISBN: 978–1-78735–589-7 (Pbk.)
ISBN: 978–1-78735–588-0 (PDF)
ISBN: 978–1-78735–591-0 (epub)
ISBN: 978–1-78735–592-7 (mobi)
ISBN: 978–1-78735–593-4 (html)
DOI: https://doi.org/10.14324/111.9781787355880

To my parents and Jake Jacques

Contents

List of figures

List of tables

Acknowledgements

Many more people have contributed to this book than I remember. To anyone I have left unmentioned, please forgive me. I am indebted to the people who agreed to be interviewed and observed for this study; its funders, the National Science Foundation, University of Missouri Research Board, and the Netherlands Institute for the Study of Crime and Law Enforcement (NSCR), which also gave me a 'work home' in Amsterdam; the Department of Criminology and Criminal Justice at the University of Missouri–St Louis for its support; Rick Rosenfeld and Richard Wright, who are the grants' 'PIs' and helped in various capacities, as did Margit Averdijk, Wim Bernasco, Frank van Gemert, Danielle Reynald and Benny de Vries; Chris Penfold, the anonymous reviewers and all at UCL Press for turning a monograph into this book. Finally I would like to thank my best mentors, Lynn and Tom Jacques, and my best colleague, Andrea Allen Jacques, for dealing with me.

Preface

Visiting coffeeshops

My first trip to Amsterdam was for a couple of days in the autumn of 2003. A second-year student at the University of Georgia, I was studying abroad at Oxford, just a few hours by air from Amsterdam. Years before, I had learned how to smoke marijuana and enjoy its effects, probably too much so.[1] For stoners like my former self, visiting Amsterdam's coffeeshops is a recreational pilgrimage.[2] There a smoker can purchase cannabis and get high without fear of legal trouble, despite it being an illegal activity.[3] This was a welcome change from the accustomed stress of acquiring weed in the United States.[4]

I arrived at Amsterdam's Schiphol Airport in the early afternoon and boarded a train to Central Station. I exited its main doors, walked across Prins Hendrikkade and set off down Damrak. This wide avenue is lined with stone buildings about six storeys in height. These are occupied by establishments normal to a city centre: hotels, souvenir shops, restaurants, sex museum. Nearing the end of this avenue, a young woman of about my age asked for spare change to buy food. I offered to get her a McDonald's, which I saw a few doors down, but she turned her back and walked away. I guessed that what she really wanted was money to buy drugs, but who was I to judge?

Damrak ends at Dam Square, about a couple football pitches in size. Straight ahead is Madame Tussauds and another avenue, Rokin, which leads toward the Flower Market. Further down is the Rijksmuseum, Van Gogh Museum and Heineken Factory. To the right are two impressive buildings, New Church and Royal Palace. Going in that direction eventually takes you to Anne Frank's House. Heading in the other direction, as I did, brings you past a massive shopping mall on the left, De Bijenkorf. In the square's centre is the National Monument, a 72-foot high pillar. People gather on its steps to people-watch, sometimes while smoking a joint.[5] The spot has changed quite a bit since the city executed criminals here, a few centuries ago.[6]

Following the map to my hostel, The Bulldog, I ventured past the National Monument to Damstraat. This short street is a gateway into the city's red light district, the birthplace of coffeeshops.[7] These little establishments are a big deal, having sown the seeds for drug policy reform in Portugal, Australia, the United States, Uruguay, Canada and beyond.[8] About half way down Damstraat, I noticed Coffeeshop Paradise on my right. Above the door was a green and red neon sign, its name surrounded by palm trees.[9] I went inside and took in the atmosphere: a Rasta motif of Pan-African colours and Bob Marley posters on the wall, with his music playing over the speakers.

I noticed a sales counter in the back left corner. Unsure how 'this' worked, I walked up, admitted my ignorance to the dealer and humbly requested assistance. He showed me two menus, one for cannabis, the other for drinks and food. The cannabis menu had several types of marijuana and hashish, ranging in price from about €10 to €20 per gram. He offered to let me inspect the options by taking a close look and a whiff. I made a selection, purchased provisions (rolling papers, lighter, green tea) and took a seat at a small round table by the window.

The subsequent details of my trip are hazy, but it was an informative experience. From afar, I saw Amsterdam's coffeeshops as an exotic feature of the drug market landscape. Yet once the novelty wore off, coffeeshops appeared mundane, even boring. Emma, the manager of a coffeeshop whom I interviewed years later, joked that 'passing out is usually the most excitement you get'. Coffeeshops are under control. At the time, I gave this little consideration. If anything, I assumed it is a byproduct of people being high.[10] Years later I discovered that the civilised atmosphere is more than a secondhand effect.[11] Rather, order in the midst of smoke is key to Dutch drug policy. Coffeeshops do not have a *carte blanche* to sell cannabis. The government allows them to break the law, but not the rules.

*****

Coffeeshops are known internationally as the most famous example of Dutch tolerance.[12] Yet the Netherlands does not in fact tolerate coffeeshops.[13] Inaction is not the policy lever. Actually, coffeeshops are highly regulated.[14] Surveillance and punishment make the policy work. Those tools are used to enforce the rules. The rules specify what coffeeshops can do, and cannot do, to be 'tolerated'. This book examines the rules in Amsterdam's coffeeshops: what they are; why they exist; how they are enforced; how they are broken – and to what effect. What are the benefits? What are the problems? Does this strategy of control have utility?

I describe and explore the perspective of coffeeshop personnel, including owners, managers, dealers of cannabis and servers of drink and food.[15] I interviewed and observed them while living in Amsterdam from September 2008 to May 2010,[16] returning for the summers of 2011 and 2016 to keep in touch with the scene.[17] Geographically, I focus on coffeeshops in the 1012 postal code of Amsterdam. It is the city's centre and its oldest part.[18] 'The 1012', for short, is about a square kilometre in size (Figure 0.1). It is bordered on the north by the Prins Hendrikkade, which recall runs along Central Station; on the east by the Geldersekade and Kloveniersburgwal Canals; and, on the south and west by the Singel Canal. Damrak and Rokin constitute the area's spine, with an oversized heart made up of the infamous red light district. I also looked at Haarlemmerstraat, which technically lies outside the 1012 postal code, but is geographically and socially contiguous.

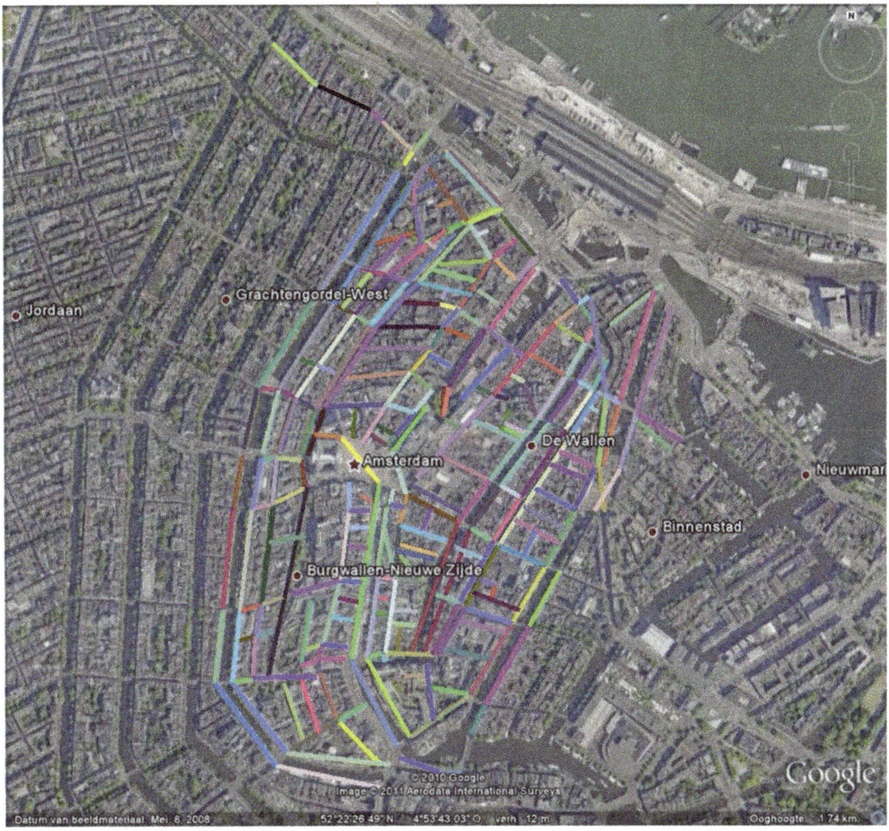

Figure 0.1 Map of the 1012. Google, Aerodata International Surveys. Street segment lines added by Wim Bernasco

By walking every street in the 1012, I learned that it contained 84 coffeeshops, about one-third of the city's total.[19] I spent countless hours observing coffeeshops while hanging out.[20] I visited each one on multiple occasions, becoming a regular at some. My field notes documented routine practices and unusual events. This mostly involved recording how personnel managed their stock, patrons and the rules, all of which are interrelated. The nice thing about taking field notes in coffeeshops is that I could do so in plain sight without impeding the social scene, as it is entirely normal for someone to be on their laptop computer there. However, that is not always appropriate, such as at weekends, evenings, or other busy times. In those circumstances I took short notes on my phone and then expanded them later. In bits of this book, I give precise, observation-based percentages and counts. These data were collected near the end of my time in Amsterdam with the help of a colleague, Danielle Reynald, and a team of students who collected numbers on every coffeeshop in the sample.

In addition I convinced personnel of 50 coffeeshops to do an interview in exchange for €50.[21] The data thus gathered lies behind most of the findings presented throughout this book. Interviews lasted between one and two hours and covered a variety of topics, including the rules. I asked each participant for permission to record the interview so that our conversation could be transcribed word for word.[22] Seven respondents refused and one conversation was conducted in a place too loud to be recorded; for these interviews, I made written notes. Table 0.1 provides an overview of the interviewees' characteristics; Table 0.2 provides one of all personnel at their respective coffeeshops.[23]

Table 0.1 Interviewee characteristics

Participant name (#)	Coffeeshop	Position	Tenure	Age	Race/ ethnicity	NL born
Adam (41)	Howling Man	Dealer	<1	30	White	Yes
Amani (30)	Stop	Owner	24	48	Black	No
Amir (21)	Mirror Image	Dealer	1	30	Arab	Yes
Anna (22)	Maple Street	Manager	2	40	White	Yes
Charlotte (43)	Nick of Time	Server	<1	23	White	No
Claire (14)	Sun	Dealer	<1	28	Multi	No
Dean (39)	Dollar Room	Manager	<1	32	White	Yes
Elias (32)	Passage	Dealer	2	34	White	Yes
Emir (4)	Walking Distance	Dealer		40	Arab	No

(Continued)

Table 0.1 (Continued)

Participant name (#)	Coffeeshop	Position	Tenure	Age	Race/ ethnicity	NL born
Emma (19)	Purple Testament	Manager	7	38	White	Yes
Fabian (46)	Most Unusual	Dealer	5	30	White	No
Finn (26)	Execution	Owner	23	53	White	No
Gijs (6)	Escape Clause	Manager	2	46	White	Yes
Guus (36)	World of His Own	Dealer	20	48	Multi	No
Gwen (29)	Like a Child	Manager	1.5	32	White	Yes
Hanna (47)	Meek	Dealer	<1	31	White	No
Hassan (5)	Shrine	Manager	4	25	Arab	Yes
Helen (18)	Last Flight	Manager	<1	38	White	No
Imran (42)	Eye of the Beholder	Owner	15	45	Multi	No
Jack (25)	Alike All Over	Manager	3.5	35	White	No
James (37)	No Return	Dealer	4	31	White	No
Jana (23)	World of Difference	Dealer	6	26	White	Yes
Jasper (44)	The Hour	Manager	5	28	White	Yes
Jens (28)	Nice Place to Visit	Dealer	1.5	28	White	Yes
Joseph (11)	Open Sky	Manager	6	55	Black	No
Kamila (15)	Arrow in the Air	Server	2	32	White	No
Keven (13)	Four of Us	Dealer	10	39	White	Yes
Lizzie (50)	Whole Truth	Manager	3.5	35	White	Yes
Lola (17)	Fever	Server	9	30	White	Yes
Luca (7)	The Lonely	Dealer	5	38	White	Yes
Lucia (3)	Doomsday	Server	<1	20	White	No
Luuk (2)	Angels	Owner	16	50	White	Yes
Maikel (40)	Thing	Owner	4	38	Black	Yes
Mara (27)	Wish	Owner	6	35	White	Yes
Maud (8)	At Last	Dealer	1	27	Asian	Yes
Max (1)	Everybody	Manager		37	White	Yes
Mike (10)	Judgement Night	Dealer	<1	19	White	No

(Continued)

Table 0.1 (Continued)

Participant name (#)	Coffeeshop	Position	Tenure	Age	Race/ ethnicity	NL born
Noah (12)	What You Need	Dealer	5	35	White	Yes
Noortje (48)	Dust	Dealer	10	34	White	Yes
Olivia (20)	Elegy	Dealer	3	24	White	Yes
Omar (49)	Back There	Manager	8	25	Arab	Yes
Ruben (35)	The Mighty	Dealer	10	45	White	Yes
Selma (38)	Man in the Bottle	Dealer	<1	27	Multi	Yes
Sophie (16)	Hitch-Hiker	Server	2.5	25	Multi	Yes
Stefan (34)	After Hours	Dealer	5	40	White	No
Stijn (33)	Mr. Bevis	Dealer	8	35	White	No
Thomas (45)	Buzz	Manager	3.5	32	White	No
Victor (31)	Chaser	Dealer	<1	30	Multi	Yes
Willem (9)	Perchance	Owner	1.5	27	Asian	Yes
Wouter (24)	Live Long	Dealer	<1	44	White	No
Modal category or average	-	Dealer	5	34	White	Yes

Note: An empty cell denotes 'Don't know'. '#' refers to a participant's order in study, from first interviewed (1) to last (50). 'Tenure' reflects a participant's time, measured in years, serving in a specific position at the coffeeshop, not their *total* time working there or other coffeeshops. 'NL born' shows whether an individual participant was born in the Netherlands. Overall averages may be slightly different from those reported in Jacques et al. 2016, due to rounding. To calculate average tenure, employees with less than one year in the position are counted as 0.5 year or 6 months.

Table 0.2 Personnel characteristics of interviewed coffeeshops

Coffeeshop	# Personnel	# Male (per cent)	Age range	# White (per cent)	# Immigrant (per cent NL born)
After Hours	11	5 (45)	21–40	10 (90)	1 (91)
Alike All Over	11	4 (36)	24–50	11 (100)	4 (64)
Angels	D/k	11 (D/k)	20–44	14 (D/k)	14 (D/k)
Arrow in the Air	7	4 (57)	24–40	7 (100)	7 (0)
At Last	4	2 (50)	21–34	2 (50)	1 (75)
Back There	6	6 (67)	25–41	5 (83)	1 (83)

(*Continued*)

Table 0.2 (Continued)

Coffeeshop	# Personnel	# Male (per cent)	Age range	# White (per cent)	# Immigrant (per cent NL born)
Buzz	7	7 (100)	23–43	6 (86)	3 (57)
Chaser	9	9 (100)	D/k	5 (56)	D/k (D/k)
Dollar Room	12	11 (92)	22–36	12 (100)	2 (83)
Doomsday	D/k	4 (D/k)	18–36	18 (D/k)	14 (D/k)
Dust	9	6 (67)	32–45	8 (89)	0 (100)
Elegy	13	7 (54)	24–49	12 (92)	12 (8)
Escape Clause	9	8 (88)	25–46	9 (100)	8 (11)
Everybody	19	11 (58)	20–45	19 (100)	1 (95)
Execution	12	7 (58)	25–53	12 (100)	6 (50)
Eye of the Beholder	8	7 (88)	22–46	4 (50)	6 (25)
Fever	5	4 (80)	25–33	3 (60)	4 (20)
Four of Us	7	6 (86)	27–50	7 (100)	0 (100)
Hitch-Hiker	17	12 (71)	21–52	14 (82)	1 (94)
Howling Man	15	12 (80)	20–51	12 (80)	2 (87)
Judgement Night	23	15 (65)	19–50	D/k (D/k)	6 (74)
Last Flight	19	10 (53)	20–38	10 (53)	10 (47)
Like a Child	20	9 (45)	18–44	18 (90)	10 (50)
Live Long	7	7 (100)	22–50	7 (100)	0 (100)
Man in the Bottle	4	3 (75)	27–41	4 (100)	3 (25)
Maple Street	9	4 (44)	23–42	9 (100)	2 (78)
Meek	4	1 (25)	21–46	3 (75)	3 (25)
Mirror Image	D/k	2 (D/k)	30–33	3 (D/k)	3 (D/k)
Most Unusual	5	0 (0)	30–60	5 (100)	5 (0)
Mr. Bevis	18	2 (11)	19–50	8 (44)	14 (22)
Nice Place to Visit	18	9 (50)	21–43	14 (78)	4 (78)
Nick of Time	13	9 (69)	23–44	13 (100)	12 (8)
No Return	9	9 (100)	28–47	8 (89)	4 (56)
Open Sky	3	3 (100)	33–55	1 (33)	3 (0)
Passage	3	3 (100)	25–34	3 (100)	2 (33)

(Continued)

Table 0.2 (Continued)

Coffeeshop	# Personnel	# Male (per cent)	Age range	# White (per cent)	# Immigrant (per cent NL born)
Perchance	4	3 (75)	27–32	2 (50)	3 (25)
Purple Testament	5	2 (40)	20–38	2 (40)	3 (40)
Shrine	6	5 (83)	22–36	4 (67)	2 (67)
Stop	2	2 (100)	48	0 (0)	2 (0)
Sun	9	2 (22)	25–50	8 (89)	8 (11)
The Hour	21	13 (62)	20–40	20 (95)	1 (95)
The Lonely	D/k	6 (D/k)	32–40	7 (D/k)	0 (D/k)
The Mighty	9	8 (89)	20–46	8 (89)	9 (0)
Thing	4	3 (75)	21–38	1 (25)	1 (75)
Walking Distance	4	4 (100)	31–48	0 (0)	4 (0)
What You Need	11	6 (55)	21–50	11 (100)	0 (100)
Whole Truth	27	7 (26)	21–43	25 (93)	10 (63)
Wish	8	5 (63)	24–41	8 (100)	3 (63)
World of Difference	15	10 (67)	23–50	12 (80)	15 (0)
World of His Own	10	6 (60)	21–60	1 (10)	8 (20)
Average	10	6 (60)	24–44	8 (80)	5 (50)

Note: 'D/k' denotes do not know. 'Per cent NL born' shows the percentage of personnel born in the Netherlands. Overall averages may be slightly different from those reported in Jacques et al. 2016, due to rounding and number of cases in denominator. In this work overall average percentages are calculated by dividing the variable's mean by the average number of total personnel across coffeeshops, which is 10. Especially for coffeeshops with more personnel, these numbers may not perfectly reflect the actual characteristics because they are based on interviewees' knowledge and recall.

Notes

1. See Becker 2015. For information on the drug scene I grew up in, see Jacques and Wright 2015.
2. Grapendaal, Leuw and Nelen 1995.
3. Leuw and Marshall 1994.
4. For information on the risks associated with drug use and distribution, see MacCoun and Reuter 2001; Musto 1999; Nutt 2012; Zimring and Hawkins 1992. Since my first trip to Amsterdam a trend toward legalisation has begun, see Caulkins 2017; Caulkins, Kilmer and Kleiman 2016; Reinarman 2016; Reuter 2013.

5. For the history of this monument in the Amsterdam drug scene, see Cuskey, Klein and Krasner 1972.
6. See Spierenburg 1984. For historical information on deviance, crime and social control in Amsterdam and Netherlands, see Roberts 2017; Spierenburg 1984, 2007, 2013. In the contemporary period, see van Swaaningen 2006; Tonry and Bijleveld 2007; Tonry and Farrington 2005. In Europe widely, see Eisner 2001, 2003; Elias 1994; Emsley, Johnson and Spierenburg 2004; Geltner 2008, 2014; Pinker 2011; Roodenburg and Spierenburg 2004.
7. Grapendaal, Leuw and Nelen 1995.
8. For information on the causes and consequences of cannabis policy reform, see Hawken et al. 2013; MacCoun and Reuter 2001; Pardo 2014; Room 2014.
9. All person and business names are pseudonyms, with a few exceptions. I use a coffeeshop's real name when referring to information found in a public source. I also use a coffeeshop's real name if discussing something unique to and publicly associated with it (see, for example, 'Amsterdam Coffee' invertisements). Use of a coffeeshop's real name is unrelated to whether or not its personnel participated in an interview.
10. See Boles and Miotto 2003; Meyerscough and Taylor 1985.
11. For a classic work on civilised behaviour, see Elias 1994.
12. For information on Dutch tolerance and law, see Buruma 2007; Mascini and Houtman 2011; Pakes 2005; Reinarman 2010.
13. 'Tolerance is inaction when a grievance might otherwise be handled' (Black 1998: 88).
14. For information on regulation and crime control, see Clarke 2018; Eck 2010, 2017, 2018; Felson 2018; Fisse and Braithwaite 1988; Freilich and Newman 2018; Gill 2002; Laycock 2005; Scott 2018.
15. For information on ethnographic and qualitative criminology, see Copes and Miller 2015; Miller and Palacios 2015. Classic examples are Du Bois 1899; Shaw 1930; Sutherland 1937; Thomas and Znaniecki 1920a, 1920b; Whyte 1943. More contemporary examples are Anderson 1999; Duneier 1999; Goffman 2014; Maruna 2001; Venkatesh 2006. Works on drug use and distribution include Bourgois and Schonberg 2009; Briggs 2011; Jacobs 1999, 2000; Sandberg and Pedersen 2009.
16. I moved to Amsterdam to complete a project on victimisation and reactive social control among Amsterdam's bars, coffeeshops, and street dealers (for findings, see Jacques et al. 2016). The Institutional Review Board of the University of Missouri–St Louis approved this research. From the start the project involved Richard Rosenfeld, Richard Wright and Frank van Gemert. Later on Wim Bernasco, Danielle Reynald and student assistants, especially Benny de Vries, became involved.
17. Also during the summer of 2011 I collected data for a study of robbers (see Lindegaard, Beransco and Jacques 2015; Lindegaard et al. 2013).
18. For a history of Amsterdam, see Mak 2001. For information on Amsterdam and Netherlands during the approximate study period, see City of Amsterdam 2011; Lindeman et al. 2005; Nordholt, Hartgers and Gircour 2004.
19. See Bieleman et al. 2008. Since the mid-1990s the number of coffeeshops in the Netherlands and Amsterdam has been in decline (MacCoun 2011; S.N. 2017).
20. For information on conducting ethnographic observation, see Emerson, Fretz and Shaw 2011; Spradley 1980.
21. For information on conducting interviews, see Spradley 1979; Weiss 1994.
22. To improve readability I edited some quotes by rearranging or deleting words. When making such changes, I preserved each statement's original meaning, of course. For a discussion of editing quotes, see Weiss 1994.
23. For further methodological details, see Bernasco and Jacques 2015; Jacques and Bernasco 2013; Jacques et al. 2016.

Introduction
The law and rules

In Amsterdam's coffeeshops, the worldwide prohibition on cannabis sales is void.[1] Kamila, a server at Arrow in the Air, described these retail establishments as 'where you can come and socialise, and don't be scared that the police will get you. You go to the bar [counter], you take your coffee, you roll your joint, and see how it is – and you don't get punishment for it'. The manager of Purple Testament, Emma, nonchalantly stated, 'We just sell weed here. It is normal'.[2]

Many municipalities in the Netherlands, not only Amsterdam, allow licensed coffeeshops to sell cannabis.[3] But on the books, and confusingly, this business is outlawed. 'I keep on telling people', said Selma, who deals at Man in the Bottle, 'it is still illegal because the law never allowed it. It has been tolerated because, at the moment, it is still illegal: if the government decide they want to put a stop behind it, they can do it.'

It is a crime to sell cannabis in the Netherlands. There are severe sanctions for breaking the law. At the time of my study, the maximum penalties for possession, cultivation, sale, transport and production of cannabis for commercial purposes are six years' imprisonment or a fine of €67,000.[4] The penalties apply to cannabis sales outside a licensed coffeeshop. Once a supply enters a coffeeshop, it transforms from a serious risk to a taxed good.[5] In the words of Jack, who manages Alike All Over: 'Everything coming in the back door is black. It is all off the books, and then everything out the front door goes through the books, so is taxed.'

As a national policy, the Dutch government's allowance of coffeeshops stems from its distinction between 'hard' and 'soft' drugs.[6] The former refers to illicit substances deemed to have an unacceptable health risk (for example, cocaine or heroin), whereas the latter includes drugs considered to be less harmful, such as cannabis.[7] These categories inform harm reduction: doing less about one problem to avoid causing worse problems.[8] The rationale of allowing coffeeshops is to 'protect cannabis users ... from exposure to hard drugs and the criminal elements who traffic in them'.[9] If people are allowed to buy cannabis from coffeeshops, the thinking goes, they are less likely to use hard drugs sold by dealers with a diversified product line.

Dutch drug policy is set at the national level, but municipal governments, such as that of Amsterdam, decide whether to permit coffeeshops in their jurisdiction.[10] Where allowed, the local government issues a sort of business licence to coffeeshops, albeit not a traditional licence because cannabis distribution is a crime. Finn, the owner of Execution, described the licence in this way:

> It is a warning letter from the mayor in which he allows me to break the law unless I break the [rules]. It is a really strange document because it is signed by the mayor, it is printed on paper from the local government, but it doesn't have any status. In other words, I can never take it to court. That is the tension in the Dutch coffeeshop system. Owners of coffeeshops always feel harassed and blackmailed, and in fact they are, because they know that the government can suspend that drug supply [licence] at any time.

As alluded to by Finn, the privilege to break the law comes with a catch – a set of strictly enforced rules or regulations.[11] Everyone inside a coffeeshop must be at least 18 years of age. No customer can be sold more than 5 grams of cannabis per day, nor can there be more than 500 grams on the premises. Hard drugs are strictly prohibited. Nuisance is not allowed and cannabis advertisements are forbidden. In short, Dutch policy is meant not only to separate the markets for cannabis and hard drugs from one another, but also to restrict sales by coffeeshops and prevent them from becoming an intolerable problem.

Police checks

To ensure that coffeeshops adhere to the rules, the police conduct surprise checks.[12] The prospect of these visits is a constant concern for coffeeshop personnel. '"When [are] the police coming?" That's the only worry', complained Luuk, the owner of Angels. The fear is that police surveillance will lead to punishment. As Jack explained: 'You get a licence and you agree to let the police in the door whenever they come. So you make sure you are doing nothing wrong, ever. We get checked up [on] very regularly. We have far more checks on our business than any other sort of business in the country. We have police checking for all sort of stipulations they can shut us down for.'

According to Dutch policy, police checks are supposed to occur at each coffeeshop at least twice a year. 'They always come around, for sure, twice a year', stated Stijn, a dealer at Mr. Bevis. He added: 'I know two or three months [ago] they came in [here] after the summer, and then again at the end of the year or the beginning of the year. There are loads of coffeeshops, though.' Some coffeeshops are subject to fewer police searches than dictated. Mara, the owner of Wish, recounted: 'In the last year we didn't have one [check]. They did it every year in August, always in August. The last week of August, they always come in, but the last four years there was nothing wrong, so I think they [stopped coming].' I remarked, 'Well, it hasn't hit the last week of August yet', to which she responded: 'Maybe today, tomorrow [they will come], but last year in August they didn't come in, also. It's quiet.' I asked when the last check was, to which she replied: 'It seems about 18 months ago, or something like that. We normally know [they come] two times a year, but maybe because it's quiet [they don't come], maybe because they wait.'

It is atypical for coffeeshops to have had only one or no police checks in the previous 12 months. For those in my sample, the average number is about two and a half. This means some establishments are subject to more than the requisite couple checks. Jack talked about this happening at Alike All Over:

> I would say for checks, we have probably averaged one a month, so 12 in the past 12 months. It is ridiculous, and we kind of feel unfairly done, but my mate down the road is starting to get the same [at his coffeeshop]. They didn't have any [checks] for ages and ages and ages, and then they are suddenly getting them every two weeks. And it is almost like these [police] units aren't communicating with each other, they are like two different units. 'You were only here 10 days ago and we were perfect then!' It's like [from them], 'Ah, we are going to catch you out now! You weren't expecting us!' When they come really regularly, it sometimes seems like they are expecting you to relax and let your standards slip. But you don't do that, and [therefore] you can welcome the police when they come in to do their checks. It is annoying because you shut the shop for three hours, sometimes.

I am uncertain why coffeeshops are inspected more or less. Possibly a researcher could interview officers in charge of these searches to learn the answers, but I did not try this.[13] However, the answer is more complicated than establishments that are perceived to be 'bad' coming under greater surveillance. Indeed, the police regularly visit some coffeeshops due to perceiving them as good. Olivia, who deals at Elegy, told me: 'They actually take the trainee cops here because we always have our licences and everything in order, and we are supposed to be very nice for the police to come in and do their checking things. They do come in, but we never get in trouble. They take their trainees and say, "Now this is how it works".' Local police also bring foreign colleagues to good coffeeshops to demonstrate Dutch drug policy in action. Stijn described these visits as follows:

> We always work with the police. Here everything is cool. When the police come, we work always together. And even sometimes, police come here from Germany, America, China, and they [local Dutch police] show you their badge and say, 'Listen, we have colleagues across the road, and they don't know how it works in Holland. Can you show them stuff?' Then I show them the weed. I show them the hash. I show them what we sell. Tell them the rules.

Coffeeshops' proximity to police stations may also increase the number of inspections. This situation was mentioned by Jack, who talked about the stress involved in being a training dummy:

> It is very funny, and I think this may be because we are right across the road from the station, but we seem to get all the juniors being trained how to do the coffeeshop checks. So there are a bunch of kids with guns, younger than me, telling me what to do. It freaks me out because I come from a place where police don't carry guns, and certainly not fucking children. A bunch of 20-year-olds, armed, coming in my shop, [screaming] 'Don't touch that!' They freak out, they are really sketchy, because they have this idea that we are trying to pull one over on them.

When police checks occur, there is a standard procedure. First, they are unnanounced. 'They just come in and "poof"' is how Luke put it. He went on to describe what happens next: 'They come down and search. You have to do everything in the law, but it's always a fuss. They come in with 15 [officers], and search everything. They check everything, look everywhere, opening everything, and asking everything.' Imran, who owns Eye of the Beholder, further detailed the investigative steps:

> They never come [by] to say they are coming [later]. They just come. They put everything on the scale, they see if the scale is right,

> and then they see how much [cannabis] you have [in total]. Then they check the ID of the [person] who is working, then they check the money – what you have sold already that day, and what you started with. Then they start checking every area, sometimes with a dog.

Police and coffeeshop personnel are not the only parties involved in checks. Customers get entangled in the surveillance web too. Are they minors? Do they have hard drugs? Does the cannabis in their possession add up to more than 500 grams in the coffeeshop? Evidence of such amounts to a rule violation and trouble for the business. It is easy to imagine that patrons, especially tourists, are taken aback by the sight of several officers barging inside. I asked Anna, manager of Maple Street, if customers seem worried when that occurs. 'No, I don't think so', she replied. 'Well, maybe in the first place. But it is no problem if they see that I think it is normal that they are coming in.' Still, a problem for customers is they cannot simply walk out of the door when the police arrive. Maud mentioned this happened at the most recent check of At Last: 'At the time, there were two customers, and they couldn't leave. They [officers] said they had to stay there while they were investigating. They were here for their break and they were like, "Hey we have to go back to work", and they were like, "Our boss is not going to be happy".'

Some personnel, such as Emma, claim to 'like the fact that they come in and check us'. But most owners and employees have a negative view of inspections. This is not only because of the inconvenience and risk. Even if everything is in order, these are tenuous encounters because the duty of officers is to search for wrongdoing.[14] It is unsurprising, then, that personnel express displeasure with how checks unfold – although they complain less about the process than officers' demeanour.[15] For example, Anna, the manager of Maple Street, told me: 'We have had them in here probably three times, and they were so impolite to us, and they are really stupid.'

No matter how officers behave, there is little personnel can do at the time to improve their position, other than be respectful.[16] Jack explained why it is good to exhibit a positive demeanour to officers, even when facing a negative one:

> When they come, they are just doing their job. They can be rude and aggressive, sometimes. One of the young girls here opened the shop one morning, and literally two customers had walked in the door, and then there were 10 policemen in the door, all armed and

> in her face demanding to see things. She had to ring me up and talk to me for half an hour so I could explain. 'Show them this, show them that'. I told her not to take shit off them, just to be nice and tell them to relax. They shout at the little girl expecting her to crack and say, 'Yes, we've got 6 kilos of cocaine under here! Sorry!'
>
> Sometimes they come in with this attitude, like you are really up to no good. I know we are doing nothing wrong, so my reaction is just like, 'Come in, chill out, relax'. They want to take all our names and check all our passports. One of my friends in another coffeeshop now has a form that he prints out to try and get the name of the chief of the search, and all of your [officer] names and which station you work, and [will say to them], 'If you can write that down for me, then we can all sit down, have a cup of coffee and get started, and speak like civilised people'. Then they are like, 'Oh, all right, you are just another business'.

As touched on by Jack, personnel use humour to relieve the strain of interaction with officers.[17] Another example was mentioned by Gijs, who manages Escape Clause: 'They just showed up. I say laughing, "Hi, guys. Want a coffee?" It sort of breaks the ice and then we do our thing, they do their thing. Everyone is doing their job. And, yeah, it's basically vice versa. "OK, you do your job, we do our job".'

Punishment

The attitude of coffeeshop personnel towards police also matters because detected violations do not invariably result in punishment. By treating officers with respect, personnel may reduce the sanction risk, if a violation is detected. The same effect results from earning a reputation as a coffeeshop that generally abides by the rules.[18] Gijs talked about this when I asked if there had ever been more than 500 grams on his premises:

> That has happened in the past. It is sometimes hard to check. Now, there is not more than 500 grams in the shop because a little while ago in the [shop], there was a bust from the police and they found like 540 grams. Because we have a good relationship with the police – they like the way we work, they like the way we stick to the rules and all that – they were milder [with the punishment].

'So what did they do?' I asked. His answer was surprising:

> Well, they didn't do anything, really. They didn't give us any closing or whatever, but it might have to do with we have good contact with the police. We have better contact with the police than other shops, so we are standing in a better daylight because when they come in with a bust it is always fairly normal, fairly mild, and almost a good atmosphere.

For violating the rules coffeeshops may be shut down, temporarily or permanently, and fined. In addition personnel may be arrested, prosecuted and accordingly punished, though this seems rare. Typically punishments are administered on an escalating basis, such that more infractions lead to more severe penalties, although this does not apply invariably. Jasper, who manages The Hour, described how the escalation process works: 'Yellow cards are like you get a bust, they fine it [the business] and get one yellow card [on your record]. Two yellow cards: you go for a week, you close. Three yellow [cards]: a month. And then four: you're done.'

Punishment is not a frequent occurrence, but personnel know the risk is real. This is because the coffeeshop community is close-knit. When a member is punished for a violation, personnel learn about it.[19] Anna had heard of coffeeshops where the police 'came and found hard drugs on the customers, then they closed'. The owner of Perchance, Willem, told me about a 'coffeeshop [that] is closed down now – I heard rumours that they were selling other things inside'. And a popular website devoted to the coffeeshop scene, www.smokersguide.com, posted a story with the headline: 'ABRAXAS COFFEESHOP AMSTERDAM FORCED TO CLOSE ITS DOORS!' The story reported:

> Due to the strict policies regarding possession of any hard drugs on coffeeshop premises, Abraxas Coffeeshop was forced to close its doors. The employee who caused this situation was a recently employed women [*sic*] from Italy, who had less than a gram of cocaine and a bit over a gram of MDMA in her bag, left over from the previous night. Her carelessness has cost this fine establishment it's [*sic*] life.[20]

Being closed, even temporarily, is bad for business. Speaking purely in financial terms, coffeeshop owners have the most to lose from closure. In the short term, the punishment equals the sum of missed sales profit.

The loss is greater if the business is closed for good because the owner is prohibited from selling it as well. In both the short and long term, how much is lost depends on the coffeeshop, as some obviously make more sales and so are worth money more than others.

To gain a rudimentary sense of coffeeshop economics,[21] I asked personnel to estimate their coffeeshop's annual profit, a fair sale price for the whole business and the normal weekly number of customers and sales (Table 0.3). On average, the annual profit is about €535,000, with

Table 0.3 Economic estimates for interviewed coffeeshops

Coffeeshop	Annual profit	For sale price	# Weekly customers	# Weekly sales
After Hours		€100,000	200	200
Alike All Over	€730,000		1,400	1,400
Angels	€200,000			
Arrow in the Air	€353,600	€300,000	560	1,400
At Last	€365,000	€750,000		100
Back There		€150,000	350	140
Buzz	€1,277,500	€2,250,000	1,500	2,500
Chaser	€1,095,000	€500,000	200	200
Dollar Room	€730,000		1,050	1,575
Doomsday	€100,000	€1,000,000		
Dust		€1,000,000	490	280
Elegy		€1,000,000	1,400	840
Escape Clause				2,100
Everybody	€500,000	€5,000,000		
Execution	€250,000	€1,800,000	700	700
Eye of the Beholder	€300,000	€2,000,000	875	1,575
Fever	€65,700	€400,000	420	329
Four of Us			300	300
Hitch-Hiker	€547,500	€1,500,000	1,400	4,200
Howling Man	€1,095,000	€1,000,000	1,400	2,100
Judgement Night				2,800
Last Flight		€1,000,000	600	1,000
Like a Child		€500,000	1,225	2,450
Live Long	€547,500	€500,000	1,050	1,575
Man in the Bottle	€547,500	€200,000	700	1,260
Maple Street	€547,500		1,225	1,225

(Continued)

Table 0.3 (Continued)

Coffeeshop	Annual profit	For sale price	# Weekly customers	# Weekly sales
Meek	€255,500	€500,000	560	350
Mirror Image	€711,750	€1,000,000	420	1,330
Most Unusual		€300,000	1,400	1,400
Mr. Bevis		€1,000,000	1,000	850
Nice Place to Visit	€1,277,500	€1,000,000	1,400	1,400
Nick of Time	€912,500	€50,000		
No Return	€1,095,000	€750,000	200	150
Open Sky		€350,000		1,240
Passage			55	
Perchance	0			350
Purple Testament	€310,250	€200,000	1,190	1,190
Shrine		€100,000		
Stop	€310,250	€300,000	43	130
Sun	€328,500	€5,000,000	350	350
The Hour		€2,000,000	7,000	7700
The Lonely				
The Mighty	€104,000	0	250	250
Thing	€219,000	€400,000	175	420
Walking Distance				
What You Need	€547,500		1,050	1,400
Whole Truth				
Wish	€730,000	€4,000,000	1,050	1,050
World of Difference		€5,000,000	2,100	273
World of His Own			90	180
Average (range)	€535,118 (€0–1,277,500)	€1,191,667 (€0–5,000,000)	956 (43–7,000)	1,286 (100–7,700)

Note: An empty cell denotes 'Don't know'. 'For sale price' presents answers to the question 'If the business was for sale, what would be the approximate asking price?' Especially for interviewees who are not in ownership or management positions, the profit and sale price estimates may not accurately reflect the actual economics. At the time of the study US$1 = ~€1.30–1.40; AU$1 = ~€1.40–1.80; £1 = ~€0.85–0.90.

a range from zero to more than €1.25 million.[22] For reasons I get into shortly, the 'for sale' price estimates are all over the place: they range from zero to €5 million, with an average of about €1.2 million. As might be expected, those amounts positively correlate with the number of weekly customers and sales. The average of the former is €950, with a range from €43 to €7,000. The sales average is €1,300 and ranges from €100 to more than €7,700.

Not all personnel are able to answer questions about the business; owners have the most valid information. Mara gave a ballpark '€400,000' as the price for her coffeeshop, while Imran estimated, 'More or less €2 million because if you calculate the 20 years' profit [that's what it is worth]." Managers know the numbers, too. Joseph, who manages Open Sky, recounted:

> Two or three years ago, I know this place was roughly half a million because there was a girl who offered 250,000 [euros] [for the coffeeshop next door] and she [the owner] refused. That was about four or five years ago, and here is a lot upgraded, so I think a lot more than that [now].

A factor in calculating coffeeshop worth is whether the licence can be sold. If not, these establishments are far less valuable, especially since the Amsterdam government is no longer issuing new licences. When I asked respondents about the sale price, some thought it was effectively zero because, to their knowledge, a coffeeshop licence cannot be sold. Jack's view was that:

> A coffeeshop licence is not worth fuck all. You can have one, but you can't sell it. You can't change the name and it can't change address. It is only there for as long as they give it, and there is no guarantee that they will renew the licence. So to sell it, it is very hard to say what it is worth.

A couple days later I interviewed Finn and admitted my confusion to him. Could places sell their licences? He explained the legal situation as follows:

> They can. There are two addresses in Amsterdam that cannot be sold. In 1996 when the Amsterdam coffeeshop policy was put to papers, there were six addresses of coffeeshops that were catering to high school kids. They were allowed to stay, but when the shops closed there were to be no new coffeeshops on those locations. Of those six, there are two left. So in reality, unless the school goes away or is upgraded to a university, they cannot sell their licence. So out of [all] the coffeeshops [in Amsterdam], only two cannot sell.

Next, I asked about the worth of Finn's business. He was not entirely sure. 'You can get the licence and the inventory, I would say a million [euros]; it all depends. If it is some filthy rich former freedom fighter who comes with a suitcase with 2 million [euros in it], then fine!'

Closure of a coffeeshop has a serious effect on the lives of employees, not just owners. As seen in Table 0.4, the average coffeeshop has

Table 0.4 Personnel positions of interviewed coffeeshops

Coffeeshop (# of personnel)	# Owner (per cent)	# Manager (per cent)	# Dealer (per cent)	# Servers (per cent)	# Runners (per cent)	# Other (per cent)
After Hours (11)	1 (9)	1 (9)	6 (55)	0 (0)	2 (18)	1 (9)
Alike All Over (11)	2 (18)	1 (9)	8 (73)	0 (0)	0 (0)	0 (0)
Angels (D/k)	1 (D/k)	D/k (D/k)	D/k (D/k)	D/k (D/k)	D/k (D/k)	D/k (D/k)
Arrow in the Air (7)	1 (14)	2 (29)	3 (43)	0 (0)	0 (0)	1 (14)
At Last (4)	1 (25)	0 (0)	3 (75)	0 (0)	0 (0)	0 (0)
Back There (6)	1 (16)	2 (33)	3 (50)	0 (0)	0 (0)	0 (0)
Buzz (7)	1 (14)	1 (14)	5 (71)	0 (0)	0 (0)	0 (0)
Chaser (9)	1 (11)	2 (22)	2 (22)	2 (22)	1 (11)	1 (11)
Dollar Room (12)	1 (8)	2 (17)	6 (50)	0 (0)	3 (25)	0 (0)
Doomsday (D/k)	2 (D/k)	1 (D/k)	4 (D/k)	10 (D/k)	D/k (D/k)	1 (D/k)
Dust (9)	4 (44)	1 (11)	4 (44)	0 (0)	0 (0)	0 (0)
Elegy (13)	1 (8)	2 (15)	8 (62)	0 (0)	2 (15)	0 (0)
Escape Clause (9)	1 (11)	2 (22)	6 (67)	0 (0)	0 (0)	0 (0)
Everybody (19)	1 (5)	1 (5)	7 (37)	7 (37)	2 (11)	1 (5)
Execution (12)	1 (8)	1 (8)	10 (83)	0 (0)	0 (0)	0 (0)
Eye of the Beholder (8)	1 (13)	1 (13)	6 (75)	0 (0)	0 (0)	0 (0)
Fever (5)	1 (20)	0 (0)	4 (80)	0 (0)	0 (0)	0 (0)
Four of Us (7)	2 (29)	0 (0)	5 (71)	0 (0)	0 (0)	0 (0)

(Continued)

Table 0.4 (Continued)

Coffeeshop (# of personnel)	# Owner (per cent)	# Manager (per cent)	# Dealer (per cent)	# Servers (per cent)	# Runners (per cent)	# Other (per cent)
Hitch-Hiker (17)	1 (6)	3 (18)	5 (29)	5 (29)	3 (18)	0 (0)
Howling Man (15)	2 (13)	1 (7)	4 (27)	3 (20)	3 (20)	2 (13)
Judgement Night (23)	2 (9)	3 (13)	15 (65)	0 (0)	3 (13)	0 (0)
Last Flight (19)	1 (5)	2 (11)	8 (42)	8 (42)	0 (0)	0 (0)
Like a Child (20)	1 (5)	4 (20)	4 (20)	8 (40)	0 (0)	3 (15)
Live Long (7)	2 (29)	0 (0)	4 (57)	0 (0)	0 (0)	1 (14)
Man in the Bottle (4)	2 (50)	0 (0)	2 (50)	0 (0)	0 (0)	0 (0)
Maple Street (9)	1 (11)	1 (11)	6 (67)	0 (0)	0 (0)	1 (11)
Meek (4)	1 (25)	0 (0)	3 (75)	0 (0)	0 (0)	0 (0)
Mirror Image (D/k)	D/k (D/k)	1 (D/k)	1 (D/k)	1 (D/k)	0 (0)	0 (0)
Most Unusual (5)	1 (20)	1 (20)	3 (60)	0 (0)	0 (0)	0 (0)
Mr. Bevis (18)	1 (6)	2 (11)	14 (78)	0 (0)	0 (0)	1 (6)
Nice Place to Visit (18)	1 (6)	4 (22)	6 (33)	6 (33)	0 (0)	1 (6)
Nick of Time (13)	1 (8)	0 (0)	4 (29)	3 (23)	3 (23)	2 (15)
No Return (9)	1 (11)	4 (44)	3 (33)	0 (0)	0 (0)	1 (11)
Open Sky (3)	1 (33)	1 (33)	1 (33)	0 (0)	0 (0)	0 (0)
Passage (3)	1 (33)	0 (0)	2 (67)	0 (0)	0 (0)	0 (0)
Perchance (4)	2 (50)	0 (0)	2 (50)	0 (0)	0 (0)	0 (0)
Purple Testament (5)	1 (20)	0 (0)	3 (60)	0 (0)	0 (0)	1 (20)
Shrine (6)	1 (17)	1 (17)	4 (67)	0 (0)	0 (0)	0 (0)
Stop (2)	2 (100)	0 (0)	0 (0)	0 (0)	0 (0)	0 (0)
Sun (9)	1 (11)	0 (0)	3 (33)	5 (56)	0 (0)	0 (0)

(Continued)

Table 0.4 (Continued)

Coffeeshop (# of personnel)	**# Owner (per cent)**	**# Manager (per cent)**	**# Dealer (per cent)**	**# Servers (per cent)**	**# Runners (per cent)**	**# Other (per cent)**
The Hour (21)	3 (14)	1 (5)	6 (29)	8 (38)	2 (10)	1 (5)
The Lonely (D/k)	1 (D/k)	0 (0)	6 (D/k)	0 (0)	D/k (D/k)	0 (0)
The Mighty (9)	1 (11)	1 (11)	6 (67)	0 (0)	0 (0)	1 (11)
Thing (4)	1 (25)	1 (25)	1 (25)	0 (0)	0 (0)	1 (25)
Walking Distance (4)	2 (50)	0 (0)	2 (50)	0 (0)	0 (0)	0 (0)
What You Need (11)	3 (27)	0 (0)	4 (36)	3 (27)	1 (9)	0 (0)
Whole Truth (27)	2 (7)	6 (22)	8 (30)	8 (30)	2 (7)	1 (4)
Wish (8)	1 (13)	2 (25)	4 (50)	0 (0)	0 (0)	1 (13)
World of Difference (15)	1 (7)	2 (13)	9 (6)	0 (0)	3 (2)	0 (0)
World of His Own (10)	1 (10)	1 (10)	4 (40)	4 (40)	0 (0)	0 (0)
Average (10)	1 (10)	1 (10)	5 (50)	2 (20)	1 (10)	0 (0)

Note: 'D/k' denotes 'do not know'. Dealers may serve drink and food in addition to selling cannabis, but servers do not sell cannabis except, perhaps, in a rare circumstance. 'Other' largely includes cleaners, who perform their role outside open hours. Totals may not add up to 100 per cent due to rounding. Average percentages are calculated by dividing the variable's mean by the average number of total personnel across coffeeshops, which is 10. In particular, for coffeeshops with more personnel, these numbers may not perfectly reflect the actual characteristics because they are based on interviewees' knowledge and recall.

about 10 personnel, so at least 500 individuals depend financially on the 1012's coffeeshops.[23] Some coffeeshops are small operations with just a few personnel; others have around a couple of dozen. These individuals fill different roles, or positions, which are not always mutually exclusive. The average coffeeshop has one owner, one manager, five dealers who focus on selling cannabis but may also serve drink and food, two servers who only serve the latter, a runner who brings the cannabis stock and maybe another dedicated employee, such as a cleaner or a doorman.[24]

Violations put the entire existence of a coffeeshop at risk – and, by extension, jeopardise the livelihoods of its personnel. Interviewees consistently put the average salary of workers at €1,000 to €2,000 a month.[25] For instance, when I asked Ruben, a dealer at The Mighty, what they earn, he answered, 'Approximately 1,600 euros a month, with bonuses'. And Gwen, who manages Like a Child, told me, 'The average working income, everybody here makes between 1,000 and 1,300 euros a month net. That depends [on] how much you work [in hours].'

Understanding how coffeeshop workers approach their work relates to employment contracts.[26] Many employees have a contract with the business that guarantees a certain number of hours on the job and specifies a salary. Such a contract also protects them from being arbitrarily laid off or fired. For those reasons, owners and managers hand out contracts selectively. As Gijs explains:

> People who start working their first contract of three months, in those three months we can say, or after the three months [ends], we can say, 'No, it's not going to work, we are not going to extend your contract'. But in the first two months you [also] have the possibility of saying, 'I don't even want to have to think about it. Sorry, you have to go. This is not your job'.

Because owners and managers are careful about giving contracts, it may be more difficult to land a job in the first place. But once an employee has a contract, it can work to the benefit of the entire business. This is because the contract secures the employee's stake in conformity and the business.[27] To protect their reliable source of income, contracted employees do more to protect the coffeeshop from violations. To quote Kamila: 'I have a long-term contract for my future and I have my rent to pay, so you have to be smart. Don't cut your wings!'

Not all employees have contracts, however. Some also work off the books, at least partially.[28] One reason that owners and managers make this arrangement with workers is to avoid the legal restraints commensurate with contracts. Another reason is it can reduce the taxes paid by all parties. This issue came up when Sophie, a server, told me about the extent to which Hitch-Hiker follows the rules: 'We don't get hired, how do you call it, "under the table"? We don't do that here.' I asked, 'Is that a big thing?' She answered, 'In coffeeshops? Yeah. Most girls and guys, they have jobs in this area and you get paid without taxes. That is the main reason to work in this kind of job.'

Selma was partially paid 'under the table'. I learned of her situation when asking how many hours she works each week. Looking for clarification, she asked me, 'Officially?' I told her, 'No, in reality', to which she replied:

> 45 hours a week. Like €1,500 a month. I signed a contract for 10 hours a week, so I work officially 10 hours, so he has to pay tax for 10 hours a week for his employee, me. Through my salary slip I earn €346 a month [officially]. I work 6 or 7 days a week, so when you put all the numbers together you divide them into a couple of weeks, that's what we did here. I get paid under the table. My salary, I take €8 an hour. I just work a normal day, it is €65 from 9 till 5.

She went on to describe how this arrangement benefited the owner but cost her, which she tolerated to keep her job:

> If I would be working 36 hours a week officially then I would be building up holiday money [that the business has to give its employees for time off]. Everything you build up. With 10 hours a week, you build up shit. Then for sure he pays the government less because he does not have to pay tax for an employee working that amount of hours. I would rather have a contract of 36 hours, of course, because at the end of the year that is the days I have been building up to be free [for holiday].

Obeying and breaking rules

The prospect of punishment coupled with regular police checks motivate coffeeshop personnel to obey the rules.[29] 'There are things they [police] could find that would shut you straight away', said Jack, 'so you just make sure those things are always fucking dealt with. You make sure you are on top of those things. We stay within the rules because we know how easy it is for them to shut us down.' Similarly, Sophie described her workplace as: 'a very good coffeeshop. My boss is very strict. The owner, she is very strict. She does not want to break any rules: don't do anything illegal.' Meanwhile Emir, a dealer at Walking Distance, told me, 'It is my business. I try to keep it clean [of violations].'

Personnel stay on top of rule enforcement because everyone has something to lose from the closure of their coffeeshop. When I asked

Thomas, who manages Buzz, about why they follow the rules, he asserted, 'We love our shop, we love our job and we would be at risk of the coffeeshop being closed down'. Likewise Luca, a dealer at The Lonely, stated the rules are enforced because otherwise 'these seven people are out of a job, and I don't want that responsibility. It is not worth it. This is our job. This is our way of paying our living. You have to work. You have to pay your rent. You have to live.'

Though a coffeeshop may not be punished for a violation, an employee risks termination if a misdeed happens on his or her watch. Jens, who deals at Nice Place to Visit, talked about this pressure:

> Under-aged people, young kids with [fake] ID, drunk and disorderly people and street dealers, we don't want them in our coffeeshops. Street dealers can cost you your licence; so can underage children and young kids. They are not allowed. If they are in there and the police come in on my fucking watch, I would be fired – if the coffeeshop is not closed down.

Clearly, personnel have reason to play within the rules. Indeed, and as intended by Dutch policy, the rules create order in coffeeshops. Jens continued:

> Cannabis is still illegal in most of the world, so it is still a little bit of a taboo thing. And they [the government] do feel that they have to regulate it more. So you get all these extra little rules because you have got this whole grey area thing. It leads to more control in the coffeeshops themselves, and you should have staff who take care because you are playing with your licence.

At a glance, the rules appear uncomplicated and easy to handle. For that reason some personnel, such as Emir, worry about checks, but reckon no harm will come from them. 'If police come in, they are always happy with us. Always, everything is perfect, always perfect.'[30] 'They give you rules', said Stijn, a dealer at Mr. Bevis, 'and they are simple to follow. You would be very idiotic if you didn't follow the rules because the rules are simple.'[31]

The mechanisms for enforcing the rules – again, police checks and punishments – are part deterrence, part 'proterrence'.[32] Deterrence entails scaring people out of doing something 'bad', however this is defined.[33] Proterrence involves scaring people *into* doing something to stop others from doing something bad. In coffeeshops, the rules scare personnel out of making violations (deterrence) and into preventing other persons from making them (proterrence). This whole book focuses on the rules and enforcement mechanisms as deterrents, but the second half, starting with the chapter on minors, also examines how those shape proterrence.

Deterrence and proterrence effects are not absolute, but rather restrictive.[34] In other words, fear of police checks and punishment does not prevent all violations, but it does suppress their frequency and seriousness. This outcome is evident from what personnel disclosed about violations at their respective coffeeshops in the prior 12 months (Table 0.5).

Table 0.5 Rule violation among interviewed coffeeshops

Coffeeshop	>500 grams	Advertise	Sold to minors	Sold >5 grams	Hard drugs	Nuisance (fight)
After Hours		D/k				
Alike All Over				X	X	
Angels						
Arrow in the Air	D/k					
At Last	X			X		
Back There						
Buzz				X	X	
Chaser		X		X	X	
Dollar Room		X				
Doomsday	D/k	D/k		X		
Dust						
Elegy			X	X	X	X
Escape Clause	X					
Everybody	X			X		X
Execution					X	
Eye of the Beholder					X	
Fever						
Four of Us						
Hitch-Hiker	D/k	X			X	
Howling Man				X	X	
Judgement Night	X	X		X		
Last Flight		X				
Like a Child						
Live Long		X				X
Man in the Bottle				X		
Maple Street				X		

(*Continued*)

Table 0.5 (Continued)

Coffeeshop	>500 grams	Advertise	Sold to minors	Sold >5 grams	Hard drugs	Nuisance (fight)
Meek				X		X
Mirror Image	D/k					
Most Unusual					X	
Mr. Bevis						
Nice Place to Visit		D/k	X	X	X	
Nick of Time			X	X	X	
No Return					X	
Open Sky					X	
Passage						
Perchance						
Purple Testament				X		
Shrine						
Stop						
Sun				D/k	X	
The Hour		X				X
The Lonely						
The Mighty				X	X	
Thing						
Walking Distance						
What You Need	D/k			X	X	
Whole Truth				X		X
Wish				X		
World of Difference						
World of His Own						
Per cent violated	11	15	6	43	32	12

Note: 'X' denotes violation of rule. 'D/k' denotes 'do not know', meaning the interviewee neither confirmed nor denied violation. For each coffeeshop the following labels refer to whether the following occurred in the 12 months before the interview: '>500 grams' – more than 500 grams of cannabis on the premises; 'Advertise' – advertisement of coffeeshop; 'Sold to minor' – a person under 18 years of age was sold cannabis; 'Sold >5 grams' – a person was sold more than 5 grams of cannabis in a single day; 'Hard drugs' – hard drugs were on the premises; 'Nuisance' – a physical altercation between customers.

Almost two-fifths reported no violations. Another one-fifth reported that only one rule had been broken. Nearly 90 per cent of those interviewed reported breaking two rules or fewer. The other 10 per cent reported violating three of the six rules, with the exception of Elegy, which violated four. Across the 50 coffeeshops, 6 per cent disclosed selling to a minor; 11 per cent had more than 500 grams inside; 12 per cent admitted to a fight taking place between customers (prohibited under the 'nuisance' rule); 15 per cent had advertised; hard drugs were inside 32 per cent; and 43 per cent sold more than 5 grams to a person in a single day.[35]

Those statistics should be taken with a pinch of salt as it is unlikely that they perfectly reflect reality. I see no good reason for personnel to make up violations, but it makes sense to lie by denying they occurred. My guess is the statistics thus undercount infractions, much in the same way there is a dark figure of crime.[36] It is impossible to know for sure, however, as there is no foolproof source of information on the issue. Police reports are even more problematic because officers detect only a very small portion of all violations. For instance, only three of the 50 participants said their coffeeshop had been punished in the 12 months leading up to the interview.

From a quantitative perspective, the dark figure of violation is a serious problem. But it is less bad, even good, when examined through an ethnographic lens. It is possible to learn from lies, withholdings and other sorts of invalid information, so long as they are recognised as potentially being such.[37] To that point, there are a few reasons why my data probably undercounts coffeeshop violation. The most obvious is some participants are not fully forthcoming. If true, this reflects the concern of personnel that admitting to violations could lead to punishment. Why else would they lie? And in addition to lying, how else do they prevent being discredited as a violator?

It is also possible that denials are not lies, but invalid due to a lack of information. An owner or employee may not know what other personnel are doing. Superiors may warn subordinates to obey the rules, but this may not fully deter them from bringing hard drugs to work, selling to minors or dealing more than 5 grams to a person in a day. Conversely, workers may follow the rules while their superiors secretly store more than 500 grams on the premises or make large sales. Such secrets, like lies, suggest all coffeeshop personnel are concerned about the risk of violations. Otherwise a greater flow of information would be expected between the interviewees and myself.

Furthermore, personnel do not know about everything and everyone in their establishment. My educated guess is that hard drugs go inside every coffeeshop, stowed inside patrons' pockets and bags. And though personnel do not sell to known minors, few coffeeshops have a doorman stopping them from walking inside, though even entry is forbidden by the government. In addition, detecting fake IDs is not that easy, especially when IDs are not consistently checked. These possibilities are only a few of the daily difficulties faced by coffeeshop personnel.

Mistakes are another cause of violations. For example, the 500 grams limit is breached when a runner accidentally brings too much cannabis to the coffeeshop; this may happen if a dealer accidentally orders too much due to miscounting the stock on hand. When such events occur, personnel break the rules by accident, despite being fearful of punishment. These violations are logically impossible to report to a researcher, unless subsequently discovered, perhaps by police. This also illustrates the regular problems that personnel worry about, lest they risk their business and livelihood.

*****

> There is no business like a coffeeshop that has to stick to so many rules. The coffeeshop owner has the most worries of every businessman basically because you have so many rules. It's too much to comprehend sometimes.
>
> –Gijs

Having outlined the rules and risks, the book turns to more specific questions: How do personnel go about obeying the rules? How are they violated? What are the causes and consequences? Each chapter examines a different rule, with the goal being to comprehend better how each rule shapes the social life of coffeeshops. First is how personnel stock the coffeeshop, a process complicated by the 500 grams limit and the illegality of the back door. Next is attracting customers by advertising, which can land a coffeeshop in hot water. Nor are all customers welcome: coffeeshops are obliged to keep out persons who are under the legal age limit, in possession of hard drugs or a source of nuisance. While handling those troubles, personnel try to maximise profit by selling customers as much as possible, though the government limit is 5 grams per person per day. The book closes by looking at how the rules cause violence, and considers their utility.

Notes

1. For information on drugs and drug policy in Amsterdam and the Netherlands, see Booth 2003; Buruma 2007; van der Gouwe, Ehrlich and Van Laar 2009; Jansen 1991; Korf 1995; de Kort and Korf 1992; Leuw 1991; Leuw and Marshall 1994; Monshouwer, van Laar and Vollebergh 2011; NMFA 2008; NMHWS 2003; Ooyen-Houben and Kleemans 2015; Reinarman 2016; Spapens, Müller and van de Bunt 2015; van Solinge 1999; Trimbos Institute 2010; Uitermark 2004.
2. For information on stigmatised versus normal traits and behaviour, see Goffman 1963.
3. See Bieleman et al. 2008; Bieleman, Nijkamp and Bak 2012; MacCoun 2011; Wouters, Benschop and Korf 2010.
4. NMFA 2008.
5. See MacCoun 2011.
6. Hard drugs and soft drugs are also referred to respectively as Category I and Category II illicit substances (NMFA 2008).
7. There is evidence to support this distinction (Trimbos Institute 2010; Nutt, King and Phillips 2010). For information on the health effects of cannabis use, see Hall and Degenhardt 2009; Moore et al. 2007; Volkow et al. 2014; Whiting et al. 2015. Of drug use more generally, see Kleiman, Caulkins and Hawken 2011; Nutt 2012; Nutt, King and Phillips 2010; Zinberg 1984.
8. On harm reduction and drugs, see Denning, Little and Glickman 2003; Marlatt 1996; Rhodes 2009; Zinberg 1984. As a philosophical principle in formal control, see Bentham 1970 (1789).
9. NMFA 2008.
10. Several government bodies have sway over coffeeshops. The national policy is coordinated by the Ministry of Health, Welfare and Sport because drug taking is cast as a health issue rather than a moralistic one. The Ministry of Justice, in particular the public prosecutor, handles law enforcement. The Ministry of the Interior and Kingdom Relations is in charge of more local matters. Within municipalities, policy and law enforcement practices are determined by the so-called 'three way consultations' between the mayor, chief of police and a role akin to a public prosecutor. Olivia, a dealer at Elegy, shed some light on the rationality behind the coffeeshop political landscape: 'In Holland, "politics" is a lot of stuff that is decided by the City and not by the government. I am quite a big fan of the Amsterdam policies, but the national policies are a bit different, which is logical. You have to decide about coffeeshops all through the country, and we are just a shop in the centre of Amsterdam selling weed to tourists. It is a big difference if you are somewhere down South selling weed to French dealers, where the crime rates are a lot higher, of course, and that is much more like organised crime; this is still quite innocent compared to that.'
11. Nor does the licence last indefinitely. 'Every three years you have to renew your new licence. You have to go to the city house and have a new one [made]', explained Mara, owner of Wish. For information on regulating crime and disorder, see articles in *The Annals* issue edited by Freilich and Newman (2018).
12. For a classic work on inspection as a deterrent, see Bentham 1843. In contemporary criminology (including penology), see Clarke 1995, 2009; Clarke and Felson 1993; Felson 2006; Freilich and Newman 2016, 2018; Foucault 1975; Marx 2016; Reynald 2010. In addition, the police checks reflect the notion of focused deterrence otherwise known as 'pulling levers policing'; see Braga and Weisburd 2012, 2015; Braga, Weisburd and Turchan 2018; Corsaro et al. 2012; Kennedy 2006; Kennedy, Kleiman and Braga 2017.
13. There are a few reasons why I did not interview officers about their searches of coffeeshops. First, I did not want coffeeshop personnel to fear that I was 'snitching' to police. Second, I did not have enough time. Third, my colleague Frank van Gemert did undertake such interviews. Because that is his data and the interviews were conducted in Dutch (which I am not fluent in), the findings are not analysed in this book.
14. For information on stigmatised individuals as discreditable versus discredited, see Goffman 1963.
15. For information on officers' demeanour in police-citizen encounters, see Mastrofski, Reisig and McCluskey 2002; Tyler 2003, 2004.
16. For information on citizens' demeanour in police–citizen encounters, see Alpert, Dunham and MacDonald 2004; Sykes and Clark 1975; Worden and Shepard 1996.

17. See Goffman (1963) on out-group alignments. For information on the use of humour by drug dealers, see Dickinson and Wright 2017; more generally among criminals, see Sandberg and Tutenges 2018.
18. For information on the relationship between respectability and punishment, see Black 1976; Cooney 2009.
19. For information on personal and vicarious experiences relating to deterrence and punishment, see Bentham 1970 (1789); Stafford and Warr 1993.
20. Smokers Guide 2015, http://smokersguide.com
21. See also MacCoun 2011.
22. Booth (2003, p. 339) reports 'that the average cannabis café [i.e. coffeeshop] by the late 1990s had a turnover of about $450,000'. He suggests this profitability is why 'café owners were rigorous in their application of the law'.
23. See also MacCoun 2011.
24. I refer to a doorman as such, rather than as a 'doorperson', because this role is almost always filled by a man.
25. I did not systematically gather quantitative data about this issue; rather, it came up during unscripted follow-up questions.
26. For information on employee contracts, see Bassanini, Nunziata and Venn 2009; Engellandt and Riphahn 2005; Gebel 2009; Ichino and Riphahn 2005. I thank Jake Rosenfeld for leading me to this literature.
27. See Toby 1957.
28. For information on off-the-books labour, see Bourgois and Schonberg; Venkatesh 2006.
29. On the perceived certainty and severity of punishment as a deterrent, see Beccaria 1995 (1764); Bentham 1970 (1789); Gibbs 1975. I also recommend the bodies of work produced by Bruce Jacobs, David Kennedy, Thomas Loughran, Ray Paternoster, Alex Piquero, Greg Pogarsky and Daniel Nagin, among others; for example, see Jacobs 2010; Kennedy 2012; Loughran et al. 2011; Nagin 2013a, 2013b.
30. This reflects a general tendency of people, including drug dealers, to recognise risk but think it is unlikely to become real (Jacques and Wright 2015).
31. Tying back to the risk of being personally at fault, Stijn further commented: 'If this guy has drugs on him, some people are under 18, they [police will] give me the fine under my name. My boss will be very pissed off with me.'
32. This distinction relates to that of Bentham between 'direct legislation' and 'indirect legislation' (see Bozzo-Rey, Brunon-Ernst and Quinn 2016). I thank Philip Schofield for pointing this out to me. For an introduction to Bentham, I recommend Schofield 2009.
33. For perspectives on defining what is 'bad', 'wrong', etcetera, see Black 1998; Bentham 1970 (1789).
34. For information on rational choice and crime, see Cornish and Clarke 2014. On restrictive deterrence, see Gibbs 1975; Jacobs 1993, 1996; Jacques and Allen 2014; Moeller, Copes and Hochstetler 2016.
35. For information on self-disclosure of stigmatised traits, see Goffman 1963.
36. For information on the dark figure of crime, see Biderman and Reiss 1967; Coleman and Moynihan 1996; Morrison 1897. On offenders as a better source of crime data than other sources, including policing, see Jacques 2018a; Polsky 1969.
37. For information on lying and withholding information as a general feature of social life, see Goffman 1963. As a methodological issue, see Copes et al. 2015; Dean and Whyte 1958; Sandberg 2010. On the kinds and importance of negative evidence (that is, the absence of data and non-events), see Lewis and Lewis 1980.

1
500 grams

'Never, never. That is the biggest rule we have', answered Gwen when asked if her coffeeshop exceeded the 500 grams limit. To the same query, Luca also responded: 'No, not allowed. If it is too much, we are fucked.' As explained in the Introduction, coffeeshops obey the rule in case police come to check. Selma put it this way: 'Never more than 500 grams because I never want to take the risk of having a control [check] inside. If you have more than 500 then they can close your shop.' Maikel, the owner of Thing, addressed my question by saying: 'No, because I would have to explain myself if the police came to check. I would lose my registration and that would be it, over.' And Stijn stated: 'When they come in and you have more than 500 grams, you are fucked. You have a fine [the first time] and it [if] is two times you are closed.' Personnel must stay vigilant because the police checks occur without warning. To quote Joseph: 'Usually about 450 [is the most it gets up to in here]. We have to be very serious because anything can happen. We don't know when the police are coming. They could come today or come tomorrow, so you have to be alert.'

Early one Tuesday morning, I caught a glimpse of what checks entail. I walked up to At Last to meet its dealer, Maud, with whom I had a scheduled interview. I opened the front door. Standing there was a uniformed officer. His colleague was 10 metres away at the sales counter. The officer at the door said something to me in Dutch. With no idea what he was saying, I requested we speak in English. 'Sorry', he said, 'you have to leave. The shop is closed.' I asked if it would be that way for long. He guessed another 10 minutes.

I walked along a nearby street to pass the time and returned a quarter of an hour later. I went inside, saw both officers at the counter and did a 180-degree turn. However, the policeman who had been at the door shouted that it was OK to stay, so I completed the 360-degree turn, went up to the counter and greeted Maud. She asked 'Isn't this interesting?' 'Yeah, very interesting', I responded. The officer looked confused, so I told him 'I'm a criminologist', thinking that would clarify things. He must have heard me incorrectly, as he replied 'Yeah, I'm a criminal, too.' I emphasised 'No, I'm a crimin*ologist*'. A funny guy, he stayed with his original response of 'Oh, well, I'm a criminal', and joked about why police make good crooks. I did not argue.

The officers left a few minutes later. Maud made me a cup of coffee as I reviewed the informed consent form with her, which I did with every participant.[1] Then the interview commenced. I started the conversation by asking about the officers' visit.

> **Maud:** They came a few minutes before you. I was working and then boom, suddenly they were here. They came [in] like I did something [wrong]. They give you that feeling. They come with so many police officers, I don't know why. This is crazy [I thought]. That was why it felt so like 'boom'. There was one woman, I think, and six or seven guys checking everything: the toilet, the craziest places; weighing the weed.
> **Me:** And do you know what [gram] total they came up with?
> **Maud:** Less than I counted. They said, 'Oh, you have less than you were counting'. I said, 'Oh, so how did you get more? Maybe I did something wrong'. So then I got nervous from it because I did not know.
> **Me:** What was your number?
> **Maud:** 464 grams, I think, and he said we had about 423 grams. He said he did not know how come we had more [listed] than we have [in actuality]. Now we know [what explains] the difference. My boss says [to me after], 'You count the list from yesterday and you make a new list from today [and added them together, but you shouldn't have].' I said, 'Oh, that's why.' I was so nervous. He [the officer who was still here] was waiting for my boss because my boss also has a closet. My boss has the only key of it and they want to know what is inside.

The numbers were off, which may have raised officers' suspicion; ditto the locked closet. Maud was understandably stressed by the encounter with police, given what was at stake.[2] In the end, however, the police found the coffeeshop to be in compliance with the rules. Unlike Maud's arithmetic, that outcome was not a mistake. 'My boss does not take the risk', she asserted. 'You don't take the risk for that, in case they come checking.'

Weighing risk

To give a mental picture, 500 grams of cannabis fills more than a few gallon-size plastic re-sealable bags. It is a lot of cannabis by conventional standards, enough to provide 100 customers with 5 grams each, though few buy that much at once. Most coffeeshops have no pressing need to keep more than 500 grams on the premises. Indeed, about 90 per cent of my participants reported that they did not exceed that amount. To understand further how the supply is managed, I asked personnel to specify the largest amount of cannabis that had been inside their coffeeshops in the past 12 months (Table 1.1).

Table 1.1 Aspects of coffeeshop supply

Coffeeshop	Max. gram count	# Suppliers	# Monthly buys
After Hours	400		
Alike All Over	470	35	4
Angels	<500		
Arrow in the Air		1	8
At Last	500.1		1
Back There	390	5	1
Buzz	497	6	
Chaser	500		
Dollar Room	450	5	8
Doomsday			
Dust	500		
Elegy	500		
Escape Clause	>500		
Everybody	>500		
Execution	800	10	
Eye of the Beholder	450	60	5
Fever	450	4	1
Four of Us	500	1	30
Hitch-Hiker			
Howling Man	500	15	
Judgement Night	>500		
Last Flight	450		
Like a Child	495		
Live Long	500	15	3

(Continued)

Table 1.1 (Continued)

Coffeeshop	Max. gram count	# Suppliers	# Monthly buys
Man in the Bottle	500	16	8
Maple Street	200	1	30
Meek	350	24	2
Mirror Image		2	
Most Unusual	400		
Mr. Bevis	450		
Nice Place to Visit	500	4	5
Nick of Time	500		
No Return	500	20	1
Open Sky	450		
Passage	420		
Perchance	450	1	15
Purple Testament	350	2	
Shrine	<500		
Stop	350	4	30
Sun	460		
The Hour	470	6	1
The Lonely	<500		
The Mighty	480	25	3
Thing	200	1	0
Walking Distance	<500		
What You Need			2
Whole Truth	500		
Wish	480	1	4
World of Difference	500		
World of His Own	400	50	10
Mean (median)	454	13 (5)	8 (4)

Note: An empty cell denotes 'Don't know'. 'Max gram count' refers to largest amount in coffeeshop in the previous 12 months. During first seven interviews I asked only if the 500 grams limit had been exceeded. For these coffeeshops '<500' denotes 'No' and '>500' denotes 'Yes'. Also, Mike knew the limit had exceeded 500 grams, but not by how much; thus his answer for Judgement Night is recorded as '>500'.

Some establishments come nowhere near exceeding the limit. The lowest total is 200 grams, a number given to me for Thing and Maple Street. Anna said of the latter: 'Never, ever more than 500 grams. We keep it lower, 200 or something. We don't want to be over it because [of the risk].' The next lowest amount is 350 grams at Meek, Purple Testament and Stop. Other coffeeshops set the absolute maximum closer to 500 grams, but leave breathing room. The safe space ranges from a couple of scores to a few grams below the government-set limit. 'About 460 grams' is the figure gave by Claire, who deals at Sun. Mara put the figure at 'Almost 5[00], 480 I believe it is'. And a manager of Whole Truth, Lizzie, told me: '490 [is the maximum we go to], but it never goes over. It always stays under [500]. We are not allowed [to have more].'

Coffeeshops do violate this rule, however. The finding that about 90 per cent fully complied means, of course, that about 10 per cent did not. Also, 11 of the coffeeshops reportedly bring their supply up to the very maximum allowable limit of 500 grams. They, too, probably break the rule, without being aware of it. This is because drug tourists[3] purchase cannabis at one coffeeshop, smoke some of it and venture to another coffeeshop with the residual in their pockets or bags – a process that repeats several times in a day or across several days. Thus coffeeshops that stock te maximum 500 grams of cannabis are susceptible to being pushed over the limit by customers who bring their own stock inside.

Personnel also choose to violate the 500 grams rule – something not always approved of by owners or managers. I talked with Charlotte, a server at Nick of Time, about how a coffeeshop can be in violation because of business 'under the table'. Though her coffeeshop never intentionally overstocked *per se*, she appreciated that the limit could be broken: 'Some [dealers] do other [side] deals. The dealers do their own things, not really from the coffeeshop. If someone comes and checks, sometimes there is 100 [grams not accounted for, potentially].' Charlotte is saying that dealers selfishly sell their own cannabis instead of the coffeeshop's stock, thereby increasing, in effect, their hourly wage and the risk to the establishment.

In other cases, exceeding the 500 grams rule is a management decision. Finn reported the largest amount during the preceding year, specifically 800 grams in Execution. He also told me of a time the police found even more there. It happened a few years ago,[4] and resulted in 'an extremely pleasant altercation with a judge'. He was being sarcastic. 'I had more than 500 grams on the premises and they found it, 900 [grams].' The violation was punished with 'a fine, about €1,200'. He took the loss in his stride, comparing it to the life of a sports professional: 'If you are a professional football player, you can get injured. You might not like it, but that is what you chose to do.'

Clearly that experience failed to deter Finn from keeping more stock on hand than allowed, as he continues to do so.[5] Other coffeeshops change trajectory after being caught and punished.[6] Jana, a dealer at World of Difference, described an incident that led to its reformed operation:

> They [police] come to check that all things are right, and to check [that] you have no more than 500 grams in the shop. They found 30 grams too much. They kept me responsible for that 30 grams too much. It was a lot of things coming together. First, they get irritated because I didn't have my ID on me. Then they get irritated because there was too much. And then I didn't have a key for the safe, so there were a lot of things. I didn't really agree with the way it went because I am not responsible for the things that go on around here. If my boss had too much they [police] should not try to make me responsible because I am the only one in the shop.

The series of calamities resulted in Jana being jailed 'until somebody – my former boyfriend – brought my passport to the station'. I asked Jana, 'Do you guys ever have more than 500 grams here any more?' Her answer demonstrates that coffeeshops become obedient because of sanction experiences:

> No, never again. Before we start, we always count how much we have, and that is about 450. It was really, really bad [being in jail], because in the beginning I was always thinking, 'Yeah, If I go to the station it is not nice, but it is not that bad'. Then I was there for eight hours and then I was thinking, 'Yeah, I appreciate my freedom of smoking a cigarette or drinking a coffee when I want'. Also, the station where they put me was with a lot of junkies and it was really, really bad that you cannot go where you want to go.

Checking

Personnel keep within the 500 grams through constant accounting, or what they refer to as 'checking'.[7] Ruben, for example, said the shop's supply is kept 'a little bit under [500], like 480. We check a lot'. When I asked Wouter, a dealer at Live Long, if the total ever breaches 500 grams, he answered: 'No, because we check that, we check that. Between 4 and 5 hundred [is what it gets to], but we check it.'

Checking occurs where cannabis is sold: the dealer counter. In some coffeeshops this counter stands apart from that for food and drink. In others, the counters for cannabis, food and drink are adjacent or one and the same.[8] Either way, coffeeshops store stock on, under or behind the dealer counter, where the cannabis menu tends to be found too. Menus are discussed further in the next chapter.

Checking in the old days was a pen-and-paper process, but this method still persists at less prosperous or old-fashioned coffeeshops. It works by personnel starting the day or shift with a known number of grams in the shop, for example 450. They subtract each gram as it is sold and add each gram delivered by a runner, owner or manager, or a supplier. I often watched Selma do this at Man in the Bottle, where I was a regular. When a customer ordered marijuana or hashish, or 'hash' for short, she grabbed her pen and a single sheet of paper divided into many rows and three columns labelled with type, quantity and price. For each sale, that information is recorded in a different row. As needed, the entries are subtracted from the starting amount to determine how much cannabis is inside the coffeeshop. This shows the types and quantities required to restock up to the self-imposed or government limit.

By the time of my study, many coffeeshops had transitioned from the pen-and-paper method to electronic accounting. This is done with a special computer, or computers, connected to the coffeeshop's digital scale(s). To use these, a dealer tells the computer which type of cannabis is being sold; this looks the same as servers tapping screens in restaurants. Before or after communicating information to the computer, the dealer puts the selection on the scale, aiming to parcel out precisely the amount ordered by the customer. The scale relays that amount to the computer, which then multiples that number by the pre-programmed price and displays it on the monitor.

Though more expensive than the old-school accounting method, the electronic method is easier for personnel to deal with; it is also more accurate. In James's words, the benefit of computer-based checking is knowing 'exactly to .00 [grams] how much you have in stock at all times'. Jack described the system in more detail:

> The legal limit is 500 grams, everything included, and that includes our cakes, our joints, our weed and our hash. We keep it at about 470, just to be on the safe side, just in case one of the staff members has a 10 gram bag in their pocket. We are very strict. When we got this whole computerised system, we [now] have a system and spreadsheets and all sorts. I can push a button now and see exactly how many grams are in the building.

Figure 1.1 A piece of marijuana weighing about 0.5 to 1 gram. Coffeeshops using the pre-weigh system would have this 'nug' ready for sale in a plastic bag, labelled with weight and price. Coffeeshops using the free-weigh system would select one or more 'nugs' from a plastic or metal container to build up the correct weight on the scale. *Source*: author

As Jack mentions, the cannabis products of coffeeshops include loose marijuana and hash, pre-rolled joints and cakes – or, more generally, 'space' food. Marijuana is a green plant substance while hash is a hard, clay-like substance made from the resin of marijuana (Figures 1.1 and 1.2). Across coffeeshops in the 1012, more than a 100 marijuana strains and 50 kinds of hash were available during my time in Amsterdam. Twenty-two is the largest number of marijuana strains that I saw sold at an establishment: four is the fewest, and about 10 is typical. For hash, the most I noticed being sold at a single coffeeshop is 13 types, with four being the least and about six the norm.

There are two ways in which coffeeshops sell 'loose' cannabis, meaning cannabis not already rolled into joints or baked into food. One is the 'free-weigh system', in which marijuana and hash are weighed and bagged in front of the customer. Until sold, each variety of loose marijuana is stored in its own plastic or metal container that can comfortably hold between 10 and 20 grams. When a customer orders a strain, the dealer reaches into the appropriate container and weighs out the requested amount. With a computerised system, this is automatically subtracted from the gram total; if pen and paper are used, it is written down.

The 'pre-weigh system' is different. The weighing and bagging of loose cannabis is done off-site. There are two ways of storing and selling

Figure 1.2 Two large blocks of hash, each weighing several grams. Coffeeshops using the pre-weigh system cut this hash into small portions and place them in labelled plastic bags. Coffeeshops using the free-weigh system cut these blocks with a large kitchen knife when a customer places an order. The dealer seeks to cut off the exact amount ordered to give the customer a solid piece. *Source*: author

pre-weighed bags. The more common of the two resembles the free-weigh process in that the bags are stored in containers, each of a single variety. The other way resembles a jewellers where items are displayed in a glass case, except that here the items are cannabis in plastic bags. Customers look it over until they spot what they want and then inform the dealer. I asked Luca why they do it that way at The Lonely. 'Because you want to see what you are buying', he explained. 'You want to see what you buy. That is the whole idea.'

In addition to loose marijuana and hash, coffeeshops sell pre-rolled joints. Three types are found on menus: marijuana mixed with tobacco; hash mixed with tobacco; and marijuana alone, referred to as 'pure'.[9] Edibles are another option. When ingested, these produce a psychoactive effect, albeit a slightly different high to that experienced by smoking. In addition, the effect of edibles takes longer to feel and lasts for longer. In Amsterdam, the word 'space' is added to their name to denote psychopharmacological properties. Customers can find space cookies, space cakes, space muffins and space brownies in a few flavours, but mostly chocolate.

Pre-rolled joints and edibles count toward the 500 grams limit. Emma mentioned how pre-rolled joints weigh into their accounting: 'We will have a maximum of maybe 350 [grams], but we usually try to keep well under it, because they count 0.3 grams for a joint, so you have to be well under the 500 grams, so we always make sure.'[10] Stijn commented on how edibles add up: 'We do 400 [grams maximum] because we have space cakes, and we have about 100 [of them] and that is 40 grams. Max in the shop is 450. Yeah man, no more than 500 grams.'

From a business standpoint, offering a greater variety is good, to the extent it generates sales. Yet it increases the difficulty of checking and restocking. For instance, Dean initially said of Dollar Room's supply, 'There are no problems getting it', but then corrected himself: 'Well, that is not really true. Sometimes you have problems, [such as] that we don't have that kind of [variety of] weed or something. Special strains, sometimes you have it, sometimes you don't have it.'

Because of such difficulties, coffeeshops wind up listing more products on their respective menus than can be reliably restocked. This is evident by looking at how menus evolve over time. As of November 2009, for example, that of one coffeeshop listed nine marijuana strains, eight types of hash, five pre-rolled joint varieties and 13 flavours of space cake – by far the most I ever saw. A year later, that menu showed one less marijuana strain, one less hash option and no space cake; all were crossed out with a pen.

Restocking

As with any retail business, running out of items may result in missed sales.[11] To prevent this problem, businesses stock more than needed to fill the immediate demand. Yet coffeeshops, especially the most successful ones, have their hands tied by the 500 grams rule. They cannot simply overstock cannabis on the premises, so instead they regularly restock. This occurs daily during closing time. At the end of each night, staff check how much cannabis remains to determine what needs to be replenished before reopening. Selma, who opened Man in the Bottle most days, told me how the restocking process worked there:

> I wait for a text [message] from my colleague at 11 o'clock at night, or 12 before we close. He would put for me on the text the amount we have in total, the total after closing time. So like [if] he had left 220 grams that means I can fill it up with 280 grams [in the morning when I open]. And then he makes a list of the stuff we need, and then I make the whole calculation of what I take, yeah because it is always 500 or less.

Man in the Bottle is not one of the busiest coffeeshops, so they usually wait to restock after their door has shut for the evening. Other establishments make many more sales and are in constant jeopardy of selling out – a problem exacerbated by offering more variety. Though good for the bottom line, it causes a restocking problem. As Gijs explained:

> You can only have 500 grams in the shop. You can imagine that we have 27 kinds of weed and 20 kinds of hash – so basically you can have 10 grams from every kind roughly in the shop to stay under the 500. So you can imagine if somebody comes in, buys 5 grams from that kind [of variety], and the next person says they want 5 [of the same], then that's finished.

When a coffeeshop sells out of a variety, one option is to '86' it (i.e. remove it from the menu) for the day and restock once the door shuts. The cost of that choice is lost sales, so instead coffeeshops restock the supply while still open. A role strictly dedicated to restocking, day or night, is that of the runner.[12] 'One goes, one comes, one goes, one comes', Imran said of them. If you keep your eyes open in a busy coffeeshop, it is easy enough to see them at work. Based on appearance alone, they look like many of the customers: casually dressed, often wearing a backpack. But runners take their bag behind the dealer counter and unload tens to hundreds of grams. Before leaving they put the new goods in their proper place and add them to the books, or hand over those tasks to an on-duty dealer or manager.

Though usually Man in the Bottle restocked while closed, I did see a delivery there due to an emergency outage of space cakes. The boss was on holiday with his wife, who usually baked them. Selma's sister was asked to make some instead; she agreed to whip up 10 pans of space cake in exchange for €150. While I was drinking my coffee at the counter, a guy rode up on a bicycle. He came inside the shop and handed a backpack full of space cakes to Selma. She counted them, wrote down the number and stuffed the brownies into the coffeeshop's mini-fridge.

Though cannabis deliveries are made in plain sight, personnel discussed them with an air of secrecy, if they mentioned them at all. When interviewees were asked about how cannabis gets to their coffeeshop, they commonly feigned ignorance. This secretiveness is a source of insight; it shows personnel are concerned about the *de facto* risks of transporting large amounts of cannabis around Amsterdam.

But almost anyone who works in a coffeeshop must know something about the cannabis delivery process. For example, when Claire was questioned about it, her immediate reply was: 'I don't know, I don't check this.' 'But you are smart, you watch', I remarked. Then she admitted the truth: 'Yes, well, lots of times in a day.' Similarly, I asked a server, Charlotte, if it is anyone's job to bring cannabis to Nick of Time. She initially replied, 'I don't know. They don't talk about it with me', then added: 'Well, [there are] three [runners] that I know of for sure, and then maybe there are other people.' Posed with the same question, Stijn at first declared he could not answer, but continued: 'Yes, of course, there is someone bringing the stuff in, but I really don't want to say. There is always somebody coming to bring the stuff, at some parts of the day.' And Sophie, in reference to the runners who deliver to Hitch-Hiker, said simply, 'They work for my owner. It's three guys we know, but we don't really know what they do here. They just bring the weed every day.'

Runners do not simply show up randomly. That would be too risky, as it could put the coffeeshop in possession of more than 500 grams. Rather, personnel make orders that the runners fulfil. Mike, a dealer at Judgement Night, described how he and his colleagues called on runners:

> There is another form of employee who basically goes into the place where the weed is stored, and comes to the coffeeshop every now and then with a certain amount. It is about 100 grams. Basically the coffeeshop cannot have more than 500 grams of weed inside, so that's the problem when you have a lot of things to sell. For example, you have one top seller [strain] that sells like 40 grams, so you always need to have a lot of this one. You have weed that you sell almost every 15 to 30 minutes. You need to have it there because many people come just for that weed. So [imagine] a customer comes and you say it is over [out of stock], so you don't make money. So you call this guy who comes with what you want. It's on a mobile phone that stays always in the coffeeshop and is nobody's phone. This is the phone for the runners, and that is it. Just the runners have the number [for the phone], nobody else. When you order things with the runner, you cannot say to him, 'Give me 25 grams of this', so you just say the name of the product that you want. That happens twice a day on a quiet day, but on a busy day it can happen about six times. It depends how much you sell.

Runners are not the only people who deliver cannabis to coffeeshops. Owners do too. When I questioned Maikel, who recall owns Thing, about getting cannabis there, he simply told me 'I bring the stuff'. Owners rely on family to participate in the supply chain, too. 'My parents do that for me', said Mara. 'They retired and my father hates to do nothing, so he says, "OK, I bring it every morning". Sometimes, I will do it myself.' Emma's boss is normally responsible for deliveries, but she also discussed how he benefits from free family labour: 'If need be and my boss is on holiday, two of my boss's nephews and his little brother have to bring it. But they don't get paid for it because it's family. There are people bringing it, but it is not their job.'

The job description of some managers includes delivery. Speaking about the deliverers for Like a Child, Gwen told me: 'They are assistant managers. Yeah, the weed store managers, and then [there is] one large manager who takes control of everything. Those three are also for the other coffeeshop [that is under the same name].'

Instead of making delivery part of an employee's primary job description, another option is to pay them for the duty on top of their regular salary. This is how it worked at Alike All Over, according to Jack:

> Generally the boss [owner] will do it during the week when he is here. But during the weekend there is somebody, well maybe two of them, whose responsibility it is to refill. That's part of like an extra thing on top of their regular job with us [as dealers].

Independent contractors are yet another type of person involved in delivering cannabis to coffeeshops. Kamila referred to these individuals as 'private persons, like about two or three persons'. When I asked if they are considered to be personnel, she replied, 'Well, they are different'. Similarly, Adam, a dealer at Howling Man, said of the deliverers: 'The manager is one of them, and there are two or three other people who bring stuff. They don't work here. They are guys who work for the big boss and they have their own specialities.'

Storing excess grams

When a deliverer arrives with product in tow, proper accounting calls for the addition to be logged and added to the total. Like many technologies, accounting is both a way to maintain and to escape control.[13] By keeping track of what comes in and goes, personnel know with certainty how close they are to exceeding the 500 grams limit. And when they see there is too much, they can take remedial measures to reduce the risk of being caught in violation by police.

One way to prevent too much cannabis from being inside the coffeeshop is to tell the deliverer to stay outside until enough of the existing supply is sold to replenish. Adam provided an example:

> They [runners] come twice a day. Basically, every shift orders its new stock that they need, and we have to make sure that we stay under 500 grams. Well obviously they don't just 'try to': they do. You can see everything on the scales, on the computer, to tell you how much. Sometimes they bring a bit too much and then they wait for another half an hour, until you have sold enough.

It makes sense that personnel have deliverers bide their time off the premises, but that puts them at risk of prison time. This is because, remember, possession of large quantities of cannabis outside a coffeeshop is a *de facto* offence. From what I heard, though, deliverers are rarely apprehended. Two circumstances heighten the risk. One is when the police set up a road block. 'They close off the street', Selma told me, 'and everybody who goes in and out has to show their ID or passport. Then if they think you have something on you, they have the right to search you.' Luckily for deliverers, road blocks are rare. In Luca's words: 'Those are things you have to watch out for. This past weekend, they put it on the news that they were going to stop all people on bikes and check their bags. That is not very often. It is the first time I heard of it.'

The more likely problem for deliverers is a surprise police inspection at the coffeeshop. If caught at the wrong moment, such as outside the door, the person with the delivery is in hot water. If inside, the coffeeshop is at risk of exceeding the 500 grams limit. To prevent such an occurrence, personnel call to warn deliverers when the police show up. As Mike explained: 'If the police come, the first thing you have to do is call him [the deliverer]. I know for sure it happened in the past. The runner was about to come, the police came inside and the first thing you do is call him.'

Whereas those troubles are situational, the 500 grams rule presents a constant problem. Breaking it jeopardises the coffeeshop's survival, but keeping the supply elsewhere puts individuals at risk of serious punishment. To quote Sophie: 'The big problem is that we have to get supplies in a half legal and half illegal way.' As a solution, personnel store excess stock in secret places. Finn gave an example of such practice:

> Especially [on] busy days like the Cannabis Cup[14] in November or New Year's Eve, we might stash an additional 200, 300 grams [on site]. The additional inventory that I need for logistical reasons on those days is harder to find for the police.

Another coffeeshop I frequented is Everything. On a couple of occasions I observed personnel secretly store cannabis inside the back of a small vending machine.[15] These machines hang on the walls of many coffeeshops. They are about 0.5 to 1 m in height and width, and 0.25 m in depth. A glass pane reveals different items for sale, such as lighters, rolling papers, grinders and other provisions. Below each item is a price listed in euros. If a customer wants to buy one of these items, he or she presses a button to select the product and slots in the appropriate amount of coins. The product can then be collected from the hole in the bottom.

Within the machine is an area visible only when opened from the side with a key. This is the space from which items drop into the take-out port, but also where Everything stores excess cannabis. As I watched covertly, I saw an employee enter the coffeeshop and unlock the machine. He reached inside and pulled out a stack of cash. He quickly shuffled it into his large, bright blue Albert Heijn shopping bag – common in the 1012 because 'AH' is the largest Dutch supermarket chain; several of its locations are scattered in the vicinity.[16] Then the runner unloaded 10 to 20 containers into the back of the vending machine, locked it and left. These containers looked exactly like those stored behind the dealer counter: about a fist or two in size, made of hard plastic, with a re-sealable cover to keep the cannabis fresh, with a different container for each one. I think it is safe to assume that the containers in the vending machine find their way behind the dealer counter, but are stowed in the meantime so the *visible* gram total stays under 500.

Coffeeshops also store extra stock in adjacent space outside the legally defined confines of the coffeeshop. Technically this is off the premises and so not checkable by police. Mike told me about such a spot:

> In the boxes [out of which the cannabis is sold], there is always less than 500 grams. But, for example, it happened in the past they had it in the basement because the runner comes. What happens is you have to guess [what] they are going to sell in half an hour, so that he brings you [all] the weed [you will need]. If he comes with more [than you end up needing] and you have 510 grams in the coffeeshop at that moment [for example,] the first thing you do is take the 5 or 10 grams more into the basement or somewhere else, never into the boxes. It is like everything [is] hidden.

Off-premises stash spots reduce a coffeeshop's risk of being found in violation of the 500 grams rule, but do increase the risk of serious legal trouble if discovered by police. The danger is to whoever occupies or owns the space. Unless restocking is totally outsourced, coffeeshop owners and managers have to decide on the safest place to keep their stock until delivery time. Unlike deliveries, off-site storage places are not a visible part of working at a coffeeshop. Thus some personnel genuinely know nothing about it, or little more than that. Lola, for instance, told me: 'The boss, he buys [the stock], puts in a place that nobody knows, and then every day he gets [some of] it back and you have a supply for the whole day.' When I asked Mike if he knows the off-premises storage location, he answered: 'I don't really know, but I can guess it is at the house of this guy. That sounds to me logical. But I am not sure. I never ask. I have no sure information, but that is what I think.'

Again this withholding of information – from personnel and from me – is evidence that the proverbial back door of coffeeshops is risky business. A degree of common sense dictates, after all, not to tell a stranger where a large quantity of a valuable, illegal goods are stored. A few personnel gave details, however. In line with Mike's guess, the only off-premises stash spots I learned of are private residences. 'I am not supposed to have more than 500 grams in the shop, so I have to keep it at home so it is not here', Maikel admitted. Max thought that was a bad idea, noting, 'As a coffeeshop owner, it's best you don't put stuff like that in your house'. Yet he acknowledged that Everything's supply is 'always in a safe house'.

For 'eight to nine weeks', Selma kept Man in the Bottle's supply in her home. To contextualise the experience, she starts with a description of how it came to be there:

> I started working here in April, and then in May I heard they [owners] were going on holiday, so they were planning to close the shop for six weeks. That meant they would fire me and then hire me again after six weeks, when they came back again. And I couldn't handle that – six weeks, no job, no contract, nothing. Then I wanted to go and talk with my boss to say that 'OK, for me it was no problem if he wants to close for six weeks, but then I just need some money for this period, and then I can start working again and I would pay it back'. While I was saying this, I asked him is there no option to stay open and he was like 'Yeah, if you want to keep all the stuff in your house. I trust you. Then we can just stay open'.

For me to make the decision to do that was pretty easy because I would just be able to work every day and earn my money and get extra money. I had a total going through my house [of] 18.5 kilos because we had some stuff coming out of Finland. It became a big mess in that corner [of my apartment] because I made upstairs a nice table with a scale and everything. I had one box like this [*c.*16 x 12.5 x 10 in, about the size of a banker's box] and I had hash in there and then, you know, those big blue garbage bags, I had three really big blue garbage bags and my colleague was already telling me 'It's a lot, a kilo of marijuana is huge'. I didn't know how it would look like and it was just very big. For the moment I had my sister coming over one day and I was like 'Yeah, I want to show you something, look at this, look at this'. Yeah, it was really nice. Still, it was strange because I really felt I was doing something not right.

Regular suppliers

Coffeeshops sell cannabis above board, but their supply comes from the underground market. Jana described the problems caused by this paradox:

> It is very hard to work with this situation. There are so many elements of the black markets, so it is very hard. You are still sometimes being treated like criminals [by the government], but you have a business and you pay taxes, you pay rent and [do] everything that the police tell you [that] you need to do.

In general personnel were reluctant to talk about the supply side of business. For instance, when I inquired as to how Passage obtains its product, Elias, a dealer there, was apprehensive. 'I don't think my boss will like [me talking about] it, and I have to respect that' was his reply. When posed the same question about Open Sky, Joseph stated: 'That question I will not answer. It is personal and I do not want to disclose that here. I am sorry. I am not going to say anything at all.' Despite expressing trust in me, Jana was also unwilling to discuss the matter with respect to World of Difference: 'I am not going to answer that one. It is the part of the business that is in a grey area. I am not the owner of this business. I know you won't do anything with it, but I don't even want to take that risk.'

Other personnel could not talk about the supply because they knew nothing about it. 'I have no idea. I can't tell you that. I really have no clue', admitted Stefan, a dealer at After Hours. Likewise, Stijn, Victor and Noah told me, respectively, 'No idea'; 'I don't know shit about suppliers'; 'It is all done without my knowledge'. Lower-level employees looked at the back door as beyond their purview. 'I really don't know [about it]', said Luca. 'I only work here, and the rest is none of my business.' Personnel such as Olivia, a dealer at Elegy, thought ignorance is bliss: 'I don't know. I really would rather not know. They really don't tell us. I am very happy that I don't know.' And though Gwen managed Like a Child, her responsibility was more for food and drink than cannabis. So when questioned about the coffeeshop's supply, she responded cautiously: 'That I don't know. That is information I don't have.' She then detailed why not:

> It's something I don't want to know, to be honest. I think that's a bit too deep down for [me to have] information. I think that is something that has to do with the managers and people that actually make that decision, not something that the girls who stand behind the bar have to know. Like, for instance, the dealer does not know how much I pay at the grocery store to buy whatever I have to buy, you know what I mean? So, I think it is information that maybe you could know, but it is not really necessary to know, I think. Of course, I would like to know in a way, but I don't think it is our level to know.

Other employees knew a little more about their coffeeshop's supply. When asked about that of Purple Testament, Emma initially answered, 'No clue at all'. After I politely pressed her, she added, 'It is more than one [supplier], but I have no idea how many'. Then I probed for further information on how the money and cannabis are transferred at the back door. She speculated by generalising from her experience working there:

> I think it is usually a direct transfer [meaning that the business is not done on credit]. And I think maybe there are a couple of people that you work with that you can first give them the money and then get the weed, but that would be only people that you have known for a long time and that you trust. Other than that, I am pretty sure it is always direct. That is logical. It is the same here: when I sell the weed, I want the money from the people before they start smoking it. Otherwise, they forget it altogether.

Fortunately, some personnel were able and willing to talk at length about the two major issues involved in obtaining a supply for resale: who does it come from? How are transactions made with them? One of the findings is surprising and is examined in the next section. I also learned that coffeeshops have 'regular' suppliers, as many people could guess.[17] By definition, they are persons who supply a coffeeshop 'over and over', to use the words of Hassan, a manager at Shrine. Maikel told me: 'I have a regular [supplier] I order from; four years now.' Other coffeeshops, such as Dollar Room, have more than one regular supplier. To quote Dean: 'We definitely do not have just one guy. Maybe at least five or something, at least.'

Purchasers rely on regular wholesalers because it saves time and energy compared to searching for new suppliers. Victor put it this way: 'Basically, we work with the same people. If something goes good once, why wouldn't you use them again?' When in need of product, then, purchasers simply contact people with whom they successfully did business in the past. 'I call him up', said Hassan. 'I say what I need. I say I want that amount. It goes like that. He says, "OK, no problem, I'll get you that amount".' 'When I am running out of it', Maikel explained, 'then I call for it. I don't wait until it gets finished. So say 20 grams [left] for me to get more White Widow.'

I asked how long it takes to be delivered. 'There is no delay', he answered. 'Sometimes we [get a] delay because of transport – one or two hours.' Moreover, having a regular supplier ensures a steady stream of product. This was a factor mentioned by Jasper: 'If you have a couple of guys who sell you weed, that is very important that you have that, 'cause then you have the choice of taking the weed and stuff [before it is sold to others] because we sell a lot.'

Another benefit of buying from regular suppliers is that it confers better bargains. When the supply-chain question came up with Finn, he responded:

> I never buy anything. I have never engaged in any transaction larger than five grand and I have never been found with grass outside the coffeeshop. I don't want to lose my licence because of some fuck-up by the police. Our police force is getting dumber by the year. And, of course, the smart policemen do not walk in uniform. I have a specialist who knows more about these things than I do.

Then he called over the specialist, Florist, to join the conversation. Among other things, he explained how having regular suppliers stabilises fluctuations in market price:

> The grower sets the price. If the price is too high, he will not get rid of his stock, and then he has to lower his price. [However,] right now it is summer and it gets hot, so the yield is not so high and people are on holiday [so there is less supply to be had]. The price stays the same [though] because when it is easy enough they also want their price. They are not short-term thinkers. You have to think in the long term because people have so much choice and you can buy it from somebody else. So, if you sell it to me more expensive because there is not much around then I will not buy from you when there is enough around because you asked [of] me a high price.

A further advantage of dealing with regular suppliers is they are more trustworthy, having shown themselves not to be defrauders. This is especially important for businesspeople who cannot use the court system to resolve disputes.[18] When I asked Lola if her boss ever buys from strangers, she replied: 'He has his own people whom he trusts, and I think he sticks with those people. I think about three or four people. He is going to buy from one of those guys what he needs for the moment. It depends on what you are searching for because you have so many types of weed.' Meanwhile Jack told me: 'We will deal with anyone we know and trust. With strangers it takes a little while. It is less likely to happen that we will take weed off someone we don't have any knowledge of, if someone just turns up with some weed. Generally, it is the people we know and trust that we do business with.'

Some suppliers sell product that they personally grow.[19] Legend has it that there are massive fields of marijuana to be found throughout Holland, but this never came up as a direct source of supply. Instead, personnel referred to suppliers as 'house guys'. At the time of this study, the Dutch policy is to tolerate the growing of four plants at each residence.[20] Clearly visible from my apartment, for example, was a neighbour's balcony with an impressive garden of marijuana plants. It is *de facto* illegal to sell the product, but people do so anyway, with coffeeshops as prime customers.[21]

Other suppliers sell product grown by someone else. Wouter said of middlemen and women: 'People who are growers sell it, but we have also people who buy it from the growers and sell it to the coffeeshops. They are between it.' At Maple Street, Anna told me: 'We don't buy it [directly]. There is somebody in between.' Mara detailed how her coffeeshop works with an intermediary:

> I have somebody, and she takes care of that [the supply part of the business]. She is not on the list [as personnel]. When she sells

> us something, she takes something. We pay her once a week. It depends how much you buy, but every week she gets money. When she buys something for 3,000 [euros, for example,] she sells it to us for 3,100 [with 100 euros as profit]. The normal ones [strains] we buy in kilos, that's normal. Almost every time it's a kilo. But when it is the more expensive one, like a Cheese [strain] or something, then we buy half a kilo [for] between 3,000 and 3,400 [euros].

Intermediaries are part of the trade in marijuana and hash. They are especially important to the latter because it is more of an import product. Mike believed that the 'weed is grown here. I know for sure that some hash in the place that I worked, where I used to work, that was imported. For sure they are. For sure it is imported from India, Afghanistan, India, Pakistan and Nepal'. In Ruben's estimation, 'The hash is mostly from Moroccan people, the Moroccan hash, and the black hash it varies – 99 per cent is foreign: Moroccan, Nepalese, Afghani.'

A coffeeshop could grow its own cannabis. However, I only heard of this being done by one coffeeshop, which I leave unnamed because it is widely known to do so. 'The owner grows most of his stuff himself somewhere secretly', its representative admitted.

Because hash is manufactured, not simply grown, what it means to be a 'hash supplier' is slightly different. Other than making it yourself, the next closest option is to buy hash at its source, as did Selma's boss:

> With the hash it is different than with the marijuana. My boss is Moroccan. He knows what quality hash is. He wants to see it in a block, smell it, burn it to know exactly what the quality is, because he knows what the best hash is. So he will never let somebody else buy it for him. He takes it himself from Morocco. Or he gets it from Spain, he drives there, or he buys it from here when he sees it [is high quality].

A variant of the self-grow approach is for coffeeshops to cultivate relationships with their regular growers, thereby improving the profitability of all parties. Consider what Max said Everybody does:

> We work with people that we know very well, and even we give them help if they need it. We point them in a certain direction. If you have a problem with growing it then we send somebody, he can help you out. We have a guy, 'Dr. Greenthumbs' we will call him, and he will make house calls if they have a disease or anything is

> wrong. We started to work that way because sometimes there is a big crisis because of all the [police] pressure – they want to catch all the growers – and we need to protect ourselves against that. So we made arrangements with certain people so that we are sure that we will get enough products for the shop.

Something similar goes on at Escape Clause, according to Gijs:

> We have our small-time growers, who are nice people. So imagine I'm a grower. I keep my weed in the cellar, or in a cupboard in the house, and maybe I have a kilo of weed. For each type of weed there is a certain price if you grow it perfectly, so there is a minimum price and a maximum price. If it's perfect you get a maximum price; if you didn't give a fuck and you just grew your plants, then you get a minimum price. A lot of people you have good contacts with – you advise them what to do, stuff like that, so they grow good end products. That is part of our policy: we work with small-time growers. [Other shops] have around the [time of the] Cannabis Cup a nice list of things specially grown for the Cannabis Cup to impress the Americans. Soon as the Cannabis Cup is over, it's all sold out. People can't get it any more. We think differently, and this is why we have these close contacts with our growers. We try to stick with people we know.

Sample-based suppliers

Some coffeeshop purchaser–supplier relationships are based in pre-existing friendships.[22] Luuk said of his suppliers: 'Some I know already for 10, 15 years. The one I know the longest is 20 years, and the most recent is 5 years. Most are friends.' A manager at The Hour, Jasper, described the suppliers as the owner's 'friends'. 'They start [off their relationship while] little boys', he explained. Mara was friends with her supplier before owning Wish, so requested her services once it opened.

If purchasers and regular suppliers do not know each other prior to doing business together, how do they meet? There may be many ways, such as chance encounters and networking. Most commonly, though, back door relations result from the sample process.[23] You may recall that Jack remarked 'someone just turns up with some weed'. That is not a figure of speech: it is literally what happens. 'You got a lot of people doing that', to quote Lola. Wouter reported: 'sometimes people come once a week [with a sample]'. And Selma told me: 'My boss has one or two steady people he takes his marijuana from, and the rest is just people that come in [with samples].'

The sample process begins, Ruben explained, when 'people just walk in and ask if you need something'. Likewise, Mara said that sample-based suppliers 'just come in, bring a sample, [say] "I've got something nice", and they show what they have'. Maud stated: 'I see people coming and if they say, "Hey, I got some stuff, are you the one who is buying?" I say "No". It is my boss who makes the final decision.'

As touched on by Maud above, not all personnel have the authority to make purchases. If the buyer is not present at the coffeeshop, on-duty personnel ask for the supplier's information. Selma 'tell[s] them to leave the sample, write down the phone number, what it is, and how much they want to have for it. Then I give it to my boss and then he decides what to do with it'. Similarly, Hanna asked them to leave their number. 'I [will] hold it here and I give it to the owner. I will let the owner call.'

Another option is to inform the supplier of when the purchaser will be present. 'With the weed', Ruben commented, 'you always ask them to show you something, and they have to come back when the boss is here. I can take a sample, I can look to see if it is good, but he has the final say of whether to buy it.' Whereas he told suppliers to come back, other personnel, such as Gwen, told them to go elsewhere: '[I] tell them to go to the main office and then they can ask if anyone is interested. If they want it then they will have contact, but there is nothing whatsoever that I can do about that.'

Personnel do not entertain every sample-based supplier, however. When Stefan and I started talking about this issue, he said of their visits:

> It happens, people come in. If it happens, they get the same answer: 'I don't know nothing. I don't know nothing about that.' I don't like to [deal with that], so I just say I don't know anything about it. None of us [employees], as far as I'm aware, make those decisions. I never see any of that. I just work behind the bar [dealer counter], so I don't see any of that.

There are other reasons for keeping out of the sampling process. 'I don't take samples from Dutch men', explained Selma, 'because I don't trust them. They can be police officers, undercover or something. I always tell them to come back at 5 o'clock [to see my boss].'[24] I asked for a concrete example, so she gave this one:

> These Dutch men, they were like in their forties, they started coming in four months ago. They wanted to sell hash. I really didn't trust it, and then they were like at one point, because we were talking for like 10 to 15 minutes, they were like, 'Oh, let's have a cup of coffee'. So they had a cup of coffee, and then he took the big block of hash out and he started rolling [a joint] from that. Then I knew he was not undercover because you cannot walk with a block of hash like this in your pocket; nobody, even undercover police who try and catch somebody in a coffeeshop, that is impossible. I told them, 'If you want to come, you come at 5 o'clock and talk with my boss.'

'The weed supply', Jack stated, 'is very much an open market place. If someone has a sample, we will look at a sample.' Samples are not only looked at, but also evaluated with other senses.[25] Jack continued: 'The chance of me bothering to show it to the boss is pretty slim, unless it looks spectacular and the price is good, in which case I will ask the boss to have a look.' Maud's boss 'smells it, breaks it, opens it'. Personnel caught between the supplier and purchaser become involved in assessment too. 'Sometimes', Selma told me, 'if they give a really nice sample, I test it myself, then I give the rest to my boss and then I say what I think of it. I know [from smoking it] what the quality is now from the marijuana.' Humorously, Max described the good and bad parts of sampling:

> I can tell you a funny story. My boss is on holiday, people come to show me weed and I have to look at this product. I don't really know it that well, but I look at it and it looks good, smells good, but I still have to see how strong it is. But it's one o'clock in the afternoon and I have to smoke a joint. [It was really strong so] I go like, 'Oh no, I'm flipping out!' I have this [new] dealer [we hired] who is coming and I have to tell him how to do his job right. I have to do all these conversations and I don't want to be stoned then.

Not every coffeeshop bought from sample-based suppliers, but personnel still take advantage of this process. Jasper and I laughed when he said of samples: 'I show them to my boss, and he says, "Oh yeah, now I'm gonna smoke it". He doesn't buy them. He knows his own people [who are regular suppliers].'

Yet if a purchaser likes the sample, they may get back in touch with the supplier who brought it. Maud observed of her boss: 'If it is nice, he will want to know more about this guy, how much it costs, and how much he can offer.' According to James: 'They leave a sample with their phone number, how much they have got, and I tell them it will take two or three days to go through the manager to ok it, and he will call them if he likes it.'

Assuming contact is re-established, the next-to-last step is for the purchaser and supplier to discuss, sometimes negotiate, trade terms.[26] Ruben said of this stage: 'They ask you, "We have this amount, do you want it?" You say yes or no. Everybody who has something for a decent price, you buy it.' If the purchaser thinks the price is too high, they counteroffer. Hassan described the negotiation in this way:

> Sometimes it's like buying your groceries. Let's say you are going to buy coffee from him and he's asking €2, but you want only to pay €1.50. This kind of thing [negotiation], it's like normal. It's like buying beans or something, that's the way it goes here. It's not like a big thing, it's normal. If you can't agree about a price or you don't like the quality, you just don't deal with him.

I asked Ruben what a decent price is. 'That depends on the market', he replied. 'It is like gold and silver [in that price fluctuates]. It varies between €2,000 a kilo and maybe €5,000 or €5,500 a kilo. With hash it is even more variable. It is like alcohol. You have a bottle of champagne for maybe €10,000.' I did not ask everyone about purchase price, but I was quoted more or less similar numbers. When I questioned Jack about what a good bargain is at present, he answered, 'Between top of the menu and bottom of the menu' – meaning the best to least good cannabis – 'you are looking at wholesale prices of 3 to 7 euros per gram, within that range.' That multiplies up to €3,000 to €7,000 per kilo, echoing Jens' assertion that a kilo of marijuana usually costs 'between 3 and 7,000' euros.

Trust, quality and price are all factors that determine what stock a coffeeshops buys. So too do the stock levels that they have in reserve. Whereas purchasers call regular suppliers when in need of restocking, sample-based suppliers come to the coffeeshop on their own impetus. For that reason, they may arrive at an inopportune moment in which the coffeeshop does need not a particular product. Conversely, a sample-based supplier can make a lucrative deal if he or she comes at the right time with the right product at the right price. In Maud's words: 'This can happen quickly. If he [boss] thinks it is OK then it will happen all in one day. If the quality is good, we buy it. It is about the quality also and the stock [we have on hand].'

This concurrence is more common at some coffeeshops than others. At Last is among the most dependent on sample-based suppliers. Maud added to the earlier thought: 'It can be anyone. It is not always the same person; not just one guy who is doing all the stuff. We don't have to find it, we don't have to search for it. They just come. There are people that do that stuff and just sell it.' Perhaps due to their dependence on irregular suppliers, At Last is a sample hotspot.[27] 'In a week', estimated Maud, 'maybe one or two are coming.' Other personnel estimate a lower but still noticeable number. 'A lot of people just come in [with samples]', Hanna observed. 'Maybe somebody once in every two weeks' was Charlotte's guess, while 'maybe once per month' was the estimate for Nick of Time.

At the opposite extreme are coffeeshops such as After Hours. 'It rarely happens', said Stefan of visits from sample-based suppliers. 'Once every few months maybe. Yeah, it's very rare.' He theorised a plausible reason for the lack of solicitations: 'Maybe they've learned that [my coffeeshop doesn't do business with them]. I mean, if people come a few times [and] they're told, "No, we don't want to buy that", you ain't going to come a fifth time, right? They learned. It rarely happens with us.'

Making more sales and having more variety may also make a coffeeshop more dependent on sample-based suppliers. The greater those numbers, the harder it is for regular suppliers to meet the demand. To this point, Jens described the situation at Nice Place to Visit:

> They will buy at least four or five or six kilos a month, if you want to have a consistent variety on the menu. In about a month, like four or five purchases, maybe 50 or 60 kilos a year, also minimum. We've got 20 types of weed on the menu, so that starts you off with at least 20 kilos because you have to have at least a kilo of each in stock, and if you want to keep that going all year you have to buy 4 kilos a month. We probably get a couple of hundred kilos a year, maybe. There are at least four people, that I know, that come and deliver to us regularly. They are separate people, separate accounts. But people that come off the streets [with samples], we get them [too]. We may get four or five of them in a weekend.

Looking ahead to Chapter 2 on advertising, it should be asked why coffeeshops put up with the hassle of buying, restocking, storing and selling so many strains. Owing to the large number of coffeeshops in the 1012, it is important for these establishments to win market share by selling a range of quality products.[28] This was mentioned by Willem, when I asked what affects his earnings: 'Quality. Your product must be very good. Most people come for your product. If your product is shit then you are fucked. The main thing is you go to a bar for a drink, you go to a coffeeshop for a smoke. It has to be good product or they say, "What the fuck is this place?"'

Yet the offerings at coffeeshops are about more than making money. From what I heard, the wholesale and retail price for cannabis is pretty proportionate to its quality. So long as a purchaser pays the going rate, the profit margin will be similar irrespective of what is on the menu. In addition, coffeeshops in the 1012 are less dependent on turning new customers into regulars, given tourists make up much of the demand. Some visitors research where to go, but many arbitrarily end up somewhere. And countless times, I heard tourists give low- or mid-grade recommendations to fellow travellers.

Despite those mitigating factors, personnel preferred to sell higher- over lower-quality product, and more types than fewer. For people such as Jack, this is a matter of self-respect: 'I, for one, certainly want to be able to pride myself with the product I am selling. That is the point of having a menu, surely. I can say, "Look at my menu. This is the top of my menu, this is the bottom of it. This is really good, this is all right". We should all be able to take pride in it.'

Notes

1. For information on the ethics of ethnography and research more broadly, see Childress, Meslin and Shapiro 2003; Katz 2006, 2007; National Research Council 2003; Plattner 2003.
2. For information on the emotions of being stigmatised while in mixed contacts, see Goffman 1963. On emotions and wrongdoing, see Katz 1988, 1999; Jacobs and Wright 2006; Wright and Decker 1994, 1997.
3. For information on drug tourism in Amsterdam, see Belhassen, Santos and Uriely 2007; Cuskey, Klein and Krasner 1972; Uriely and Belhassen 2005. On Amsterdam versus other parts of the Netherlands, see Advisory Committee on Drugs Policy 2009.
4. Though my quantitative questions focused on the previous 12 months, the qualitative descriptions also covered earlier periods. Thus the numbers do not always match the quotes.
5. For a possible explanation of the continuation, see Pogarsky and Piquero 2003; Stafford and Warr 1993.
6. For information on a person's negative experiences leading to desistance, see Decker and Lauritsen 2002; Jacques and Wright 2015; Laub and Sampson 2003; Sampson and Laub 1993; Sutherland 1937. An issue that I do not know much about is the 'life-course of organisations' with respect to the onset, continuation and termination of crime. This topic is relevant to a number of research areas, including corporate crime (Clinard and Yeager 2006), environmental crime (Burns, Lynch and Stretesky 2008), organised crime (Lyman and Potter 2014) and state crime (Ross 2000).
7. For information on the history of accounting, see Brown 2013; Gleeson-White 2013.
8. A small number of coffeeshops have servers who take drink and food orders at tables. However, cannabis purchases always occur at the dealer counter.
9. For information on differences across countries in mixing cannabis with tobacco, see Global Drug Survey 2018.
10. For information on estimating typical joint contents, see Ridgeway and Kilmer 2016.
11. One reason why coffeeshops do not invariably lose sales is some clientele make a purchase despite the restricted product line. For information on this choice generally, see Burnham, Frels and Mahajan 2003.
12. For information on drug runners, see Coomber and Maher 2006; Curtis and Wendel 2007; Levitt and Venkatesh 2000.

13. For information on the relationship between (self-)inspection, knowledge and control, see Bentham 1843; Foucault 1975, 1980, 1985; Marx 2016.
14. 'The *High Times* Cannabis Cup is the world's leading marijuana trade show, celebrating the world of ganja through competitions, instructional seminars, expositions, celebrity appearances, concerts and product showcases' (*High Times* 2018).
15. For information on illicit drug dealers' stash spots and other techniques of preventing sanction, see Cross 2000; Knowles 1999; Jacobs 1993, 1996, 1999; Jacques and Reynald 2012; Jacques and Wright 2015; Johnson and Natarajan 1995. In Amsterdam specifically, see Bernasco and Jacques 2015; Grapendaal, Leuw and Nelen 1993; Jacques and Bernasco 2013.
16. For information on hiding deviance by using normal items as props, see Goffman 1963.
17. For information on regular and irregular suppliers, including how such relationships affect trade, see Brownstein, Mulcahy and Huessy 2014; Jacques and Wright 2015; Mohamed and Fritsvold 2010; Venkatesh 2006; Zaitch 2002. On different levels of the drug hierarchy, see Levitt and Venkatesh 2000; Sevigny and Caulkins 2004; Waldorf, Reinarman and Murphy 1991.
18. For information on how the illegality of drug markets affect trade, victimisation and social control, see Coomber 2006; Dickinson 2017; Dickinson and Wright 2015; Goldstein 1985; Jacobs 1999, 2000; Jacques and Allen 2015; Jacques, Allen and Wright 2014; Jacques and Reynald 2012; Jacques and Wright 2013, 2015; Jacques, Wright and Allen 2014; Moeller and Sandberg 2017; Morselli et al. 2017; Reinarman and Levine 1997; Reuter 2009; Taylor 2007; Werb et al. 2011.
19. For information on cannabis growers, production and importation, see Bouchard, Beauregard and Kalacska 2013; Chadillon-Farinacci, Apparicio and Morselli 2015; Giessen, Ooyen-Houben and Moolenaar 2016; Malm et al. 2017; Kleemans 2007; Ooyen-Houben and Kleemans 2015; Spapens, Müller and Bunt 2015; Toonen, Ribot and Thissen 2006.
20. Bruinsma 2007.
21. Ibid.
22. For information on the role of pre-existing relationships in drug distribution, including a lack thereof, see Bourgois and Schonberg 2009; Brownstein, Mulcahy and Huessy 2014; Coomber 2006; Jacobs 1999; Jacques and Wright 2015; Mohamed and Fritsvold 2010; Venkatesh 2006; Zaitch 2002.
23. For information on distributors giving away free drugs, see Belackova and Vaccaro 2013; Bright and Sutherland 2017; Coomber 2006; Harrison et al. 2007; Jacques and Wright 2015; Zimmerman and Wieder 1977.
24. For information on race and ethnicity as an indicator of being an undercover police officer, see Jacobs 1996, 1999. On undercover policing more broadly, see Fijnaut and Marx 1995; Marx 1989.
25. For information on evaluating the quality of drugs, see Sevigny 2013; Sevigyn, Pacula and Heaton 2014; Shukla 2016; Winstock, Wolff and Ramsey 2001.
26. For information on negotiation in determining the price of drugs and conflict management, see Jacobs 1999; Jacques and Wright 2011, 2015; Moeller and Sandberg 2017.
27. For information on crime hotspots, see Chadillon-Farinacci, Apparicio and Morselli 2015; Ratcliffe et al. 2011; Sherman, Gartin and Buerger 1989; Short et al. 2010.
28. For information on the quality of cannabis in coffeeshops, see Niesink et al. 2015; Piljman et al. 2005.

2
Advertising

During my senior year of high school I remember when a friend, Trevor, returned from Amsterdam. A committed stoner, he made good on his word to go there once he was 18. I knew about coffeeshops, but not the name of any. That changed when Trevor got back, as he proudly wore a Baba Coffeeshop T-shirt. Ever since, I have carried a mental picture of that name splayed above the eight-armed elephant logo. Many coffeeshops, not only Baba, deal in memorabilia. There is an array of products branded with their logos. 'We don't have ads', commented Linda, a server at No Return. 'What we do is like the merchandise, [like] T-shirts, sweaters.' Coffeeshops also sell sweat pants, scarves, hats, key chains, coffee cups, plates, ashtrays, grinders, lighters, rolling papers, small containers to carry cannabis, and more. They even sell copies of their cannabis menu and give away other print materials, such as posters or flyers. Customers take these home and put them up on their walls, thereby spreading the word about coffeeshops.

The problem with coffeeshop memorabilia is it can be a violation of the rule banning advertising, the purpose of which is to minimise the proliferation of cannabis use.[1] Consider what Jack told me happened at Alike All Over:

> A picture of a cannabis leaf on that flyer, that can get us shut down. That was the last offence we had. A couple of years ago we got in trouble for that, and these things do stand against you [affect sanction for further violations].

The easiest way to avoid such problems, though not the most profitable, is to shun advertising. This is the reported strategy for 85 per cent of coffeeshops. When asked if their establishment advertises, common responses were 'No, it is not allowed' (Adam), and 'You are not allowed to advertise' (Lola). In response to being questioned about why Eye of the Beholder does not advertise, Imran responded with his own question: 'We are not allowed to advertise, so why take the risk in that way?'

However, some personnel understood that the rule against advertisement is nuanced, not unconditional. That is, the ban restricts the use of certain information items in certain ways.[2] The two key factors are an advertisement's content and location. By content, I mean images and words. 'Weed leaves are not allowed', explained Lizzie. Nor is 'cannabis' or its synonyms. The word 'coffeeshop' cannot be coupled with the business address or phone number. 'We don't even use the word "coffeeshop" on lighters', reported Gwen. With respect to location, what could be considered an impermissible advertisement is not categorised as such if it is only visible from within the coffeeshop. Ruben told me of a time the police accused The Mighty of wrongly displaying "T-shirts with our phone number and address on them. It said "coffeeshop" and the phone number and the address'. The business argued in court this is within the rules. 'We won', remarked Ruben, because 'the T-shirts were in a poster frame and you couldn't see it from outside. We were not advertising them in front of the window, so you had to come inside to see them.'

Returning to content, Max clarified that advertisements are allowed to have 'coffeeshop' *or* the address and phone number. He mentioned this when trying to change police officers' minds about what is permissible:

> The guy [officer] comes [over to me] and he says, 'We have a problem'. I said, 'What's the problem?' He says, 'This!' and he showed me the match books that we have. I said, 'I'm allowed to sell gift matches to the people. What's the problem?' He said, 'No, look!' It said 'Coffeeshop' and featured our logo. I said, 'Now listen, you have to read the letter from your boss again because, actually, there are two things that I can do: I put my name on there, or I put my address and my telephone number on there, but you cannot do them both. So that's my logo and it says 'Coffeeshop Everybody Amsterdam' – that's it.

His coffeeshop also had a conflict with police over a flyer's content. When the officers first discovered the printed material, they thought it merited closing the establishment. Luckily for the coffeeshop, Max talked them out of pursuing that punishment. He argued the flyer would not leave his coffeeshop and was therefore not a violation:

> On the old flyer, it said our address [and 'Coffeeshop'], but we are not allowed to advertise [this way]. We put these flyers in the cellar. The police came in and then this smarty pants – because you always have like two detectives, and the rest [are] from the police school – this guy from the police school goes into the cellar, and he went: 'Yeah! We got them! We got them!' So that means for us, they can close us for a week, and then he comes with the flyer. 'Yeah, but what's the problem?' I asked. [He replied] 'Your address is on here.' So I said, 'Oh great, then you've got me. Yeah, you've found a kilo of coke, you know? I've got all prostitutes in the cellar, what were you making a fuss about?' Then I also said, 'The flyer I can keep wherever I like. If I want to keep it as memorabilia [but not distribute], just to have it, I can put that in my cellar.' So then the guy, this was the funny thing, he said, 'I'm going to take it all!' I was like, 'You're crazy'.

Other than the ban on nuisance (examined in Chapter 6), the rule against advertisement is the most ambiguous. This has both good and bad effects. From the perspective of government officials, including police, it is good because personnel tend to interpret the rule as a ban on all advertisement and so fully refrain. But for personnel who know how to play within the rules, the vagueness opens loopholes through which to push their advertisements.[3] The best example is a series of flyers distributed by jointly owned coffeeshops: the original Dampkring on Handboogstraat, the second Dampkring on Haarlemmerstraat and the Tweede Kamer.[4] These flyers consist of public awareness announcements about improper 'coffee use', paired with the coffeeshop's name, and a striking photoshopped image, such as smoke rings hovering above a coffee cup, with a solid black background (Figures 2.1–2.5). In order that customers notice these flyers and take them home, they are placed at conspicuous spots that lend themselves to discovery, such as near the dealer counter or front door. They are also stacked in a way to encourage the customer to 'take one'.

While having coffee, I listened to two employees discuss these flyers with a customer who admired them. One of the workers explained that coffeeshops cannot advertise, so these flyers are actually 'invertisements' – material designed to 'bring out information' about cannabis use. The other employee referred to these lessons as 'The Hints', an example being not to smoke every day. Then he pointed out that the flyers do not depict or spell out cannabis in any way because 'we are not allowed to talk about the product'. Instead the flyers refer to 'Amsterdam

Figure 2.1 Two examples of invertisement flyers (i.e. advertisements disguised as public service announcements) given away for free at the Dampkrings and Tweede Kamer. The reverse sides provide additional instructions on how best to enjoy 'Amsterdam Coffee'. *Source*: author

Coffee', though everyone knows this really means 'cannabis'. For example, the back of one flyer reads:

> You won't solve your problems by having an Amsterdam coffee. You should only use it for enjoyment.
>
> Foreign countries have different law-systems. It is illegal to take Amsterdam Coffee or related products abroad.
>
> In the Netherlands the sale of small quantities of Amsterdam Coffee is only permitted in 'tolerated' coffeeshops. You should therefore never buy Amsterdam Coffee on the streets.
>
> There are different strengths of Amsterdam Coffees, so ask the coffeeshop staff for information. If you don't know how strong it is, take a 'sip' and then wait for a few minutes before continuing.
>
> Combining alcohol and Amsterdam coffee can result in unpredictable effects, so be careful, particularly if you do not have much experience of 'drinking' Amsterdam Coffee.

Hearing all that, I decided to join the conversation. If they cannot advertise, I asked, what do the police think of these flyers? The employee quoted above answered that officers examined them, but saw nothing wrong'; one even described them as 'smart'. He added that their coffeeshops always work around the rules to see how far they can go. His colleague joined back in, saying more or less (i.e. paraphrased): 'In the back of our heads, the coffeeshop name is on it and all over the world, people know the name because of the invertisement. But it's not advertisement. This [invertisement] is allowed by law, and we stick to following those rules.' They were so confident of this that when the second Dampkring opened in 2008 a massive invertisement image was painted on its exterior wall.

Figure 2.2 Obvious as it is that this painting of a coffee cup with smoke rings amounts to a cannabis billboard, the Amsterdam police deemed it not to be a violation of the ban on advertising by coffeeshops. *Source*: author

Figure 2.3 Large bongs and hookahs are allowed in coffeeshop windows, perhaps because of their association with tobacco smoking. Words and images visible from outside the coffeeshop must be carefully controlled to avoid breaking the advertising rule. *Source*: author

Figure 2.4 A window using Rasta colours and symbols to attract customers without explicit advertising. The Rasta aesthetic is strongly associated with cannabis culture. *Source*: author

Figure 2.5 The palm tree, the most common image of coffeeshop signage, is visible in about one-fifth of those in the area of study. It is another feature of the Rasta aesthetic, as well as a more general symbol of relaxation. *Source*: author

Spreading information

People travel to Amsterdam for its coffeeshops from far and wide. Many of their itineraries are barely sketched out. People do not 'randomly' visit particular coffeeshops in the statistical sense, but rather by happenstance. It is common to see tourists walking down a street and pass a coffeeshop. They realise what it is, and then discuss – in their own minds or with companions – whether to go inside. Often they do.

To get the spontaneous customer in the door, a coffeeshop advertises itself as such on the outside.[5] The invertisement of the Haarlemmerstraat Dampkring is unique. Ubiquitous are the words 'Coffeeshop' or 'Coffee Shop' written on the exterior. The government could disallow this practice, but Max explained its public benefit:

> On every window it says 'Coffeeshop'. Why? Otherwise you get people in [who do not want to be there]. In the beginning, we didn't put 'Coffeeshop' in the window. We got people from 70 years old who came in. They came to drink coffee! No problem, but [they would be like] 'Hey look, they're smoking marijuana in here!'

To attract passersby, coffeeshops do more to the exterior than overtly label themselves. Some advertise their selection of drinks and food on the outside, or display the fact that they have amenities such as pool tables, air conditioning or Wi-Fi. Though no coffeeshop's exterior featured a marijuana leaf, presumably because this would violate the advertising ban, they incorporate other aspects of cannabis culture to attract customers.[6] For instance, a few establishments put large bongs and hookahs in the front window. Several logos made use of the animal kingdom by picturing a dog, mouse, lion, bear or grasshopper smoking a joint.[7]

Bob Marley is seen, too, which segues into another way coffeeshops signal their identity: colour choice. Though their outside walls and windows incorporate every major colour, the most common are green, red and gold. Nine of their exteriors are dominated by these Pan-African colours, which are associated with Rastafarianism and, by extension, marijuana smoking.[8] Another eight coffeeshops feature green as one of two prominent colours, typically paired with red. And green is the sole colour (other than black or white) at 25 coffeeshops. Half of exteriors, then, are the same colour as a marijuana plant.

Looking at coffeeshop signage, the most common symbol is a palm tree. Sixteen of the 84 coffeeshop exteriors incorporate it. I only noticed this long after leaving Amsterdam while looking through pictures, so I never asked personnel for an explanation. I like to think that the reason why it is so common is that a palm tree's canopy resembles a marijuana leaf in colour and shape, thereby covertly signalling its sale to customers. Or perhaps the palm tree represents relaxation, which cannabis consumption is known to induce, or is considered another symbol of Rasta culture.[9]

Not all coffeeshop visits are unplanned, of course. Tourists and locals share tips on which coffeeshops to visit and which to avoid. Joseph mentioned that customers 'always tell their friends and friends-of-friends [to visit Open Sky], so a lot of tourists know this coffeeshop'. Word-of-mouth is a major way that coffeeshops acquire customers. As explained by Willem: 'Business can't always go up. You can only do certain things, like advertising is not allowed here. So it has to be mouth to mouth.' Linking back to the previous chapter, we see this is part of why the quality and variety of a coffeeshop's stock affects their bottom line, despite a heavy reliance on tourist customers.

Advice, though, may be based on little more than haphazard visits to a few coffeeshops. On countless occasions I heard travellers praising coffeeshops I deemed overpriced, lacking quality or variety, with unfriendly personnel, poor décor or otherwise below par. Giving advice is human nature, but few tourists have the expertise to make sound recommendations.[10] My Uncle Irving is an example. Years ago he arbitrarily wandered into a few coffeeshops, and ended up liking one a lot – Coffeeshop Smokey in Rembrandtplein, which is barely outside the 1012. He told me about having a great time there; his face lit up from the happy memory and he suggested I check it out. Knowing him, he probably made the same suggestion to anyone else who told him of their impending trip to Amsterdam. My uncle means well, but in a city with many coffeeshops (that promote intoxication and foggy memories), it is easy to make invalid generalisations based on one-off experiences. In other words, someone having a good time at one place does not mean someone else will be able to replicate this. It certainly does not mean it is better than the available alternatives.

Person-to-person advice is not all word-of-mouth. Written information is shared in guidebooks, for instance. The guidebook author Rick Steves suggests visiting a coffeeshop in Leidseplein, a short walk outside the 1012 in the direction of Museumplein.[11] It is easy to dismiss the notion of taking coffeeshop counsel from Rick Steves, but many tourists will like his recommendation. I both love and hate his guidebooks because they contain so many good suggestions. I arrived at this view after my wife and I discovered a nice little bar near our Amsterdam Airbnb, where we spent the summer of 2016. While drinking, we noticed quite a few Americans there, which, for us, spolit the atmosphere. I joked that it must be Rick Steves's fault, which actually emerged as the truth. The reason I made the remark is the same thing had already happened to us in London.

The descriptively titled *Coffeeshop Guide Amsterdam* is a stoner-specific travel assistant.[12] The first edition came out after my study had finished, but it shows how coffeeshops can be 'advertised' without advertising. The guide begins with a page on what the guide is and is not, then covers, 'Do's and Don'ts/The First Time'; 'Terms and Definitions'; 'The First Coffeeshop'; 'Why are there coffeeshops in the Netherlands?'; 'The Law Situation Today'; 'Closed and Renamed Coffeeshops'; 'Prejudices! What Prejudices?'; and 'Amsterdam's Best Coffeeshops', organised by areas of the city. Among other disclaimers is the following, on page 1 of the book in size 6 font: 'This book is in no way intending to advertise any coffeeshop or the use of soft drugs.' In effect, though, the book does exactly that (and makes a pretty good job of it) by providing coffeeshops' respective names, addresses, cannabis products and prices.

A similar observation pertains to another way people learn about specific coffeeshops: the internet. The website of the aforementioned book is <https://www.coffeeshopguideamsterdam.nl>. There you can find information on how to purchase the guidebook and see a map of the city's many coffeeshops. Other websites include customer reviews of coffeeshops. Some are dedicated to cannabis, such as <https://www.coffeeshopdirect.com> and <http://www.smokersguide.com>. During my study I used the former a lot, but personnel talked more about the latter. Others are more general in scope, such as <http://www.yelp.com> and <http://www.tripadvisor.com>. By reading reviews on these websites, you see that some coffeeshops are widely lauded and others hated; most have reputations between these extremes. In addition to rating establishments, for example, on a scale of one to five stars, reviewers provide their qualitative assessments of a coffeeshop's menu (variety, price, quality), atmosphere (décor, music, clientele) and personnel (rude, helpful, attractive). Also reviewers describe specific events, both good and bad. Examples of these are examined in this chapter's final section and later in this book.

Coffeeshops are not wholly passive features of the internet. They advertise on their own websites. 'The only advertise[ment] that we have is the website', said Guus of World of His Own, 'and we only advertise [there].' James commented: 'We have a website, but advertising is a grey area because you are not legally allowed to advertise coffeeshops.' The effect of these websites may be huge – as evidenced, in part, by Dean bragging of Dollar Room: 'We have around 1 million hits a month on our website.'

As of 2010, when my study concluded, at least 28, or about one in three, of the coffeeshops in the 1012 had their own website. Some of these were barely websites at all, featuring little more than the establishment's name, email address and a message that it was 'Under Construction'. The more developed websites have information about the coffeeshop's identity, such as its history, atmosphere and location, as well as its non-cannabis products such as memorabilia, drinks and food.[13] A few coffeeshop websites display pictures of celebrities visiting the establishment, which serve as implicit endorsement by these high-status figures. Snoop Dogg seems to appear in every other image.

Coffeeshops' websites feature rule and policy statements as well. One presents a disclaimer that different countries have different cannabis laws, and that the coffeeshop does not condone or take responsibility for customers breaking them. A few websites list the rules applicable to patrons, namely restrictions on minors, hard drugs, nuisance and selling more than 5 grams to a customer in a day. Two websites touch on whether websites are a violation of the advertising rule. One states that Dutch law prohibits listing its address or cannabis products on the website; this particular coffeehouse therefore does not. This statement is interesting because many other coffeeshop websites do list the physical address (though none directly mentioned or depicted cannabis). This discrepancy further reflects that personnel held multiple interpretations of how coffeeshops are allowed to advertise, if at all.[14] The discrepancy also explains the reasons why coffeeshop websites come and go. On one home page is the following message:

> Like all Amsterdam coffeeshops, a couple of years ago we were advised [by government officials] to remove all mention of cannabis from our shop and our website. The whole of our site had to be taken down. But we were not alone. Almost all the Amsterdam coffeeshop sites disappeared from the web. Nobody, it seems, was sure whether they could mention cannabis at all and nobody was taking any risks. Confusion reigned as never before. Time and tide wait for no man, but they do make one feel a little braver. So here we are [with the current website], having another go.

The cannabis menu

No matter how customers find their way into a particular coffeeshop, they probably want to see its cannabis menu. Yet the 'no advertising' rule restricts how coffeeshops display this information item. It can only be placed on the inside of the establishment, for instance; as Selma said of the menu, 'The moment I would hang this on the door or on the window, it is illegal'. Even inside, the menu is only supposed to be positioned at certain places. Lizzie explained: 'The menu is not supposed to be very visible. So [for example], when people come in, they always ask if you have a menu [at the drink counter]. I say that we are not allowed to move the menu [over here]. They have to go to the menu [which is located at the separate dealer counter].' Some personnel, such as Ruben, think it is a violation to show the menu preemptively to customers: 'You cannot even show the menu to people. They have to ask for the menu. It is illegal to have a menu on the bar. You can only have a menu on the place where you sell the weed. They have to ask for the smoking menu.' For this reason, a few coffeeshops hide their menu behind a dark screen. The only way a customer can view it is to press a button below the blackout screen that reveals the options. But the vast majority of coffeeshops are less strict or creative. They simply put the cannabis menu on the dealer counter for people to look at as they please.

Cannabis menus are remarkably similar across coffeeshops. Pretty much all of them are a single page, or two pages at most. Other than maybe the coffeeshop's logo, these menus have no pictures; they simply spell out what is available and give prices for a certain quantity.[15] Commonly seen marijuana strains include Amnesia, Bubblegum, Cheese, Jack Herer, Northern Lights, Super Silver Haze and White Widow. For a gram, these and others sell from about €10 to €12. The lowest price I saw is €5 for vague varieties such as Colombia Outdoor, Jamaica or a 'Salad Bowl' of scraps dumped together. The highest prices tend to be €15 to €20 for varieties including Amnesia Haze, OG Kush and Head Band, though some coffeeshops sell the same product for less. Several coffeeshops offer discounts for buying larger quantities at once, such as 5 grams. More will be said about this in Chapter 4.

Hash is listed separately on the menu from marijuana, located either beside, above or below it. Caramello, Charras, Ice-o-later, Ketama, Super Polm, Water Works and Zero Zero are some of the most commonly offered types of hash. Compared to marijuana, there are fewer types of hash on the market, but they have a greater price range. At the low end, a gram of hash costs €4 for Afghan, while the highest price I came across is

€70 for 100 per cent Sativa Ice-o-later. The normal price for hash is about €10 per gram.

Recall that there are a couple of other cannabis products on coffeeshop menus. One is pre-rolled joints, which are sold for €3 to €10 a pop, though a few coffeeshops sell packs of three for €10, four for €12 or six for €16. Coffeeshops sell edibles in the form of space cookies, space cakes, space muffins and space brownies. They cost €4.50 to €7.50 each, with €5 as the standard.

To help sell items, some menus include a short description of each option. For example, the place of origin is listed as Morocco, Nepal, Lebanon or the Netherlands. The means of production is specified as 'bio/organic' or 'hydro'. The 'flowering time' required to produce the plant is given as between 9 and 16 weeks. Descriptions of smell and taste are 'sweet', 'smooth', 'spicy', and of the expected high 'stoned', 'strong stoned' or 'very strong stoned'.[16] A few coffeeshops advertise that the item won an award, like those given at the annual Cannabis Cup.[17] Almost all menus specify whether each marijuana strain is indica or sativa. Jens described the difference between these two subspecies:

> You have got two basic types: indica and sativa. Indica makes you stoned, sativa makes you high. Stoned is the sleepy feeling in your head with the heavy eyelids and the sedation where you just want to mellow out and feel like a couch potato. Sativas are the ones that lift you up, make you a little bit more energetic, a bit more like helium type of thing like you are puffing balloons, you have a really tweaky feeling. The sativas usually cost more because they are plants from closer to the equator, so they are used to longer summer cycles; they grow longer, and sativas flower in 12 to 18 weeks. Indicas, because they are used to colder climates and shorter summers, flower in six to eight weeks. So there is variation in having to keep the plant alive for 8 to 10 weeks longer than another, so the fact is that you pay more for the weed. They also run twice the risk [per growth cycle], of course.

Consumption required

The menu of one coffeeshop reads 'Drinks, Hash, Weed purchased elsewhere may not be consumed in our coffeeshop'. A similar message is on coffeeshops' websites, such as 'No outside drinks allowed inside' and 'food we do not sell is NOT allowed'. The same is posted inside and outside coffeeshops on rule signs, a means of control examined in the next chapter. It is understandable that staff frown on customers consuming items brought from elsewhere. After all, coffeeshops make money from selling food and drinks. Indeed, what makes some coffeeshops more popular – and more profitable – is the variety and quality of their non-cannabis consumables. 'We are just a coffeeshop that sells better food than many of them', said Lizzie. She continued: 'Actually, older people don't even think it is a coffeeshop. They actually come in, order two cups of coffee and go home again.'

In addition to forbidding outside products, coffeeshops require visitors to purchase something to stay inside. Fourteen per cent of the coffeeshops have a sign indicating consumption is required. This rule is used in part to control homeless individuals who use coffeeshops for daytime shelter.[18] Personnel work to keep homeless people outside because they tend to buy as little as possible, as well as for other reasons discussed in Chapter 6. Claire and her colleagues, for example, remove 'people just sitting there all afternoon and not consuming anything, then they ask you for a glass of water. We end up having people that have no roofs. They tell other people that don't have a roof to come here [too], then they come here for a sleep.' Dean described how a former customer lost his right to be at Dollar Room: 'We had a guy, he was a good customer. But after he tells me a story that now he is sleeping on the streets, now we don't let him in any more.' Referring to homeless people generally, he explained: 'They don't spend anything, and that is why they are not allowed.'

On its face, the notion that businesses can require customers to make purchases or go elsewhere is uncontroversial. Yet this causes conflict between personnel and customers, depending on what must be purchased and how often. Some personnel require frequent purchases, say every half hour, by every customer. Linda is an example: 'I force people to drink! I harass people so my efforts [sales] are higher than everybody else's!' Other personnel accept a single purchase by a single member of the group. Victor provided an example of tolerating Italian customers, stereotyped as 'want[ing] to sit there in the best places for the least amount of money'. He described how: 'Twenty of them come in, they order one drink and they just stay there for hours and hours and hours doing nothing.'

Coffeeshop personnel require customers to buy a drink, cannabis or both. Some coffeeshops, such as Angels, are fine with customers only buying drinks – and even tolerate them smoking cannabis bought elsewhere. As Luuk told me: 'We have the "drinks necessary" [sign] because otherwise they come in and sit for hours and don't drink anything. You can bring your own weed, we don't care. Our policy is you can bring your own weed, but not your own drink. You have to buy something.' However, personnel at other coffeeshops do ask customers to leave unless they purchase cannabis. I was frequently told that I have to buy something off the cannabis menu if I wanted to stay. One afternoon, for instance, I walked into After Hours and ordered a coffee. The dealer asked, 'Something to smoke?' 'No, thank you', I replied. She told me that is the cost of having a seat inside. I questioned this policy. In response, she claimed it is required of everyone. I left it at that.

Right or wrong, personnel have reasons for requiring patrons to buy cannabis. When interviewing Olivia, I told her of my experiences: 'I go to all the coffeeshops and write down stuff. What is interesting about you, actually, is that you kicked me out because I wasn't buying weed.' 'Only because this shop is so tiny', she explained. 'If people come in for only drinks, I usually say "No" in this shop because it is so tiny and I need the space for my smokers. But if people buy something to smoke, I am not going to make them buy something to drink as well. Smoking is always more important than drink because it makes more money.' When discussing the issue, Ruben told me: 'In the big coffeeshops, where you can stack 500 or 600 people, there is nobody who watches who is doing what [so customers can get away without buying anything].'

In addition to a coffeeshop's size, timing affects who is required to buy what and how often. In busier periods of a day, week or year, personnel are more likely to require customers to buy cannabis if they want to stay. 'Sometimes people have to buy weed', Elias said, 'like on a Saturday when it is busy. But on a Monday morning you could come in, roll your joint and leave without anything. You have to buy a drink, but if you want to skin up real quick because it is raining outside, you can sit down. I don't really care. On a Saturday, yes, you got to smoke.'

I saw this in action one early afternoon in July when I visited Selma at Man in the Bottle. Two customers walked inside and asked for drinks, but they left once Selma stated they must buy marijuana to stay. Once gone, she commented that were it a Tuesday or Wednesday, not Thursday, she might have let them stay with only a drink purchase, implying it was too busy at present. Days later, I asked her to give me more detail on her thinking:

> Depends on the situation on the day you are in. Like now it is Wednesday, it is very quiet. If five people come inside, and they don't want to buy marijuana, but just a drink, that is not a problem; at least they have to buy all five a drink. But then if we have a group

> of eight people coming in on Saturday, and one person buys a bag of weed, I don't accept it because it doesn't go like that.

We continued to talk through the variables. First I asked, 'What if one person bought weed but all eight buy drinks?' She said, 'That is OK.' 'What if all eight just wanted drinks and it is really busy?' I questioned. She told me:

> No, because it is a coffeeshop, and I am here to sell weed and let people smoke. If eight people come and take space and it is already busy, and they only take drinks, other people will not come in because it is full, and they are the people who may buy some marijuana. In here we are a coffeeshop. You don't go into a bar in the night time and get something to eat, not drink something. If I would be working in a coffeeshop three times as big as this one, then I won't care if people buy marijuana or not. At least they have to buy a drink because it is not a public open place for everybody, so you have to buy something, but this place is very small. There are only four tables. So, for me in the end, I would appreciate it if everybody sitting at those four tables at least buys a bag of weed, because I am a coffeeshop.

An issue that comes up for tourists and locals alike, but especially for the former, is how many days of entry a cannabis purchase buys. For example, a reviewer on *Coffeeshop Directory* shared: 'I was even told they wouldn't serve me unless I purchased some weed. When I told them that I had bought a sizeable quantity only the day before, they let me stay, but at that point I was too bummed to bother.'[19] Some personnel see the contract as expiring on a daily basis. Joseph rationalised: 'In a beer shop, [can] you say "I bought this beer last night and this is half of it, so can I drink it here?"' To that I commented: 'But wouldn't you say weed is fundamentally different from alcohol, in that alcohol you do drink right there, but weed is the kind of thing you hold on to?' His answer was rhetorical: 'Then can you buy the weed and go in your country [the USA] for one month, then come home [here in Amsterdam] and say you bought it one month ago and say, "Can I [stay in here without buying anything]?"'

It may make economic sense for personnel to require cannabis purchases during busy times. However, asking patrons to do so violates the advertising rule, as I understand it, because it requires patrons to be told about their illegal wares. I discussed this issue with Ruben, who commented: 'You cannot make people buy. We do, though. It depends how busy it is. If I just have nobody in the shop, it is crazy to not sell a cup of coffee. But when it is very crowded and we have limited space, you have to buy some smoke. If they don't want to, then they go. That's what we do, but it is not legal.' 'So there is something saying you can't force people to do that?' I queried. 'I think there is a law', he replied. I tried a direct question: 'I have always wondered when I go into a coffeeshop, "Can they even legally tell me I have to buy weed?"' He answered: 'No, no, they cannot. If people just buy a drink, you cannot tell them they have to buy weed.'

Selma and I also discussed the issue. She was uncertain of what is allowed: 'I don't know if I can tell the people that they have to buy a bag of weed. I don't know if it is the law that I can do that, but it is my place [of business] and so I think I can.' 'What if it was illegal to do that?' I asked. 'Would you keep doing it?' 'I would have to ask my boss what he wanted', she responded, to which I asked, 'What do you think he would say?' She guessed that he would tell her to carry on: 'Probably just keep on going because if everybody came in the coffeeshop and nobody bought a bag of weed, why are we open? I don't earn my money off coffee and juice.'

Perhaps that mindset explains why personnel may refuse to make non-cannabis sales, even when they have plenty of room to spare for non-smoking customers. This happened to me with great frequency. Once I went into At Last when it was almost entirely empty, except for a table with eight people crowded around it. There were at least 30 open seats and 10 open tables. When I requested a latte from the only on-site member of personnel, who I think was the owner, he asked, 'Like something to take for smoke?' I declined, but he said it is the rule. I asked if he could even have that rule, which took him by surprise. He argued that it was like a restaurant requiring the purchase of food, which I counter-argued by saying coffeeshops are different in that the business is only half-legal. His facial expression showed he was unimpressed, so I questioned whether it is better to sell a latte or nothing at all. 'Nothing at all' was his answer.

If improperly executed, turning away customers is detrimental to a coffeeshop's profit. It can also hurt their business in the long run if it angers patrons who then complain and gossip about the place.[20] Disgruntled customers do so to retaliate against the establishment, or simply because they want to help their fellow smokers. Many examples are found on *Coffeeshop Directory*, such as:

> - Not allowed to smoke your own ganja brought by you! So if you don't buy ganja there, it will be not allowed you to smoke there. Don't wanna go there again.

> - Was forced to buy drinks from very rude staff. Will not be going back.
>
> - Removed my bag, jacket, hat etc., all being watched by the guy behind the bar, I would point out, only to be told as I asked for a coffee that I had to buy hash/weed to get a coffee!!! I have not returned.
>
> - I was told that one HAD to purchase hash/weed to stay in the coffeeshop, purchase of a drink was not enough. I decided not to stay and left.
>
> - Very rude waitress, not helpful and disdainful. She refused to serve us just a tea, we had to buy weed! So we left.

Those reviews suggest that conflict over obligatory consumption is more likely to occur when personnel have a rude demeanour. Another reviewer described his take:

> We walked in and were greeted by a guy behind the counter who asked what we would like. We said 'coffee'. Without any acknowledgment, he asked what herb we wanted to buy. We said we had some already and he then asked us to leave. He was amazingly rude and we were polite. It's about 10 feet to another shop so it wasn't a big loss, but I would have been happy to buy some herb from him had it just been nice about it, e.g. 'Hi guys, this is a small place. I really only sell herb. If you want to smoke, I have some great stuff'.

When asked to buy something or leave, all customers do one or the other, eventually. But this may involve nasty words, threats or physical violence. Some of the reviews reveal that when customers take offence, their mind turns to vengeance. Consider a reviewer's description of a contentious incident:

> I got to the shop not too long after they opened on a frosty Saturday morning mid-January. I was the only person in the shop besides the dealer and his mates sitting at the bar, and they were all well pissed up [drunk]. I got a gram of weed, sat down, rolled it up and was in the process of smoking it when the bloke who sold me the weed came over to my table and started yelling at me, 'Gee, so are you going to buy anything to drink, or are you just going to smoke that and fuck off, eh?' I'm quite mellow and non-confrontational, so I didn't respond. I simply stood up, and started gathering my things to head outside with my spliff. Again, he started shouting at me, 'Fucking tourists

> come in here and think they don't have to buy anything to drink', and then [said] some rather harsh sounding Dutch to his mates at the bar. At this point I had had enough, so I simply told him to fuck off. He flew into a rage, slapped the joint right out of my mouth onto the floor, gave me a push towards the door and told me, 'Fuck off and don't fucking come back in here'. I paused for a moment, but his dodgy mates were already getting up from their barstools. I decided it would be best to leave at that point.

Such conflicts are also a problem from the personnel's perspective. Luca told me about one troublesome individual:

> This guy is always shouting, always drunk, comes in the morning, wants to sit here and there are a lot of customers inside, but he doesn't want to order anything. If you don't order something you have to go out, right. So he didn't want to go out, so I shoved him out and that's it, end of the story. If you ask a person about five times, politely, to go out and he still doesn't go out and he starts shouting, it is very simple for me: push him out. For me it is the solution.

And Lizzie described a story in which the rule requiring purchases led to tangible conflict:

> We had a fight with this guy who works at [a nearby bar] because everyone that stays [here] is supposed to drink something. He told me he just wanted a drag of his water pipe and then he was going to go. Then he went to sit down like more elaborate, and I said to him, 'Look, you know you have to drink something because that's the rule'. He looked at me like I was air. He didn't react to anything. So I said, 'If you want to drink something can you please answer!' Nothing, no reaction, no look, nothing. Then I got a little bit pissed off. 'OK, fine, that's it. Go!' Still no reaction. So then I thought to myself, 'Yes, I could ask the guy [who is my colleague] to kick him out', but I thought, 'I can fix my own problem I because I want to be taken seriously, also'. So I told him: 'Now, look, if you don't answer me I want you to leave.' No answer.
>
> He was sitting here [at a nearby table], I took the chair and then he was on the floor. Then he all of a sudden realised he was on the floor and then he got up and was pissed off that I threw him on the floor. I said, 'Look, I had to do something because you don't

> react. You are not hurt, but now we can talk. But because you don't answer I have to do something, you know?' But then I said, 'Look, it is finished now and you have to go.' Then the dealer guy came to help me. He asked 'What is going on?' and I said 'This guy has to go out'. It was very nice that the dealer didn't make a story or ask about the story, he went straight away: 'You – out, out, out!' And that was it. Then he went to the other [coffeeshop under the same ownership] to complain about me. He complained to the people there that 'This girl threw him on the floor'.

She went on to explain her reaction as a matter of keeping Whole Truth under control:

> I try to remind people that they are a guest here. This is not your house, this is a business. We have rules. You are very welcome. You can do almost anything you like within the rules. Be polite: we are all people. And if you cannot be then go to one of the other 250 coffee shops. Get lost. I mean I give [tolerate and compromise] a lot, but if you start to take the piss then [things are too out of control]. I don't want people who mess with the atmosphere. The customer is king, yes. But I am the empress. In other words, you have to behave yourself.

Notes

1. For information on tobacco and alcohol advertisement, including bans of them, see Gunter, Hansen and Touri 2010; Pennock 2009; National Cancer Institute 2008; Pacula et al. 2014; Petrone 1997; WHO 2013.
2. For information on advertisements and identity, see Goffman 1979.
3. For information on managing one's stigma by covering it, see Goffman 1963, 1969.
4. Since leaving Amsterdam, it is my understanding that these coffeeshops are now under different ownership.
5. For information on identity pegs and discrediting oneself as stigmatised, see Goffman 1963.
6. For information on cannabis culture, see Sandberg 2012, 2013.
7. Some logos are not obviously related to cannabis culture. Examples include a rhinoceros, bulldog, bird, crown and heart.
8. For information on Rastafarianism, see Barrett 1997; Helene 2004.
9. See Becker 2015.
10. For information on storytelling as human nature, see Boyd 2012; Gottschall 2012. On social scientists as storytellers, see Becker 2007; Geertz 1988; Gehman and Basboll 2014; Van Maanen 1988.
11. Steves 2003.
12. *Coffeeshop Guide Amsterdam* 2015.
13. For information on how actors construct their identity, see Goffman 1959.
14. Some coffeeshop websites are neither wholly review sites nor directly maintained by personnel. To this point, Joseph remarked: 'We are on the internet, but we have not put ourselves on

there.' A coffeeshop website may appear to be run by the business, but claim to be maintained by a 'fan' of the establishment. To my knowledge the latter situation is not a violation of the ban on advertising because it is out of the coffeeshop's control. It is possible that coffeeshops intentionally circumvent the rule by supporting such 'fans', though no personnel ever admitted doing so.

15. For information on the price of cannabis in coffeeshops, see MacCoun 2011.
16. But see Becker 2015.
17. Back in high school I often read about these competitions while perusing issues of *High Times*. While living in Amsterdam, however, I never attended due to the participation fee.
18. For information on retail establishments excluding persons perceived to be homeless, see Duneier 1999.
19. As with interview quotes, I have edited some *Coffeeshop Directory* reviews to improve readability.
20. For information on gossip as a form of social control among drug market participants, see Dickinson and Wright 2015.

3
Minors

Coffeeshops are forbidden to have minors on the premises.[1] There are no exceptions. As Elias told me: 'A lot of parents think they can bring their kid. They say like, 'They are with me". I don't give a shit! Nobody under 18 means nobody under 18. That's just the rules. We can lose our permit for that.'[2] Complying with this rule is particularly stressful for personnel. Unlike the bans on 500-plus grams and advertising, they are not wholly in control of violating the 'no minors' rule. This is because underage persons do walk into coffeeshops, or at least try to, despite the wishes of the coffeeshop's personnel.

For example, Mara feared this scenario: 'three [underage] guys [come] in, and behind them two cops [come in to do their check]. They come in, they stop the guys, they close the door, and then they say "Are you 18?" When you are working behind the bar, you haven't had the time to ask them that [yet]. When they are inside, I have the problem because they [police] say they're inside.' Her hypothetical example is based on real experience: 'it happened in the past, then we got problems. They were police problems.' James described an incident in which the 'police caught someone [underage] in the other [coffeeshop under the same ownership]. The police went in, there was a guy of like 16 with a guy of 17 who had actually bought weed. They were sat at some table.' Asked about the punishment, he answered, 'The dealer got fired. The police were very good [in that] they didn't give them [the coffeeshop] a warning'. The Mighty was less lucky. After the police found underage persons on the premises, Ruben told me they 'were closed for a week'. Of course, the worst-case scenario is that 'you can be closed down forever, ever and ever and ever', to use Gwen's words.

It is good for a coffeeshop to have more customers, unless they overwhelm personnel and thereby put the business in jeopardy. To that point, situational constraints make it difficult for personnel to stay fully within the rules that are examined in this chapter and subsequently.[3] A well-known theory is people commit less deviance if busy,[4] but people also exert less control for the same reason.[5] In addition to enforcing rules, personnel have other tasks to complete, such as weighing product, taking money, making drinks and cleaning up. An owner or employee will do all that alone, or with the help of at most a few others. Successful control is all the more difficult when it involves keeping an eye on many people in a large space not entirely visible from their primary workstation, such as the dealer counter.[6] In short, when fewer personnel are working in a bigger, busier or less open coffeeshop, it is harder to keep track of who is inside and what they are doing.

Even in the smallest establishments, personnel become too preoccupied to guard against violations. Consider what happens at the tiniest coffeeshop in the area, no bigger than a few small office cubicles. It is a popular joint, so, semi-regularly, the line grows to 10 people deep or more, at which point it starts to stretch out of the door into a tiny alleyway. In turn, the personnel speed up their service, but this comes at the inevitable cost of less thorough surveillance. This increases the opportunity for minors and other unwanted persons to idle inside until their turn at the counter, as a doorman was rarely present.

On that note, coffeeshops sometimes place an employee at the entrance to keep problematic people outside. Probably the busiest and certainly the largest coffeeshop – with more than 100 seats across three floors – has a doorman positioned throughout the day, almost every day of the year.[7] This is uncommon, though. My student observers only encountered a doorman on 4 per cent of their visits, and just 12 per cent of personnel told me that their establishment employed a person solely to fulfil this role. But the coffeeshops that did so perceived the cost as worthwhile, as it prevented underage people, among others, from gaining access. Mara explained why she pays someone to guard the entrance of Wish, the coffeeshop she owns:

> He helps in the shop [a little], but he's checking IDs and things like that because busy days it's difficult – because you [otherwise] work alone – to check IDs and everything. It's better [to have him here] because you, how do you explain it, keeps it a little bit quieter? It just stays quiet because when people come in, he watches and asks for ID. Gives a rest for people behind the bar.

House rules

As alluded to by Mara, the major technique by which personnel prevent minors from being on the premises is to check their ID (short for identification) cards.[8] Requiring customers to show their ID is a 'house rule' in every coffeeshop. Whereas government rules are enforced by police against coffeeshops, house rules are enforced by personnel against non-personnel, including customers and other people on their territory. 'These rules are for you to have a good time' reads one coffeeshop sign. That may be true. Yet their more fundamental purpose is to keep coffeeshops orderly. This is where proterrence (scaring people into preventing others from doing something bad) becomes important. The government rules, associated checks and punishments deter personnel from certain acts, but also proter them into stopping non-personnel from participating in those acts and others. So in order to understand how personnel stay in compliance with the government rules, or at least appear to do so, it is necessary to understand the house rules.

There are many house rules but, abstractly speaking, they come in three forms distinguished by their content and rationale. Government-based house rules are those with content conveying a government rule. Their rationale is to make non-personnel aware of the government rules and thereby reduce the risk of them being unknowingly broken.[9] Examples include signs at coffeeshops specifying 'Minimum age of 18 years', 'No entry under 18 years', 'Attention!!! No entry under 18 years', and, in case that is unclear, 'Under 18 no entre and dont [*sic*] fuck around'. Other signs convey messages such as 'No hard drugs' or, more specifically, 'No use or sale of hard drugs'. In addition, signs display bans on nuisance, such as 'No aggression', 'No violence', 'No verbal or physical abuse' and 'No dealing in stolen goods'.

Another type of house rules are government-inspired. Similar to government-based house rules, the inspired type are meant to reduce the odds of government rules being violated. But government-inspired rules do not directly refer to government rules. Instead, they pertain to actions that affect the risk of violating them. An example is requiring patrons to show ID. Dutch policy does not require coffeeshops to check ID, but they institute this rule to reduce the risk of selling to minors. More about this is examined in the next section of this chapter.

Not all government-inspired rules have an obvious relationship to the government rules. A seemingly trivial house rule, such as a ban on wearing a hat or sunglasses, can serve to minimise violation of the government rules. A motive for this rule is to get a better look at who is inside and thereby be in a better position to confirm their age. The dealer Stijn told me: 'Most of the time if you have sunglasses on, you have to take them off. If you have a hat on, I tell you to get the hat off just to see your face for the ID [check]. Then you can put it on again.' He further explained the rule:

> I know the main reason people use it [the rule], because my friend is manager at Mind and Matter. It is because [if] they have one more fine [then] they are closed. Yeah, and it has just opened, because once they [police] came in and they found a guy under 18 there, and you can only get two [violations]. With two you are closed man. With a hat they cannot see good if you are old enough. The same at [my coffeeshop,] the Mirror Image. At Mirror Image, you have to get your hat off.

Some coffeeshops entirely ban wearing hats and sunglasses inside, not just on entry. For these establishments, the rule is also geared towards getting rid of street dealers of hard drugs, who are stereotyped as wearing these accessories.[10] When I asked Jasper why they have a 'no hat' rule, he answered: 'For the [street] dealers. We have a lot of cameras and when we see people with a hat, I cannot see your face. Hats off. And some people don't like [that rule, so] they go away. That kind of people we don't want. Please go somewhere else.'

This rule reflects the suspicion white personnel hold of youngsters who are ethnically Moroccan, Antillean or Surinamese.[11] These minorities are perceived as a disproportionately high source of misbehaviour, including not only street dealing but also nuisance, especially aggression. Having them inside, then, is deemed a threat to compliance with the government rules. Consider the perspective of Gijs, a white *Nederlander*:

> You will understand that there is a problem with the Moroccan community, there is a problem with Antillean community, the Surinamese community. The Antilleans, they are behaving badly most of the time, and a lot of Moroccans do. This is not generalising. This is a small group of the Moroccans, a small group of the Antilleans, because all my friends who are Antillean or Moroccan, they don't like it either. You have to deal with these people. If they want to come into your shop, you are welcome if you behave to our rules, if you are nice.

Because the customary style of these 'problem' people includes a hat and sunglasses, personnel ban everyone from sporting these items.[12] Consider how Max explained the origin of Everybody's 'no hat' rule:

> A few years ago, about three or four years ago, there was a coffeeshop on the [Rembrandtplein] square and they [the government] closed it down. That was next to the Metro station. A lot of guys from the Bilmer [which is about a 30-minute ride on the subway from there], they went to that shop because it was next to the Metro station. When that shop was closed, they started to look for different shops. They heard about the quality we sell, so we had a lot of these guys coming in. I don't want groups of Moroccans, you know Moroccan kids, inside. And so we thought up a few rules to make it a little bit uncomfortable for them.

Max added that this ban helps personnel to identify who is on hard drugs and, by logical extension, in possession of them: 'You can't even watch someone in the face because he has his cap on, his hoodie on. And also in the summer, you have to take your sunglasses off, and that's because we want to see your eyes [to see] if you use hard drugs, or [to ensure] you are not totally wasted.'

In short, outlawing hats and sunglasses is a subtle tool for pushing unwanted customers outside. To the extent these stereotypes are correct, the rule stops (some) minors, people who may create nuisance, and hard drugs from being in coffeeshops. To quote Gijs again:

> There are a lot of local youths with attitudes, let's put it that way. This is not a racist or discrimination thing, but in the [shop] there are a lot of these kids living there that don't care about anyone else. They are like street gangsters. They check out the American LA gangsters, and they think they can do the same thing here. Well, not in our shop! That's basically why we have this [no hat or sunglasses] rule. When these guys come into the shop, other people get scared and they go away; they feel intimidated. So we have these house rules like you can't wear a [winter] cap inside or any hat. When you take it off, you say, 'Hello, good afternoon', and [then] you are really welcome. Some say, 'Oh, I don't want to take it off'. 'Then you go somewhere else, my friend.'

Of course, this rule is not absolutely effective at keeping out unwanted people. After all, they simply have to take off their hat and sunglasses. However, the process is useful for sorting the deterrable offenders from incorrigible ones who prefer to go elsewhere than follow a rule.[13] By enforcing this ban, moreover, personnel send a clear and early signal about who is in control, and that they are on the lookout.[14] In Max's words:

> If you have a quarrel about anything [at the coffeeshop], it's really like [with] people [who] have to take off their hats. There are only a few people who want to make a fuss about it, but those are really the people that you don't want in. When they want to make a problem I say, 'It's just my rule. That's how I want it. You can take it or leave it'.

It is critical for coffeeshops to create and enforce house rules to remain compliant with the government rules. Not all house rules have that rationale, however. The third type of house rules are unrelated to the government. Unlike government-based and -inspired rules, unrelated ones are not facets of proterrence. Instead they are wholly informal mores. Personnel gave me examples such as 'No telephones' (Jasper), 'No dogs' (Joseph) and 'No food' (Kamila). These prohibitions are seen in signs too. They spell out, for instance, 'Do not hang on doors or windows' and 'Please clean your table when you leave'. Other signs get their point across by pairing the universal 'no' symbol – a red circle with a diagonal line through it – with an image of the prohibited item or behaviour.[15] And tying back to Chapter 2, a commonly seen house rule is 'mandatory', 'required' or 'obligatory' consumption. Perhaps to avoid violating the advertising ban, none of those signs specify that a customer must purchase cannabis, though some read 'Drinks are required'.

The origin of government-unrelated house rules are based in personnel's preferences and experiences, both personal and vicarious.[16] For example, when asked why mobile phones are prohibited at After Hours, Stefan cited two factors, including one that could affect the bottom line:

> Because you want to come in there and escape it a little bit, right? People are like [yelling], 'Yeah, we're in the coffeeshop!' That's not nice for anybody, especially the people working there. But generally, the music is up, [so] if I don't hear someone talking on the phone, I don't mind. But as soon as I hear someone having a telephone conversation and if it's annoying me, [then] it could be annoying other people, right? You want to be in a nice atmosphere.

> It can also fuck with the scales. The scales can react to that [phone signal somehow and start incorrectly weighing the cannabis]. And you don't want that, you don't want that. Especially in the one little shop [that is part of our coffeeshop chain], if you see someone on [their mobile phone], you'll see the scale vibrating, the digital reading changes. But yeah, it's more the fact you want to keep a nice atmosphere. People generally raise their voice when they're talking on a telephone. It's like, what are you coming in here for? Go outside and make your telephone call.

A single house rule may be found across coffeeshops, but have different rationales from one to the other. An example is hats and sunglasses are also forbidden as a matter of respect and politeness. For Ruben, 'Shades, they have to take them off when you talk to me. I want to look somebody in the eye. I am not working behind the counter with sunglasses'. I commented, 'It is rude', to which he responded, 'It is. I like treating people the way I like to be treated'. At Thing, Maikel explained, the ban on these accessories is a matter of security: 'You have to take your hat off so that we can see their face, to see who comes in. It is my place, and I need to know who comes in here, and who goes out.'

Furthermore, a house rule may have multiple rationales within any given coffeeshop. In addition to forbidding hats and sunglasses to keep out so-called 'problem' people, Max cast the rule as a matter of sociability:

> This is not very social [to wear a hat and sunglasses inside], and I think a coffeeshop is a very social place. It [the rule] started for the [problem] guys, but now I don't even want to see it any more. Most people, when I explain it then they think about it and say, 'Well, you are right [that those accessories are somewhat antisocial]', and then they understand and they are OK with it.

That quote brings up an important distinction, namely between the 'communicated' and 'actual' reason for a rule.[17] Sometimes, they are one in the same; in others, with partial overlap; still in others, entirely different. Recall that Gijs explained that the major reason for banning hats and sunglasses in Escape Clause is to keep out the 'problem' people. However, while visiting his coffeeshop, I observed him explaining the rule to people as a mechanism of surveillance. A guy came in wearing a hat and then stood in line for the dealer counter, where Gijs was working. When the hat wearer approached the counter Gijs asked him to take off his hat 'for the security'. During our interview, he told me that the security-based explanation causes less conflict than the other:[18]

> There are more shops who have a 'no hat' rule. Already five years ago, I walked into a shop, and they asked me to remove my cap. I said, 'Why?' He said, 'Because we want to see faces on the camera. In case anybody robs anything or whatever, then we can find this person back or we can show the police'. That's part of the reason, and I use this to explain to people as well: 'It's to see faces in case somebody robs you, then we can find them back, etcetera.' That's what I tell people. I am not going to tell people, 'Look, you look like a gang member and you have attitude', because then you create problems. You don't want to do that. You want to have this person feeling welcome as well, as long as he is nice.

Personnel frequently communicate house rules to non-personnel. 'They asked my brother', commented a reviewer on *Coffeeshop Directory*, 'to remove his hat. Why?' How people react to instruction depends on how it is delivered. A positive reaction is more likely when personnel's demeanour is friendly, whereas rudeness is apt to produce responses like that of the following reviewer:

> The dealer came over and demanded that my fiancée remove her hat, as it interfered with their videotape security system. I thought it was a joke. No, he insisted. I got the impression that he was convinced that two 50-year-[old] accountants with grandkids posed a serious security threat to their organisation. We had enjoyed just about all the stinkin' hospitality we could stomach, thanked them and marched off.

To avoid negative interactions, owners and managers teach more junior employees how to convey rules to customers. Gijs described how he educates workers:

> I do guide them in how to act, and how to communicate with people. I do regular talks with them on the shop floor, but also we have a talk in the office or something. I just [recently] have been going through [this] with all the dealers. There are about 20 to 22 dealers. I discuss with them any new working scheme, some points for attention, some house rules, things they might not be doing right, steer things the right way again. Then I take any points they want to make about it.
>
> If there are things happening, like people keep their hats on [when asked to take it off] or whatever, I talk it through with them like, 'Say it in this way' or 'Say it in that way'. Always say it nicely,

be friendly. In a professional way, you have to be nice to people where the customer is king. If the customer is a nice king, then he should be treated as king. If he is not a nice king then, you have to go my man.

Like verbal instructions, rule signs are used to inform and thereby control non-personnel.[19] They specify government-based, -inspired and -unrelated rules, usually in English and Dutch, but sometimes in Italian, German or French. Rule signs are a pervasive feature of coffeeshops, found at 86 per cent of the 50 coffeeshops in the sample (Tables 3.1, 3.2 and 3.3).[20] The signs are affixed to the outside of a door or window, an inside wall or placed on the dealer counter or tables. The biggest sign is

Table 3.1 Rule signs of interviewed coffeeshops

Coffeeshop	Government-based		Non-government-based		Any
	Outside	Inside	Outside	Inside	Out or in
After Hours		X		X	X
Alike All Over					
Angels		X		X	X
Arrow in the Air				X	X
At Last	X	X	X	X	X
Back There					
Buzz		X		X	X
Chaser		X		X	X
Dollar Room	X		X		X
Doomsday	X				X
Dust	X		X		X
Elegy	X	X	X	X	X
Escape Clause	X		X	X	X
Everybody	X		X	X	X
Execution	X				X
Eye of the Beholder		X		X	X
Fever		X			X
Four of Us	X		X		X
Hitch-Hiker	X	X		X	X
Howling Man					
Judgement Night	X		X		X

(Continued)

Table 3.1 (Continued)

Coffeeshop	**Government-based**		**Non-government-based**		**Any**
	Outside	Inside	Outside	Inside	Out or in
Last Flight	X	X	X	X	X
Like a Child	X		X		X
Live Long	X		X		X
Man in the Bottle	X		X		X
Maple Street	X		X		X
Meek	X	X	X	X	X
Mirror Image	X	X	X	X	X
Most Unusual	X				X
Mr. Bevis	X		X		X
Nice Place to Visit					
Nick of Time				X	X
No Return		X		X	X
Open Sky					
Passage					
Perchance	X			X	X
Purple Testament	X		X		X
Shrine					
Stop	X		X		X
Sun	X			X	X
The Hour	X	X	X	X	X
The Lonely	X				X
The Mighty		X		X	X
Thing	X				X
Walking Distance	X	X	X	X	X
What You Need		X			X
Whole Truth	X		X		X
Wish	X		X		X
World of Difference	X	X	X	X	X
World of His Own	X				X
Per centage with sign	66	36	46	46	86

Note: 'X' denotes that the coffeeshop has at least one sign. For information on the types of signs included in 'Government-based' and 'Non-government-based' columns, see, respectively, Tables 3.2 and 3.3.

Table 3.2 Government-based rule signs of interviewed coffeeshops

Coffeeshop	**No minors**		**No hard drugs**		**No nuisance**	
	Outside	Inside	Outside	Inside	Outside	Inside
After Hours		X		X		X
Alike All Over						
Angels		X				
Arrow in the Air						
At Last	X	X	X	X		
Back There						
Buzz		X		X		X
Chaser		X		X		X
Dollar Room	X		X		X	
Doomsday	X		X			
Dust	X		X			
Elegy	X	X		X		X
Escape Clause			X		X	
Everybody			X		X	
Execution	X					
Eye of the Beholder		X		X		X
Fever		X				
Four of Us	X					
Hitch-Hiker	X	X				X
Howling Man						
Judgement Night	X					
Last Flight	X	X	X	X	X	X
Like a Child					X	
Live Long	X		X			
Man in the Bottle			X		X	
Maple Street	X		X			
Meek	X	X				
Mirror Image		X	X	X		X
Most Unusual					X	
Mr. Bevis	X		X			
Nice Place to Visit						
Nick of Time						
No Return				X		
Open Sky						

(Continued)

Table 3.2 (Continued)

Coffeeshop	No minors		No hard drugs		No nuisance	
	Outside	Inside	Outside	Inside	Outside	Inside
Passage						
Perchance	X					
Purple Testament	X					
Shrine						
Stop	X					
Sun	X					
The Hour	X	X	X	X	X	X
The Lonely	X					
The Mighty		X		X		X
Thing	X					
Walking Distance	X	X	X		X	
What You Need				X		
Whole Truth	X		X			
Wish	X		X			
World of Difference	X	X		X		X
World of His Own					X	
Percentage with sign	50	32	32	26	20	22

Note: 'X' denotes that the coffeeshop has a sign. 'No nuisance' includes signs to that effect and also signs of 'No aggression'.

Table 3.3 Non-government-based rule signs of interviewed coffeeshops

Coffeeshop	ID required		No hats or sunglasses		No mobile phones		No weapons		Consumption required	
	Outside	Inside	Outside	Inside	Outside	Inside	Outside	Inside	Outside	Inside
After Hours		X				X		X		X
Alike All Over										
Angels										X
Arrow in the Air						X				

(Continued)

Table 3.3 (Continued)

Coffeeshop	ID required		No hats or sunglasses		No mobile phones		No weapons		Consumption required	
	Outside	Inside	Outside	Inside	Outside	Inside	Outside	Inside	Outside	Inside
At Last							X	X		
Back There										
Buzz						X				
Chaser										X
Dollar Room			X		X		X		X	
Doomsday										
Dust	X									
Elegy		X			X			X		X
Escape Clause	X		X	X	X					
Everybody	X		X	X	X				X	
Execution										
Eye of the Beholder		X								
Fever										
Four of Us	X									
Hitch-Hiker		X				X				X
Howling Man										
Judgement Night	X								X	
Last Flight	X	X	X	X	X	X	X	X	X	
Like a Child					X					
Live Long	X									
Man in the Bottle									X	
Maple Street	X									
Meek	X	X								
Mirror Image	X	X	X		X	X		X		
Most Unusual										

(Continued)

Table 3.3 (Continued)

Coffeeshop	**ID required**		**No hats or sunglasses**		**No mobile phones**		**No weapons**		**Con-sumption required**	
	Out-side	In-side	Out-side	In-side	Out-side	In-side	Out-side	In-side	Out-side	In-side
Mr. Bevis	X								X	
Nice Place to Visit										
Nick of Time		X				X				
No Return		X				X		X		
Open Sky										
Passage										
Perchance						X				
Purple Testament	X				X		X			
Shrine										
Stop	X									
Sun						X				
The Hour									X	X
The Lonely										
The Mighty		X								
Thing										
Walking Distance	X	X			X					
What You Need										
Whole Truth					X					
Wish	X				X					
World of Difference		X			X	X		X		X
World of His Own										
Percentage with sign	30	24	10	6	24	22	8	14	12	14

Note: 'X' denotes that the coffeeshop has at least one sign. Because some of these signs may (not) be intended to prevent breaking the government rules, they are not distinguished as government-inspired or -unrelated, but simply as non-government-based.

Figure 3.1 Signs such as these display a variety of house rules that are government-based (e.g. 'No hard drugs'), government-inspired (e.g. 'ID required') and government-unrelated (for examples see Figure 3.2). *Source*: author

about 2.5 metres in height, hung on the wall next to the windows looking out onto the street, with rules spelled out in red capital letters about the size of a hand palm (Figures 3.1–3.4).

A benefit of having signs is that personnel can point to them when people question or break a rule. To quote Olivia: 'There are some house rules. It is mainly that if somebody does something, we can say, "The rule sign is over there".' This is useful for maintaining order by demonstrating the rules are not being made up on the spot, which could be interpreted as unfair treatment and cause further trouble.[21]

Written or spoken, house rules are part information item, part impression management.[22] They signal to police and public that rules are taken seriously in this establishment. An example concerns Wish, which

Figure 3.2 Because not all patrons can read Dutch or English, signs use the universal 'no' symbol to convey government-based, -inspired, or -unrelated house rules. In these signs customers are notified that mobile phone use and dogs are prohibited inside. *Source*: author

you may remember had 'police problems' because of minors. Following these events Mara posted about 10 signs on the windows and door. Half of these signs explicitly banned persons under 18 years of age, while the other half stated that ID is required upon entry. Anyone who walked by could see that minors were not welcome at Wish.

Signs inform non-personnel of what is forbidden, with some conveying implicit or explicit threats. 'When rules are broken, you will be asked to leave', one sign reads. Another says at the bottom: 'These are the rules. You can't accept them? Please leave through the same door.' Non-personnel get the sense that if they want to engage in certain prohibited behaviour, they are better off going elsewhere.[23] The choice is not always left up them, however. 'We can choose', said Claire, 'whether

Figure 3.3 Whereas some signs encompass many house rules, others are dedicated to a single one. This written sign, under the Jim Morrison memorial, combines English and French to communicate the ban on minors. It is posted at the entrance of the coffeeshop. *Source*: author

or not they can come in.' 'We are very conscious about who we let in', is how Thomas put it. Kamila stated: 'I am obliged to ask the people about their age, about [everything], you know? You understand? We don't welcome drug dealers. We do not welcome drunk people nor, of course, very young people. We don't let them in, we just stop them at the door.'

However, personnel are unable to prevent every troublemaker from getting inside. This is because coffeeshops rarely have someone working the door, as discussed above (p. 20). Once inside, then, problematic non-personnel have to be expelled. The process was discussed by Emir:

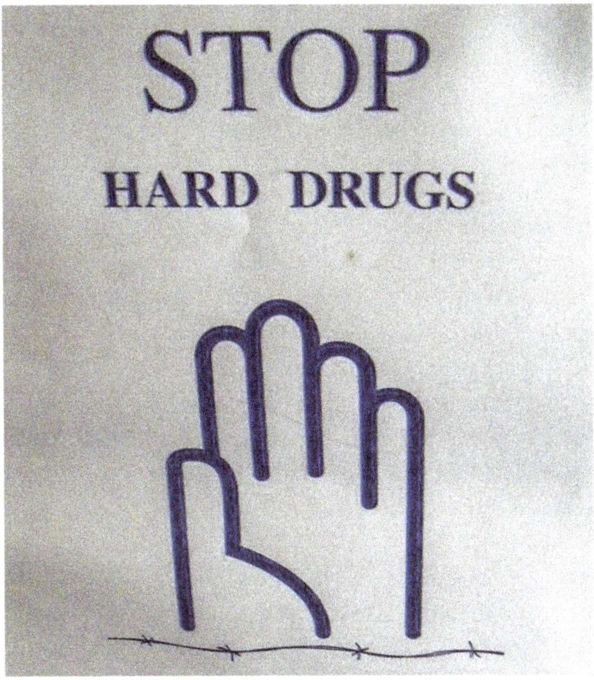

Figure 3.4 This sign is seen across numerous coffeeshops, which is unusual because rule signs tend to be individually made and posted by individual shops. *Source*: author

> Business is serious. We must ID everybody. He [the owner] wants the business to stay open. If he doesn't like someone who comes in here, then he tells them this is the last time they come in, like if someone is too loud. Only tourists, clean people, not criminals or people off the street. He has always been like that. We don't want any problems, we don't want people who might have knives, we don't want that.

House rules are not always enforced. In part, this is a consequence of discrimination.[24] The creation and enforcement of the 'no hat or sunglasses' rule is a case in point. Gijs stated the ban is enforced unless it infringes on religious practice: 'You can keep it on if you are Jewish,

Muslim or Sikh. Then it is up to them, but they can keep their hat on and everybody else get off your hat, get off your hoodie, it doesn't matter.' When entering coffeeshops, I must have been told at least two dozen times to take off my sunglasses. This would not be a problem, except that my sunglasses have prescription lenses. So I had to reach into my messenger bag, pull out my glasses case, take out my spectacles and put them on while trying not to drop them or my sunglasses. That may not seem like a big deal, but my wife will tell you that I can make a big deal out of anything. After a couple months of tolerating this inconvenience, I began to ask personnel if I could be an exception. 'These are prescription lenses', I explained. 'May I please leave them on?' No one said no, presumably because they deemed my justification acceptable.[25]

Max told me that once a year, the restriction is relaxed for Americans because enforcement is too costly: 'We don't do that [rule] with the Cannabis Cup because you have a lot of Americans coming in. These people come to the shop, and [if] they have to take off their hoodie, and they have to take off their coat, and their glasses, they won't even come in your shop any more because they think it's so ridiculous.' The Cannabis Cup is an annual competition in which coffeeshops compete to have their product voted the best. The judges are smokers who pay for the privilege. For coffeeshops, winning is good because it generates press coverage – and free advertising – in smoker-oriented publications, especially *High Times*. Plus victory provides bragging rights over neighbouring coffeeshops and a selling point for the menu. Max explained further: 'That's the only week that we say, "OK, they can keep their hat on", because otherwise they don't come in and they won't vote for you.'

Checking ID

Getting back to a focus on minors, Linda remarked: 'I check ID on everything because we are not allowed to have people under 18 in[side], and I don't want to lose the permit.' 'You have to always ask for ID anyway because you don't want anyone under 18 in your shop', Gijs told me. 'The police can close you [for that].'[26] Then referring to his employees, he added: 'Almost daily, I keep reminding them to check the fucking IDs, because what happens is if they [police] catch you with 17-year-olds inside, they can close you for a week straight away [or more]. That's a week with no profit, a week with no work for people inside the shop, customers can't go there. It's negative for everybody.'

Customers should expect to be asked for ID. A rule sign to that effect is posted in 46 per cent of coffeeshops, in addition to the two-thirds that display a sign specifying 'no minors'. Examples of these signs include 'ID required', 'ID must be shown on request', 'ID compulsory on demand', 'Keep your ID ready', and 'Show ID please'. Coffeeshops also spell out this rule on the cannabis menu, stating, for example 'Minimum age 18, only when valid ID', 'Minimum buy age = 18 years. It's necessary to show your ID-card', 'Beware for proof of age! We don't sell underneath the age of 18!' and 'Minimum age 18 I.D. required!'

Personnel assume that by checking ID, they succeed at not selling to minors. Ninety-four per cent of coffeeshops reported full compliance with the rule in the previous 12 months, or so they claimed. Typical responses to the question include: 'No, I am sure [this didn't happen]. I am very hard on [enforcing] this one' (Claire); 'No, we are very strict' (Stijn); 'No, we are very strict in this coffeeshop' (Sophie); and 'No, never, not even by accident' (Maikel). When I asked whether Arrow in the Air had sold to any underage persons, Kamila's reply was definitive: 'No, because we check everyone. We check everybody.' Imran answered the question in similar vein: 'No, never. I am 1,000 per cent sure because the girl [drink server] is there. The bar is pretty near to the entrance. It is a smaller area, and it is easier to control. Anybody that enters, she will see. She will ask straight away for identity.'

It is common for personnel to encounter persons without ID, or at least claiming such. Coffeeshops have a house rule for dealing with this problem as well. Specifically, people must leave if they cannot show ID when asked, even if they are clearly over 18. 'No entry without ID' reads one sign. And Wouter said of Live Long: 'We ask for cards, and if they don't have a card, don't have ID, they are gone.' Referring to underage persons, Jens asserted: 'If the cops come in they create a problem, and [so] you shouldn't let them in without a valid ID, even if they are old enough.'

The goal of denying entry to people without ID is to prevent punishment, of course. Emir explained why they are expelled from Walking Distance: 'The first thing [when people come inside] is ID. I always need to ask [for] ID because many times people are only 17 years [old]. If you don't have ID, then I don't serve you. It is a big problem [otherwise]. You can be fined and closed. The business has to stay good. We want to keep a clean house and keep my boss happy.' Similarly, Finn said of minors entering Execution: 'It happens often, daily. If they do not have an official ID – either a passport or European Community Card – get out! [If t]hey do not have an ID on them, and we deem them too young, we have to guide them all the way to the door, because if you leave them to walk this stretch to the door and at that moment the police walk in, you are fucked.'

Personnel are especially suspicious of Dutch people without ID. Emma and I discussed why. 'If they are Dutch', she stated, 'and they do not have ID, it is usually that they are not 18.' 'Do you always carry ID with you?' I asked. She explained: 'It is the law. Everybody over 14 has to carry ID since a couple of years [ago]. When you ride without a light on the bicycle [for example,] and you get arrested for not having a light, you get the fine for not having the light, and if you do not have ID you get a fine for not having ID, as well. I am sure that it is over 14 that you have to carry ID.'

Less clear to personnel is why foreigners claim not to have ID. There are plausible reasons. Hostels and hotels sometimes take people's passports during their stay, I assume to prevent them leaving without paying the bill. And loose border restrictions in Europe make it possible for people to travel internationally without a passport, if they stick to ground transportation. Perhaps for this reason, Kamila noted: 'French people, they don't have any ID with them. How did they come to Amsterdam with no ID? Did they swim or what? Mostly out of the five people, one only has ID. These people say, "No, I don't have one in my home [country]", so I think what are you doing here then?'

Local youth learn that foreigners are less likely to have ID, so they try to mimic them when entering coffeeshops.[27] They put on their best impression of an English-speaking tourist, made possible, in part, by the Dutch school system's emphasis on learning foreign languages. Most have a particular Dutch accent, though, which personnel use to distinguish foreigners from natives. Maud spoke about how she detected and handled such impersonators:

> The children from Holland, from Amsterdam, they want to smoke. They come here acting like they are tourist people – this is a trick. They are acting like, 'Oh, I left my passport in the hotel', but the way they speak English is very Dutch [and this gives them away]. They try to do everything to buy something. It is funny, actually. I say to them, 'Out boy! I did that trick many years ago and you are not a tourist! You are just a Dutch boy who wants to smoke. Come back at 18!'

Minors also try to buy cannabis at coffeeshops by using a fake ID. I find it amusing that four coffeeshops have a sign specifying 'No Fake

ID', as if that is not obviously forbidden. There are two types of fake ID.[28] One is government-issued IDs, so 'real', but used by someone other for whom it was originally issued. From the perspective of fake ID users, the strength of this type is that their look and feel – such as width, length, weight, thickness and material – appear correct to personnel because, after all, they are genuine ID. Yet their weakness is that the pictures may not sufficiently resemble the new user. Selma described an incident: 'A young boy came in with an identity card of somebody else. There was just a customer sitting here, and when this guy showed me the identity card, I first went to my colleague and I [also] asked this guy who was sitting here, "This is not the guy standing here?" We kept looking at him and looking at the photo, like, "Boy [you're trying to pulling a fast one]".'

The other type of fake ID is not issued by the government, but made to seem like it. Users produce these at home or purchase them at shops, physical or online, that sell shady goods.[29] The benefit of making a fake ID is that the photo can show the intended user, thereby reducing the odds of being discredited as fake. The drawback is they may not look or feel 'right' to personnel, alerting them to the possibility that the ID holder may be a minor.

Who is checked?

It may seem like a small thing to ask someone for their ID, take it from them, look it over and hand it back. To understand what a problem that can be, you have to multiply that task by the number of times it happens per day, which can be several hundred, and then multiply that number by the number of days worked in a year, which can also be several hundred. Also there is the issue of ID-related conflict, discussed shortly. For these reasons, checking ID becomes a pain. When personnel say something like, 'We check everyone', they mean it as a general expression, not an accurate literal description. They do not actually check everyone's ID, but only that of some persons.[30]

Whose ID do personnel choose to check? One group usually left alone is people who look many years past their 18th birthday. My senior colleagues, Rick Rosenfeld and Richard Wright, were never carded when visiting coffeeshops with me. On that point Emir noted, 'I always need to ask ID', though he went on to qualify this: 'If someone comes in who looks 50 years old, then I don't need ID.' Conversely, personnel seek out the ID of individuals who look young. In Stijn's words: 'It's very stupid to sell to somebody under 18. If somebody looks younger, I always check. If you look young, you have to have ID. If you don't have ID, you have to go out.' Jack agreed: 'We are very strict on ID. Anyone who comes in the door and looks like they were born in the [19]80s, I want to see their ID. That is my philosophy.' I was born in 1983, so I asked if he would card me. 'Possibly, yeah', he answered. 'I considered it when you came in the door. Then you gave me your [business] card and I was like, "OK, we can pass that one!"'

Common sense dictates whether a person is 'old' or 'young' based on their appearance.[31] Do they have wrinkles? Spots on their skin? Facial hair? Grey hair? Are they bald(ing)? How high are their pants? Personnel do not conscientiously consider these factors; they process them unconsciously to make snap decisions about age and, in turn, whether to ask for ID. Personnel also develop an instinct: they get a 'feeling' that someone may be a minor.[32] Yet because people of different ages have overlap in appearance, personnel are not always sure of a stranger's age group. Of course, it makes little difference to them if a patron appears closer to 30 versus 40 years old. But whether someone is 17 or younger versus 18 or older is very important, and this can be very hard to determine without ID, or even with it. People do look older or younger than they are. One of my childhood friends had a beard at 16 years of age, but I will never be able to grow one.

Personnel could handle age ambiguity by giving a customer the benefit of the doubt. Instead, their rule of thumb is to ask for ID when in doubt of someone's age. 'I card if I am in doubt', Noah affirmed. 'It happens all the time.' Hassan described his process as: 'I get this feeling, and I say this to my people [employees] as well, whenever you think she [or he] is a minor, immediately don't go and judge and say, "OK, maybe she is 19". Never. Someone who looks like 23 or younger, ask them immediately.'

In addition to physical appearance, doubt of age is based on how people present themselves.[33] How do they walk? Talk? Do they seem confident or apprehensive? Genuine or fake? Luca said of identifying minors: 'If I have any slight doubt, then I ask for their ID. No ID, no service. I can see on your face that you are not 18. It's to do with my feeling, and usually I am right. After five years [working here,] you should know.' 'How do you know, though?' I persisted. He stated: 'Well, if you ask people for their ID and they go like "this" [acting all uncertain of themselves], or they first walk by [the counter] looking [to see if they'll be asked]. No ID, no service, man. End of story.'

Personnel do not always ask for the ID of people who appear young. Repeat customers, if they are recognised and remembered, are not asked for ID. I saw this play out when a young female walked into Open Sky and ordered a gram of marijuana. She received it without being IDed by the dealer. I turned to Joseph and asked, 'You don't think she looks young enough to ID?' 'She is from Spain', he answered. 'Cute. I know her, already. I have seen her. This one is around 19, 20 years [old].' Assumptions can be dangerous, however – she may have initially gained access by using a fake ID, for instance. With this in mind, I commented to Joseph: 'If you just say, "Oh, I know [they are of the legal age]", sometimes that may not be not true.' He thought about it, then stated, 'You are right. I just assume I am always right. I am human, I can be wrong. It is not often, maybe once [in a year].'

The influence that knowing or recognising someone has on checking their ID also came up with Maud. She stressed: 'Now we always check IDs. When we don't know, we always check IDs. And that's what we say, we say to the person working: "You ask everyone. You have to ask everyone for ID".' 'But not really?' I queried. She responded: 'When people come every week, you [already] know they're 18 [or over]. When people come inside with a grey beard you know they're 18 [or over]. But we say the rule is you ask everyone. When we don't know and they don't have ID, they go.'

The 'ask-if-in-doubt' technique of age verification results in many false positives. This happens all the time in coffeeshops, as the vast majority of persons asked for ID are in fact 18 years of age or older. Such incidents are a waste of time and effort in the immediate moment, but in the long run it is safer to be wrong about someone being too young than about them being of legal age. Usually confirmations are uneventful, but a discussion may spring up. Maud told me about a conversation she had with a young-faced patron:

> I ask them every time. If I feel something is not right, then I follow my feelings, my instinct, and that is always right. Sometimes people look older than they are, and it happens much [of the] time. One guy had a beer, he was a redhead with freckles, and he looked old. But I had a feeling he was very young so I said, 'I want to see your ID'. He was looking at me as if to ask why I wanted to see his ID. If I ask and then they say, 'I am really 18 or 19', and you say, 'Yes, but I really want to see it'. If then they give me their card, I say, 'You look so young, what is your secret?'

Occasionally I was asked for ID when entering coffeeshops. By no stretch of the imagination did I look 17, but, apparently, looked close enough to cause doubt. Like most people, this never bothered me. A comment on *Coffeeshop Directory* illustrates the modal response: 'The budtender asked for an ID, which I was more than happy to oblige because this is Dutch law and must be followed in order for all of us to enjoy the freedoms Holland has to offer. After presenting an ID (and also showing him my receding hairline which gave him a good laugh), he opened the folder to present the menu.'

Asking for ID should be harmless, but some individuals take offence, often because they are a minor. Mara described one occasion when 'there was a guy coming in and I said "Can I see your ID?" "I have some ID, but I go somewhere else because you're asking", he said', to which she simply replied, 'OK, go'. Even if personnel are right to request ID, they dislike resultant conflict. This is the worst part of the job for Jana, who complained: 'I feel like a police person. You have to check everybody that comes in, like young kids that come in. And that is also annoying: people that make problems about their ID. There is all this discussing, you know? I just want to work, do my job.' Yet as Jana knows, watching out for young kids is part of her job.

Notes

1. For information on how Dutch drug policy affects access to and use of cannabis among minors, see Reinarman, Cohen and Kaal 2004; Simons-Morton et al. 2010; Wouters and Korf 2009. Among the general population, see MacCoun 2011; MacCoun and Reuter 1997; Monshouwer, van Laarand Vollebergh 2011; Reinarman 2009.
2. Personnel claim to be largely successful at keeping underage persons outside, though this may have the counterproductive effect of connecting marijuana-seeking teens to hard drug dealers. To quote Elias: 'If you look at someone who is 16 years old, it is easier to get coke or ecstasy than it is to get weed because they are not allowed in a coffeeshop. They can buy everything from a dealer on the street.'
3. For information on situational factors affecting crime and control, see Clarke 1995; Cohen and Felson 1979; Cornish and Clarke 2017; Felson 2006; Felson and Eckert 2015; Leclerc and Savona 2017; Hollis-Peel et al. 2011; Reynald 2010.
4. See Hirschi 1969.
5. See Cohen and Felson 1979.
6. For information on the traits of places, such as retail establishments, affecting crime and control, see Eck and Weisburd 2015; Newman 1972; Reynald 2015.
7. For information on doormen, see Bearman 2005; Hobbs et al. 2003.
8. For information on documentation and stigmatised traits, see Goffman 1963.
9. For information on the importance of people knowing the rules to obey them, see Beccaria 1995 (1764); Bentham 1830. For a sweeping analysis of why, how and to what effect rules exist, see Graeber 2018.
10. For information on the perceived relationship between appearance and stigma, see Goffman 1963, 1969.
11. For information on racial and ethnic discrimination by retail businesses against customers, see Anderson 2011; Harris, Henderson and Williams 2005; Lee 2000. On offending rates of ethnic minority groups in the Netherlands, see Crul and Doomernik 2003."
12. Personnel reported other culturally based ways of making members of these ethnic minorities feel uncomfortable in coffeeshops. For instance, Finn told me: 'If a local member of an ethnic minority comes in here they like to shake hands; total strangers, but they like to shake hands. It is part of their culture. That is strictly forbidden, handshakes with complete strangers. You can shake your hand with your brother or a friend, this is fine. It is not because we are unfriendly, but we do not shake hands with complete strangers, and we certainly do not shake hands with people that we see as a potential problem rather than a potential nice customer who will increase the atmosphere in here. And, of course, you make it extremely clear [to them] what goes on and what doesn't.'
13. See Jacobs 2010.

14. For information on guardianship as a deterrent, see Cohen and Felson 1979; Reynald 2010.
15. For information on the universality of rule signs, and on translation more broadly, see Reynolds 2016.
16. For information on the conditions leading to conflict and affecting how it is handled, see Black 2011; Emerson 2015.
17. For example, drug prohibition may be meant to protect or disadvantage particular groups (Alexander 2010).
18. For information on what is (not) said as a technique of managing stigma, see Goffman 1963, 1969.
19. For information on injunctive norms and descriptive norms, the latter of which coffeeshops signs rarely if ever communicated, see Cialdini 2003.
20. On the role of signs in crime and control, see Keizer, Lindenberg and Steg 2008; Schultz and Tabanico 2009. An old example is provided by Howard (1792, 75) in *The State of the Prisons in England and Wales:* 'Would not some public intimations of the punishment to fellow crimes be useful also in England? Notwithstanding the numbers of fishermen and loose boys about Amsterdam, the Hague and Schevelin, their public walks and beautiful plantations remain uninjured; which is owing, partly to the strictness of the police, and partly to the warnings given by *placarts* painted on boards, and hung up in different places, with representations of whippings, cutting off hands, &c.'
21. For information on procedural justice, legitimacy and obedience, see Tyler 2003, 2004.
22. See Goffman 1959, 1963.
23. This idea reflects the basic premise of order-maintenance policing. See Kelling and Coles 1996; Wilson and Kelling 1982; Zimring 2012.
24. For information on discriminatory enforcement, see Black 1976, 2011; Cooney 2009. On racial/ethnic discrimination, see Duneier 1999; Goffman 2014; Rios 2011. As relates to drug market participants, see Alexander 2010; Jacques 2017; Jacques and Wright 2015; Mohamed and Fritsvold 2010.
25. For information on excuses, justifications and neutralisations, see Scott and Lyman 1968; Sykes and Matza 1957. On talk more generally in criminology, see Presser and Sandberg 2015.
26. In addition to checking ID, Escape Clause raised the age limit from 18 to 21. As explained by Gijs, however, this had more to do with keeping out the 'problem' youth than of prohibiting minors: 'Basically the young kids come out in summer or in spring, and they try to get into the shops and so we have this policy of raising the entry age from 18 to 21. This is to keep it safe. Well, we have this thing anyway: we have a sign saying you are allowed in at [under] 21 years old. Legitimately you can come in after 18, but because there are a lot of difficult kids with attitude, and we like to keep the shop nice with nice people, we can use the 21-year-old thing. If people are not nice, then we try to make them nice, maybe a bit of education, whatever, and if they don't understand then it's best if they go to another shop. This is more a rule we have made for the locals because tourists, basically, they are always nice. I never find any tourist in the shop being obnoxious or big-mouthed. Maybe once a year, twice a year it happens [with tourists] that somebody has a bad day and then we tell them, "Look it doesn't work like that here", and if they are still like it then we ask them to go to another shop. But overall, tourists are welcome 18 and over.'
27. For information on trying to pass as normal, see Goffman 1963, 1969.
28. For information on the use of fake identification to procure alcohol and tobacco, see Arria et al. 2014; van Hoof, Gosselt and de Jong 2010; Johnston, O'Malley and Terry-McElrath 2004.
29. For example, see Goffman 2014.
30. To a degree, variation in checking ID reflects differences between personnel in a number of factors, such as social learning, self-control or perceived utility. Adam said of selling to minors: 'It is possible by accident. We are pretty straight [good] at keeping the age, but some are more fanatic about asking for ID than others.' Gijs admitted: 'It might have happened, but I say no [– minors have not been sold to]. It's very, very hard to say, of course, because I am not standing there all the time checking if the dealers are checking IDs. It might have happened.'
31. For information on common sense, see Black 1979; Geertz 1983.
32. For information on the feeling, or sixth sense, of potential victims and control agents, see de Becker 1998; Naparstek 1997; Worrall 2012.
33. For information on presentation of self and stigma management with respect to illicit drug trade, see Jacobs 1993, 1996; Jacques and Wright 2015.

4

5 grams

Basic business sense dictates it is better to sell more, yet that is not entirely true in the case of coffeeshops. This is because the government limits the amount a coffeeshop can sell to a single customer in a day. In Emir's words: 'The maximum is 5 grams. Sometimes people come in and ask [for more], and we tell them, "It is not possible. It is 5 grams [maximum]".' This limit is of little concern to most customers, but a source of conflict with some. 'One time with some English guys', recalled Kamila, 'they wanted to buy a lot from the coffeeshop. I just said I couldn't do it. And then one of them started: "But for you it is good business selling one time big, rather than selling the small packages." I told him, "No!" I think I was a little bit abrupt.' Rather than drop the issue, the customer repeated: "Do it! Do it!" It really was not nice. That was out of the question, what he asked me to do.'

Personnel restrict their sales because, as Luca explained, 'The police can just stop anybody and check your pocket here. That is allowed, and we have obvious [plastic] bags [that we put the sales into, revealing the cannabis is from us]. Five is five, not more. It's not worth it.' In other words, the extra profit does not outweigh the risk of punishment. To quote Guus: 'That's the rule. It's a risk, so I sell [only up to] 5. You have to keep on the rules.' Dean put it this way: 'We don't like to do that because if you do just one mistake like that, we have to close the shop.' And James declared: 'I know certain places do [sell more than 5 grams], but there is no point jeopardising the business for something silly like that. You play the game by the rules, and it makes it easier for you.'

To James's observation, the 5 grams limit does get exceeded. Mike described an experience in which 'this guy came around 10:30 [am] and he buys 5 grams, then he goes away, comes back at 11 [am] and buys another 5 grams, and then again at tea time buying 5 grams. I saw it all these times, like every half an hour he comes and buys 5 grams'.

According to personnel, coffeeshops violate the 5 grams rule more than any other rule (see Table 0.5). Examples are presented in the next section. First, I should note that some participants claim that *they* obey the rule, but are unsure of their colleagues' activities. When Claire was asked about selling more than 5 grams to a customer in a day, she responded: 'Me, no. The others, I don't know. I can't be sure.' To the same question, Anna responded, 'No, I don't do that' was Anna's reply to the same question, but of her colleagues she was less confident: 'I am afraid that sometimes they do, but I always tell them not to do it. It is not necessary. It can ruin their job.' Because of this, and other issues mentioned later, coffeeshops probably do break the 5 grams rule more often than reported.

Ignorance-based violations stem from misunderstanding the rule. The ban is on selling more than 5 grams per person *per day*, but some personnel think it only prohibits selling more than 5 grams *at a time*. Stijn is an example of this. He explained: 'I am not going to sell you more than 5 grams. I tell you to come back. The rule is you can go out and come back in and buy 5 grams again.' Knowing that is not true, I questioned him further. 'I thought it was in one day?' He answered adamantly: 'No, no, no. You can go to your hotel, then come back. It is a possession thing.' Presumably Stijn arrived at this idea by conflating the coffeeshop rule with the Dutch policy on personal possession. It more or less stipulates that the police will take no action against persons found with 5 grams or less.[1]

The ban is also violated by personnel who do understand it properly. Despite wanting to obey the rule, they mess up due to ignorance of colleagues' actions. Lizzie alluded to how it happens: 'It is possible that someone [a customer] comes in during the morning shift or comes in late at night, so that it is two different staff [that they buy from]. It is possible, but it is two different shifts.' What may occur is that a customer comes in during the first shift (e.g. 9 am to 4 pm) and buys, say, 3 grams of cannabis, then returns during the next shift (e.g. 4 pm to 11 pm) and purchases the same amount again. This is a violation of the rule, although the dealers are not aware of it. To try and prevent this from happening, coffeeshop menus spell out, 'Maximum 5 grams per Customer', 'Maximum 5 grams a day a person' and 'We are only allowed to sell 5 grams per person per day'.

At any given coffeeshop, multiple factors explain why the rule is broken. When I discussed the issue with Gwen, she denied knowledge of a violation – but subsequently stipulated that she does not know whether workers break the rule, then admitted she would break the rule if a customer came back at multiple points in the day, and that this may happen without her realising it. Referring to the 5 grams rule, she initially stated: 'We are very strict on that because we get punished for that really bad, so absolutely not. We really try to stick to the rules with basically everything.' Then she clarified this: 'If I say "No" [what I really mean is] it is not [broken] to my knowledge, because I can never be certain, of course.' At that point I posed a hypothetical question. What would she do if I came in and ordered 6 grams? She thought about it and hypothesised: 'I would give you 5 grams now and maybe would say if you come back in four or five hours [then I'll sell you more]. But, of course, some people may come in here four times a day and I can't tell.'

Big single purchases

Personnel cannot always blame violations on ignorance. Some do make sales despite knowing the sum exceeds the daily allowance.[2] Asked if this happened at Alike All Over, Jack admitted that 'it has been known to occur', but refused to disclose further details. Asked the same question, Ruben simply commented 'Sure'. I followed up by asking him what was the largest amount that he would sell to a customer. He smiled and said simply, 'I would rather not say'. Again such evasions are revealing, as they show that personnel worry about being sanctioned for violations.

It is doubtful that any coffeeshop fully complies with the 5 grams rule. I watched violations unfold while sitting near the dealer counter, especially on busy days at busy coffeeshops. This mostly happens when customers order a few grams of 'this' and a few grams of 'that', the total exceeding 5 grams. I never observed a dealer refuse, though sometimes I saw their facial expression change while fulfilling such orders. They had the look of someone thinking harder than they should be in this situation. Perhaps this is because they were not only weighing the cannabis, but also evaluating the risk. Sometimes dealers looked as though everything was normal – perhaps because they were too busy to think about it, better at acting or reckoned the prospect of being caught was too low to worry about.

By far the largest sales I heard about involved Man in the Bottle. When I asked Selma for the weight of their biggest sale, her reply was 'a kilo'. Then she described the largest exchange of which she had been a part: 'Me, personally, I did 400 grams' – about €4,000 worth. 'He [my boss] told me: "OK, you go get the stuff." You don't meet in the coffeeshop, you meet by McDonald's. It is like 200 metres away from here, so I walked to this [place] and there we exchanged [the cannabis and money]. I felt like a very wrong dealer! Half a criminal.'

Man in the Bottle is also the place of the largest sale I saw. I was sitting at the counter talking with Selma, her colleague Alex and their boss. A young white guy walked into the coffeeshop. Apparently a trade had been planned with him; I heard talk of 200 grams and all the personnel were aware of what was going on. Alex gathered the cannabis into a small black rubbish bag, then handed it over to the customer in exchange for cash. For some reason he wanted to pay in part with a US$100 bill. Not sure what that was worth in euros, a discussion about the current exchange rate ensued. They arrived at $1 for €0.64, until Amber pointed out that an exchange fee would be required, making the rate $1 for €0.60. The personnel were annoyed about the American money; before he walked out they told the customer to bring only euros in the future.

Unfortunately I learned only a little about the proverbial 'backstage' of coffeeshop sales.[3] I have no idea what percentage of coffeeshops make large sales, as Man in the Bottle does, nor how often, nor in what amounts. What I do know, however, is such sales rarely occur on the 'frontstage'; that is, in full view of the public. When the 5 grams rule is broken at the dealer counter, it is almost always by small amounts. Hanna unabashedly acknowledged the fact: 'More than 5 grams? Yes, of course. The most I sell, 10 grams.' Emma admitted that the most she sold was 'about 10 to 15 grams. The bags are already made; [for example] if they want some hash, that is a gram and a half. So, if somebody buys 10 bags that is 15 grams'.

Perhaps coffeeshops would visibly break the 5 grams rule more often, and in more egregious amounts, if there was greater demand. But there is little reason for locals to stock up in a city where every adult user can buy what they want for personal use daily, from many coffeeshops. The lack of desire to stockpile applies also to most customers visiting Amsterdam for a limited period. For this reason Imran did not perceive compliance with the 5 grams rule to be an issue:

> It is not even a question, it is not happening, because we do not have locals. The tourists don't buy 5 grams. It is, usually, only 1 or 2 grams. We have tourists, and they just come and try one gram here and one gram there. They will not buy a lot at one time. They are here, on average, for two or three days. How much can you smoke? Five grams is too much. So what they will do, they will buy 1 or 2 grams, try another coffeeshop and [buy more from there].

You could read into these words that if anyone is buying more than 5 grams at a time, it is locals. Yet for even the heaviest smokers, 5 grams is enough to last a few days. The quality is high, so a user does not have to consume much to get that way.[4] In jurisdictions that prohibit cannabis possession entirely, it may be rational for a user to buy larger quantities. First, this means they can make fewer purchases; second, they spend less time travelling with it, which in theory reduces apprehension risk.[5] However, that is irrelevant in Amsterdam because users do not fear being caught by police. They do not risk trouble as long as they have no more than 5 grams on their person – a further reason not to buy more than that at a coffeeshop.[6]

Those issues reduce the demand for large purchases, although other factors promote them, which I shall examine shortly. First, however, I should add that even if buyers are interested in acquiring relatively large amounts of cannabis, success does not hinge on enticing coffeeshops to break the 5 grams rule. Customers can easily sidestep the government-set limit by buying the maximum amount at multiple coffeeshops. 'If they want more than 5 grams', remarked Finn, 'they just step across the street, buy 5 grams, step around the corner, buy 5 grams more.' All of this is to say that coffeeshops are not under much pressure from purchasers to sell more than 5 grams.

Two groups are known to order larger quantities than permitted. One consists of people living in a nearby country, such as Belgium, France or Germany. I observed these tourists make prohibitively large purchases at Man in the Bottle. By train, a trip between Amsterdam and Paris or Brussels takes five or three hours respectively. I mention that because French-speaking persons wearing train uniforms (resembling those worn by airline attendants) came into the coffeeshop, stocked up on their favorite cannabis varieties, put it in their bags and headed back to Central Station for their trip home. Though I have no direct knowledge of this, it is easy to imagine that Europeans living outside the Netherlands travel to Amsterdam and buy relatively large quantities of cannabis; they then resell it upon returning home. That possibility is indeed why the 5 grams rule exists in the first place. Years before, the limit was 30 grams, but, over time, that was deemed to be too high.[7] Past and present, this international problem is much more associated with Dutch border cities than Amsterdam, located in the heart of the country.[8]

Undercover police are the other group suspected of requesting more than 5 grams from coffeeshops. 'You never know who it is', reflected Adam. 'Some people are very paranoid about it, and think there is someone spying on the coffeeshop.' Though Stijn misunderstood the rule, he said of selling more than 5 grams at a time: 'It doesn't happen because most of the time here, we are very strict. The police come in every once in a while, and we have a good name. You would be very stupid if you do that, because sometimes the police send people to buy it, to buy more than 5 grams. They just check it.' There is a belief that undercover police observe coffeeshops before conducting the formal check. This was mentioned after the police check on At Last (see Chapter 1); I overheard the owner tell Maud that he was convinced undercover officers had been inside the night before.

Personnel may worry about undercover policing, but it is clearly not an absolute deterrent. This is because they believe they can use social cues to distinguish undercover officers from normal customers.[9] Maud confessed to breaking the 5 grams rule, distributing '6 or 7 [grams], not more than that'. She thought it is harmless: 'Yeah, I have done it, but I don't take risks. I know they are not from the cops.' The type of customer cast as a potential undercover cop is white, male, middle-aged or older, with a native Dutch accent. Thinking this, Selma sold large quantities to anyone except them (and, as discussed in Chapter 1, she hesitated to take samples from them). When I asked Hanna if she sells more than allowed to anyone, she responded in similar vein: 'Depends [what] the people are like. People who are Dutch, I wouldn't do it. Maybe they are from the police or something or they go to police.' I asked what about if I asked for more than 5 grams. 'Yes', she answered, 'I would give you.'

Discounts and freebies

Related to how much customers purchase is how much they pay. Chapter 2 details the range and normal cost of coffeeshop products. Another issue is variation between customers in how much they are asked to pay for any given product, such as a particular strain of marijuana, at a given coffeeshop. Most people pay the advertised amount, but some are given discounts and freebies.[10] I learned of three circumstances in which discounts are given.

One scenario is standard business practice: charging less when a customer purchases more. 'The more you buy', said Luuk, 'the cheaper it is.' Hassan told me: 'I give deals on 5 gram bags. If you buy 5 grams, you get a deal on it: 50 cents discount per gram. Normally a gram is €8. If you take 5 grams, you are going to get €7.50 [per] gram.' Selma admitted that Man in the Bottle sells cannabis at 50 per cent fdiscount when people buy 100 grams or more. For instance, a gram of Jack Herer is listed as €12 a gram on their menu, but sold at €6 if a person purchases the requisite amount. Her coffeeshop also gave a discount for customers that 'take

5 grams. It says a discount on the menu [for that amount]'. Selma went on to say: 'But then when people take more like 15 or 20 grams, we can make even a nicer price. Then it is really cheap because instead of €70, it is going to be €60 because the normal price is €7 a gram. So if you buy 10 grams it is [usually] €70; we give it to you for €65 and we make this extra discount for €60.'

As Selma mentioned, quantity discounts are advertised on cannabis menus, such as one that reads, 'Special at 5 grams. 10% Discount'. Other coffeeshop menus offer White Widow at €8 for 1 gram or €38 for 5 grams (a saving of €2 per gram) and Juicy Fruit at €12 for a gram or €55 for 5 grams (a saving of €5 per gram).[11] Quantity discounts start lower than 5 grams in some establishments, such as one selling Vanilla Kush, among other products, at €15 for one gram or €43 for 3 grams (a saving of €2). The menu at another coffeeshop listed the amount of grams given in exchange for €10, €20, €40 or €50. For example, a customer there can buy a gram of Northern Lights for €8.50 or get 1.3 grams for €10. They can also get 3 grams for €20; 6.4 grams for €40; and 8.5 grams for €50.

That sliding scale raises the question of how coffeeshops are able to advertise selling more than 5 grams. A menu communicates the answer: 'We are only allowed to sell 5 grams per customer per day. Larger deals are for groups only.' They openly sell more than 5 grams to a person, if that customer is with someone else. Personnel calculate they can sell up to 10 grams to two customers, 15 grams to three and so on. When Charlotte asserted 'It is written clearly on the menu that you can buy more than 5 grams, but then it says in little letters' – I interrupted to comment, 'If you have more than one person' – and she responded, 'Yes, that is the trick'.

The trick is within the rules, but it does lead to violations. A person who wishes to buy more than 5 grams can simply walk in with a bunch of friends who, in fact, have nothing to do with the purchase. Or customers can lie about being with a large group of people to see if the dealer calls their bluff. Stijn said of such deceit: 'If people are with more people, then you can sell them more. Some of them lie, and say they are with 20 people upstairs, trying to buy whatever he wants.'

The other two discount scenarios are more social (than simply economic) and interrelated: coffeeshops offer cheaper prices to employees, some of whom, in turn, offer 'their discount' to their friends, workers from the area or neighbourhood residents. In addition to quantity-based discounts, Selma gave better bargains to 'the locals – they get some extra discount. I can make, instead of €14 for the bag, I can make it €12 for the bag. I can just make it myself a bit how I think the person is. I write it down just as discount. I make a line around it [on the accounting sheet,] and sometimes I write down if I know who it is or I say [it is] a neighbour.' James described his employee discount and how he passes it on to others, partially rationalising his social altruism in economic terms:

> We get 5 per cent discount as staff and, yeah, I give my staff discount to some of my friends. Five per cent is not a huge amount. I mean certainly [I give it] for all the other dealers [who work at other coffeeshops] because I've drunk and socialised in most of these places. If I am giving the dealers from Doomsday and Whole Truth their weed [for personal use], and [in return] someone [who] comes in and asks them where they buy their weed, they haven't got any qualms about saying 'No Return'. I mean, you have to promote your own coffeeshop. We have 18 or 19 weeds, whereas most places have only got like 6 or 7. So if the dealers are buying at your coffeeshop then obviously they are going to send more business when people ask for something different. So I give them a discount because it is worth it for the business, I think.

Perhaps it seems odd that personnel should buy their cannabis from coffeeshops other than the one(s) they work at. But the market is sufficiently varied in the price and quality of available products to motivate employees to buy their marijuana and hash from competitors. Probably more would do so were it not for receiving discounts from their place of work. Selma and Alex told me that without their 'special price', they would not buy from Man in the Bottle; its normal prices were too high.

Not all coffeeshops offer discounts. When I asked Wouter if any of Live Long's clients get a better bargain, he denied it. 'No, everybody gets the same. Even if they are my best friend, they get the same amount.' Maud agreed. 'No, because I have to pay it [full price] myself. Even if people are nice, I just give them the normal weight.' Gijs gave a similar response: 'No, we never do that. Everybody is equal, everybody gets the same price. There is no discount for anybody. If people say, "If I buy 5 grams can I get a discount?" the answer is "No, everybody [already] gets [a] discount. Go to the other shops, compare the prices from them with our prices, and you will see that everybody is a winner".'

Personnel can charge less for purchases, but not give more weight. This is due to the two ways in which coffeeshops sell loose cannabis: the pre-weigh and free-weigh systems (p. 30). For example, Emma, who dealt with the pre-weigh system, said of discounts, 'It is impossible [to give extra cannabis], everything is already counted. The bags are counted and I just have to come up with the money. I can't give any discounts'. The other way coffeeshops sell loose cannabis is to 'weigh it up in front of the customer, on the counter on a scale', as Hassan did at Shrine. These scales are accurate to tenths or hundredths of a gram, and personnel are accountable for every little bit. Referring to giving extra weight, Thomas observed, 'I can't do that because everything is in the system and is very specific, to 0.1 gram. So I can't do that for anyone'.

While some coffeeshops give everyone the same price, offering non-cannabis freebies is common practice among them. 'Everybody pays the normal thing', remarked Mara, though she added, 'When people come every time and they sit here and drink, they get coffee for free sometimes. They sit here, they take 4 coffees they pay for 2. But we don't make different prices for different people.' Gijs mentioned that his workers do something similar, except it comes out of their on-the-job drink allowance: 'They can give away drinks. Everybody who works on the floor has €15 to spend in his shift on drinks, coffee or whatever is available in the shop. This is hard to spend in a day. You are not going to drink eight bottles of coke. You don't do that, so you can give away some to customers. This is only with the drinks.' He also told a funny story about a promotional cannabis item that they gave away, until it got out of hand:

> We had this rule that if it is somebody's birthday you can give him a pre-rolled joint, 'Happy Birthday it's for you'. You put it in the computer as 'given away as a pre-rolled joint', but I stopped that yesterday because it was getting out of hand. I had a feeling that some of the staff working there were like, 'Oh it's my birthday today'. So that's why I put a stop to it yesterday, and that's going to be for a few weeks yet.

Rip-offs

Whereas some buyers pay a lower price per gram, others are defrauded or 'ripped off'.[12] To be clear, I am not referring to cases in which customers' experiences fall short of their expectations about quality. An example is a reviewer on *Coffeeshop Directory* who complained: 'My husband ate half a piece of hash cake and I ate only one bonbon. After waiting an hour to two hours, we felt NOTHING! Next day we ate a whole piece of cake and, again, nothing! Were we ripped off 'cause we were Americans?' Another reviewer posted: 'I was ripped off with five grams of Caramello. When burned, it bubbled, smelt really bad; no stone whatsoever, just a sore throat and headache. Will never darken their door again.' Though quality complaints might be legitimate, they could also be due to unreasonable expectations or inexperience in getting high.[13]

In this context a 'rip-off' or 'fraud' strictly refers to cannabis/money transfers in which the advertised price per unit does not match the amount received. Examples of this also appear on *Coffeeshop Directory*.[14] A customer wrote: 'He definitely under-weighed us. Their scales have been tampered with. Beware. We went in, then went out. Crap.' Another protested: 'He [a friend] purchased a gram of Maco Haze, but didn't actually see the budtender weigh it. When my mate went to roll up, he commented on the size of the deal and I must admit it looked well lightweight.' Whether customers are suspicious or certain of being ripped off depends on their ability to check the weight on a scale. 'I'm convinced', one reviewer moaned, 'the bags weren't quite the size they were meant to be. I mean we didn't have scales on us, but from my previous experience in Amsterdam that day I thought 3 grams would have been bigger.'

In contradiction to those accounts, personnel were adamant that everyone gets at least a fair deal. When I asked Hassan and Mara about defrauding customers, he and she asserted, respectively, 'No, no, I don't have the need to do that' and 'No, we don't do that'. Only one dealer, Claire, confessed to (barely) ripping off a customer:

> We weigh it. Sometimes I have customers, like before I had French people who were a real pain in the ass because they are too lazy to talk English. They talk French to me. They are very arrogant, and sometimes they think they can do everything here. They still talk French to me and then they have big attitude and I just give them 0.9 instead of 1 gram. I hate you because you don't treat me like a normal person, so I give you just 0.9! It is the wrong thing to do, but [I did it].

As with giving discounts, the manner in which coffeeshops sell loose cannabis affects opportunity to defraud clients. When questioned about giving better or worse deals, Luuk just answered, 'No, it's already in the bag', indicating that this precludes the choice. Yet depending on how long the marijuana has been bagged, and how long it is dried beforehand, preweighed bags can lose weight and thereby falsely advertise the purchase price. I asked Luca if this ever happens. 'They are dry when you buy them', he confidently replied. 'People don't want to buy wet weed. Why would you want to buy wet weed, man? It needs to be dry.' However, customers complain of this problem, which they prove valid by weighing purchases with their own scales. 'I took a scale with me', shared one reviewer.

'Got Silverhaze for €15 for 2.8 grams, but it was 2.1 plus 0.7 packaging.' 'They are selling the weed in pre-weighted bags and they try to fool you', wrote another reviewer. 'I bought some Orange Bud and some K2. Every weed in there is 3 grams. I bought two bags, didn't smoke anything. Back at home my scale showed me exactly 2 grams (Orange Bud) and 2.1 grams (K2) without the bags. With my friends' bags it was the same. Shame on them!'

Rather than weigh it themselves, customers ask personnel to do so in front of them. 'Many customers ask me "Can you just weigh it for me?"' said Kamila. 'If you don't weigh it out in front of the customer, they can ask you to weigh it for you. Some German people [for example] came in and asked to check, and I said, "Yes, let them check it". Also, we have to put one [empty] package [on the scale to see what it weighs, too]. It is about zero, but sometimes it is a bit more.' I asked her why she agrees to such requests, to which she simply said: 'You should do. It is good for your business.'[15]

Customers do the same at free-weigh establishments. I saw this at Man in the Bottle. Shortly after opening, three young French guys came in and ordered 5 grams. Selma weighed that amount, bagged it and handed it over. For whatever reason, the customer requested that she weigh it again. She put it back on the scale and invited him to have a look at the reading, but he declined. Selma re-bagged it and told him: 'If you pay for 5 grams, you get 5 grams.' He took the marijuana and left with his friends, at which point Selma turned to me and commented that it was stupid for him to have the cannabis re-weighed, but not to look at the scale.

Compared to the pre-weigh system, the free-weigh system seems less likely to result, intentionally or not, in ripping off customers. After all, the weight literally reads off at the point of sale, which eliminates the opportunity for losing weight (due to the drying process) or mislabeling bags. This openness should protect against fraud by making the amount clearly visible to anyone. Yet the free-weigh system has its own problems. Some dealers are cheeky enough to test customers. This happened to one reviewer, who wrote: 'The dealer with the baseball cap ripped me at 0.2 grams on a 5 gram deal. Even as I told him that was not enough, he just gave me a smile!'

More often, rip-offs spring from the difficulty of weighing cannabis to precise amounts, such as 1.00 gram. Exactness matters because giving even a tenth of a gram too much is bad for the bottom line, but giving too little can cause conflict with customers, which is bad for business too. Getting the weight right takes meticulousness and time. Typically the dealer starts the process by placing on the scale whatever amount of cannabis is obviously needed to get near the ordered amount, but no more. It is better to go up in weight than down because the former is less likely to annoy customers. From there, the dealer will add pinches of cannabis until the gram count is on the dot. If it is not quite there, the dealer places tiny amounts on the scale until the reading bumps up a tenth of a gram.

If a computer-based scale is used, the dealer continues that last step until satisfied with the amount, then presses a button that logs it. Sometimes a dealer jumps the gun by pressing the button too soon – from the customer's perspective. On one occasion I was near a customer who requested a gram of marijuana from the dealer. The worker proceeded to free-weigh the weed, but the highest the scale got to was 0.99 gram. Rather than keep working to get the perfect amount, the dealer simply pressed the button. He handed the bag over to the buyer, who paid for it without mentioning its low weight.

Such discrepancies rarely, if ever, work in the customer's favour. If the total is not exactly what it should be, it is almost always less. Yet at what point does a discrepancy become defined as fraud? That depends on who you ask. I suspect that many stoners frown at a dime bag weighing 0.9 gram, though this is only off by 10 per cent and practically too small to see. And most may agree that 0.99 gram is close enough. If the price per gram is €10, that is equivalent to throwing away 10 cents. Some buyers, then, will want the purchase to be no less than 0.999, which leaves a single cent on the table; even that may be wanted back.

The point here is less about transactions involving money and cannabis than the principle of fairness.[16] Still, losing a few cents may seem trivial. It is not to staff, however, as they understand that small differences add up. Gijs and I discussed this issue, a conversation that began when I asked if Escape Clause ever rips off its customers.

> **Gijs:** You don't want to do that. We don't do that, and we can't do that because we have a computer screen standing there that is linked to the scale, so the customer can see exactly what he gets. Everybody gets what he pays for. It's such an accurate system. If you want to weigh a gram [for example], I always tell people [dealers to] start from 0.8 or 0.9. If you start breaking off from higher than a gram [1.2 for example], there is always the chance it could go to 1.1 gram, and if that happens with a 100 customers you are going to miss out 0.1 gram 100 times.

Me: So how accurate do you feel a coffeeshop should be? At what point is the customer getting ripped off? I mean, maybe 0.99 isn't a rip-off, but is 0.98 or 0.97?
Gijs: You are talking about 10 cents. That can happen. Some customers, they see that and they go, 'Hey man, that's not €10, that's €9.90'. You say 'Oh fuck, sorry, here is 10 cents'. Next time he won't ask for that any more.
Me: So that actually happens?
Gijs: That has happened, yes, that has happened. So you go, 'Sorry man, here's 10 cents or would you like this little crumb of weed with it?' Then they are like, 'Oh fuck' and they feel embarrassed, like 'Why did I ask for 10 cents?'
Me: The customer could argue it both ways.
Gijs: They can, they can. In the old days, like I say I've smoked 30 years, if it was a little bit over a gram, I'd leave it. But you can't afford that if you have a shop like Escape Clause. I mean there are a lot of customers coming in. If you keep giving away to every customer, at the end of the line – because we have computer printouts of the shift – you can see exactly that you gave away too much.

Notes

1. See Verdurmen, Ketelaars and van Laar 2005.
2. For additional evidence of coffeeshops breaking this rule, see Hazekamp 2006.
3. For information on the frontstage versus backstage of social life, see Goffman 1959.
4. But see Becker 2015.
5. See Jacques and Wright 2015.
6. See Verdurmen, Ketelaars and van Laar 2005. In other sorts of retail cannabis purchases (i.e. outside coffeeshops), it is typical for buyers to limit the amount purchased (Davenport and Caulkins 2016).
7. See MHWS 2003.
8. See Advisory Committee on Drugs Policy 2009.
9. For information on drug dealers' ability to discredit supposed buyers as undercover officers, see Jacobs 1993, 1996. On discrediting stigmatised individuals generally, see Goffman 1963.
10. For information on drug dealers giving discounts and gifts to users, see Coomber 2006; Jacobs 1999; Jacques and Wright 2015.
11. For information on quantity discounts with respect to illicit drugs, see Pacula and Lundberg 2014.
12. For information on drug dealers defrauding customers, see Jacobs 1999; Jacques, Allen and Wright 2014; Jacques and Wright 2015. On rip-offs by licit retail sellers, see Blumberg 1989.
13. See Becker 2015.
14. For additional evidence of coffeeshops defrauding customers, see Hazekamp 2006.
15. For information on demonstrating one's self as not having a stigmatised trait, see Goffman 1963.
16. For information on the psychology of pricing, see Kahneman, Knetsch and Thaler 1986.

5
Hard drugs

A major goal of Dutch drug policy is to minimise hard drug consumption, such as that of cocaine, ecstasy and heroin.[1] To separate the hard drug and cannabis markets, coffeeshops are allowed to sell the latter. Otherwise, it is feared, cannabis users will be offered hard drugs by their dealers. Part of achieving market separation is the rule against hard drugs at coffeeshops. It is effective. Research shows, for example, that coffeeshops are less likely than other cannabis sellers, such as those working the streets or from home, to sell hard drugs.[2] This implies that coffeeshop clientele have less opportunity to start and continue using more serious substances. Consider how the policy shaped Jana's experiences:

> I believe very much in the system of keeping the line very big between marijuana, the soft drugs, and the other stuff, hard drugs. I really think it is a good thing that as you grow up, people see it [cannabis sold in coffeeshops]. It is open. It is not something that is really scary to do. I also hear from people from England, like the drug dealers there, that if they don't have marijuana, they have all this other stuff that you can have, 'cause you still want to get high on something. Here, where I was born, there was never a time that people said: 'I don't have it [cannabis] so take something else.' I never saw that when I was younger, and I am happy for that.

Technically, the rule is that coffeeshops cannot sell hard drugs. In practice, however, this is interpreted by personnel and police as a wholesale ban on having hard drugs on the premises. About two-thirds of personnel reported full compliance over the prior year (see Table 0.5). For example, Gijs and Claire said of hard drug use and street dealers respectively 'I never found anyone doing that [in the coffeeshop]' and 'They don't come in here'. But, as with minors, personnel are not always sure that hard drugs are absent. 'Not that I know of' is how some personnel, such as Hana and Luca, answered my question about whether hard drugs had ever been on the premises.

In part, the doubt is attributable to the 1012 being notorious for hard drug trade and use.[3] During the study period, and especially in and around the red light district, it was common to pass by people who appeared to be destitute drug addicts, or tourists high on more than cannabis and alcohol. Furthermore, an observer would hear offers of 'cocaine, ecstasy' or 'white, brown' – code words for cocaine and heroin. Street dealers are notorious for whispering this to passersby who they think may be interested in these substances. As a researcher, I used this to my advantage. When solicited by a street dealer, I solicited their participation in an interview. What they said with respect to coffeeshops is presented in this chapter's concluding section (p. 118).[4]

Given the 1012's reputation for hard drugs, personnel have good reason to believe they are brought onto the premises by non-personnel. Finn thought that 'on the whole, the coffeeshop is powder and pills free', but then added, 'I am sure some guys sniff something'. 'I am sure', Linda postulated, 'some customers might have had it in their pockets or their bags. But I haven't caught anyone, or heard of my colleagues getting anyone.'

At this stage in the book, it need not be repeated that the risk of sanction motivates personnel to obey the rule. More so than any other government rule, however, personnel perceived enforcement of the ban on hard drugs to be unjust. Part of the complaint is that coffeeshops are punished for small amounts that are tolerated on the street.[5] Adam described an occasion when police 'closed the place [a coffeeshop] down for a week. The police came in, and they found a tiny amount of cocaine and some ecstasy pills. We are talking about very small amounts'. 'The police come in and find a gram of coke on the floor', Hassan asserted, 'you are fucked! You are going to get closed. That's how it goes.'

Personnel also protested that they can be punished for non-personnel's actions. 'If you get caught in a coffeeshop with a gram of cocaine in your pocket', Jens told me, 'even if you are [just] a fucking person who comes in there and sits down and smokes a joint, that person is risking the licence of that coffeeshop, and the whole existence of the coffeeshop. They can close you down permanently for someone else having a controlled substance in their pocket in your coffeeshop.'

Coffeeshops face a similar problem with minors. Controlling hard drugs is more difficult, however, because there is no mechanism equivalent to checking someone's ID. To quote Joseph: 'I can't search you, so I don't know what is in your pocket.' Without a reasonably foolproof method of checking for hard drugs, personnel doubt that their coffeeshop is completely free of them. When I asked Jack about compliance at Alike All Over, he answered: 'Almost certainly [hard drugs have been] in people's pockets. Nobody has been caught. This is the thing: we can't search everyone coming in the door.' Elias took a similar postion: 'I have not seen it, but as long as I don't know though [there is nothing I can do]. Otherwise, I have to turn everybody's pockets around and see what they have on them [which I can't do].'

Referring to how coffeeshops are stuck between a rock and a hard place, Anna asserted it is 'very silly [to be punished by the government for this] because I cannot see what is in my customers' pockets'. Luuk stressed that it 'was not possible' to keep hard drugs out of coffeeshops, then declared why punishment for their presence is unfair: 'I heard today from somebody, they found in a coffeeshop somebody had hard drugs with them, and now they want to shut down the shop. But it's unfair because when I go to the Albert Heine [grocery store], the police come in, I have cocaine in my pocket, and [they] find cocaine with me, they don't shut down Albert Heine.'

Signs of hard drugs

Personnel are not entirely helpless, of course. 'Looking out' is their major tactic for complying with the ban on hard drugs. Looking out is important in every coffeeshop, but especially those in the 1012 because, to reiterate, it is a hotbed of hard drug distribution and consumption. 'If you know there's a lot of street dealing activity around you', Stefan asserted, 'you're a bit stupid if you're not looking out for it in your shop.' Yet, as Dean half-joked, that it is difficult because hard drug possessors 'don't have a sign [on]' to that effect. Instead, personnel must rely on social signals to identify troublemakers.[6] Finn alluded to this when he remarked: 'I have been throwing out people [for a long time] who have used heroin, cocaine or whatever, so I know when someone does not belong in here.'

Some signs of possession are behaviour-based. Personnel look out for persons acting in a way that is abnormal – or, thought of differently, a way that is normal for hard drug dealers and users. Sophie recounted an encounter with an English customer, for instance: 'He was very drunk, and I think he was on coke because he was like spaced out of his mind.' Signs are also appearance-based.[7] In Chapter 3 we discussed how coffeeshops ban anyone wearing a hat and sunglasses because they are associated with 'problem' groups – Moroccans, Antilleans and Surinamese – involved in hard drugs. A more obvious indicator is 'if you have white powder on your face', which Claire told me is indicative of cocaine use. Flour face results when people snort cocaine, as the powder can shoot in directions other than straight up the nose. If the snorter does not take care to clean up afterwards, they look as if they have been baking.

Poor hygiene is another appearance-based sign of hard drug use or dealing. 'One time we had someone here', Emir recalled, 'and he looked illegal. He looked dirty [hygienically], not clean, like a criminal. He came inside and we were busy and I saw him come in. My boss would not want [inside] dirty people from the streets, who do business on the streets; criminals.' 'For us', Thomas informed me about Buzz, 'upstairs is an area actually for tourists, and for people that want to use the vapouriser. Locals are not allowed up there [because] there have been cases of dealings going on up there, hard drugs.' I asked how he distinguishes a local from a tourist, to which he admitted: 'I am judging on appearances, if they kind of look nasty.'

In addition to what people look like, personnel use language to make inferences about involvement in hard drugs. Elias observed that 'if you are really coked up, I can see it with your speech'. Hassan took a straightforward approach: 'I have the kind of customers I want to get in, and those customers I do not. I only want tourists. That's who I want to have in. You have a lot of dealers here on the streets, and I never let them in.' I questioned how he knows the difference, to which he answered, 'Based on their looks, whether they speak Dutch'. As with suspected undercover cops (see Chapters 1 and 4) and minors (Chapter 3), speaking or sounding Dutch is a bad sign.

Some personnel have been around the 1012 long enough to recognise particular hard drug users and dealers.[8] Owners and employees use that information to keep the usual suspects at bay. As Wouter told me: 'We know the faces 'cause they are walking here all around the centre [of the city].' Lizzie said of her coffeeshop's doormen: 'Security knows exactly who the street dealers are because they have worked in this area for many years. Especially the older man, he has worked in cafés almost all his life, so he knows all of them.'

Personnel learn 'who is who' based on the aforementioned social cues. They also obtain such knowledge by witnessing people solicit interest in selling or buying hard drugs. Joseph described a time in which a street dealer 'was trying to sell something to the people outside, I think they were English guys. When he was there, he tried to ask them for a lighter and got into a conversation, but I saw what was going on was not good.' Emma told me she has 'see[n] money being exchanged. I just go up and tell them, "This is my business, and I am the only one doing business here".'

Elias estimated that '100 times in a year' street dealers try 'to push in front of the door, announcing that they have some stuff'. Their message is not always explicit, so personnel are not always sure what is said. But suspicion that hard drugs are the topic is more likely to arise, and be acted on, if the person in question looks like a street dealer in the eyes of watching personnel. Jack alluded to this cause-and-effect relationship: 'It is a matter of watching people wandering by up and down here. There are faces I know from the neighbourhood, and it is more beggars than street dealers, but anyone starting to chat with my customers on the terrace will get moved along. It is only ever, "Move along please".'

Basic economics suggests that street dealers are a problem in the 1012 because there is demand for their products.[9] Evidence of this is that customers ask personnel about buying hard drugs, presumably not realising that to do so in a coffeeshop is a massive faux pas. To quote Kamila: 'They come in and ask, "Do you know where I can buy something?"' Joseph mentioned this is particularly common of 'the British, the English guys. They come here, they ask if you have cocaine'. Once when I showed up at Man in the Bottle for a cup of coffee, Selma told me that a couple days before a German couple had asked her something. Unsure what, she asked the woman to repeat herself; she then leaned in to whisper, 'Do you have cocaine?'

Personnel's worst-case scenario is to spot hard drugs in plain sight, as the police could suddenly walk in and see the same. Jens, for example, 'found a gram of cocaine on the floor'. Remnants of consumption are a problem, too.[10] 'We have found needles in the toilet, it was hidden', Noah informed me. James reported: 'You go and check the toilets, and you might find a bit of white band around the tiles. It is probably utter bullshit that some tourist bought off an idiot out there, but [it still is a problem].'

Comically bad cases are those in which customers try to use hard drugs openly while sitting at a coffeeshop. Ruben remembered one occasion: 'these big sporty guys, like military guys, were trying to sniff on the fucking table, man. They were on the fucking front table, man! Stupid fucks.' Guus hypothesised why customers use hard drugs in the open, and described a case in which he had been involved: 'Many tourists, when they come to Holland, they think when they go into a coffeeshop they can do everything. They think everything is legal what you do. I was very surprised one time, I went upstairs to bring his drink, and he put a line on the table. And I say, "What is that?" I didn't believe it because it's unbelievable.'

Distancing possessors

When personnel think, or know, that someone is in possession of hard drugs – or is trying to acquire some – they respond with distancing techniques.[11] Street dealers loitering outside are asked to go elsewhere, for example. Finn directed them 'to piss off [from] in front of the door'. Likewise, Elias 'ask[s] them to take their business elsewhere. If you ask them to leave, they leave'. Thomas asserted: 'We have a very tight control. We are very strict on that. No loitering about whatsoever. Anybody [who] does not belong there gets asked to move along.' Joseph reacted in the following way when he observed a street dealer soliciting a customer on the terrace: 'I went to kick him out and I warned them that in my premises we don't do [hard drug] business. I told him to leave, and he just left.'

Street dealers do not always go willingly, however. 'We have a lot of screaming going on almost every day because they are in front of my door', Sophie explained. 'If they deal in front of the door, then we ask them to go away.' When they put up a verbal fight, personnel's modal response is to respond in kind. 'They can have a big mouth', Gwen stated nonchalantly, 'so you just tell them to shut the fuck up and they will go away.' Likewise Ruben 'tell[s] them to fuck off sometimes. Not out of here, but in front of the coffeeshop. They know me, most of them. Sometimes they forget where they are, and I have to tell them, "Listen man, this is my street. You have my respect so give me respect".' When I questioned him about what they say in return, Ruben replied: '"Blah, blah" – but they always walk away.'

Another facet of distancing is denying entry to possessors. 'If I know you are coked up', Stijn remarked, 'if I see it, you don't get inside. I can then tell [you] I don't want you inside.' Personnel's ability to deny entry is limited because, as we have discussed, coffeeshops tend not to have doormen, though they are effective when used. Lizzie explained that because of Whole Truth's doormen, 'We don't have a lot of problems from street dealers. And if they come anywhere near here, they are not allowed to interact inside at all. Just, "You know you cannot come here".'

When a hard drug suspect does make it inside, the method of distancing changes from denying entry to expulsion. Personnel do so before or after selling to the wrongdoer, depending on the timing of the provocation.[12] Hassan insisted that he denies service when 'I see someone and I don't trust him; when I have that feeling my senses say, "Listen, this guy is not 100 per cent", so I don't sell him stuff'. Referring to the 'dirty' person 'from the streets', Emir continued: 'He came inside and we were busy and I saw him come in. I told him, "Man, it is not OK". I had a feeling and I stopped him. I told him, "Sorry, excuse me, I don't need you to stay here". We don't want that sort of people in here.' Linda stated that suspected 'street dealers are just told, "Hey, we don't want you in". We remove them right away'. And Joseph described why he refuses selling to people he deems risky: 'People come here, and I refuse to sell to them because I don't trust them. I see them as street guys, maybe like a drug dealer. I cannot search you, but I will tell you clearly that I refuse you because I think you are a street boy.'

Other cases of expulsion occur after a sale is made to the possessor. Joseph recalled a case in which he 'kick[ed] away a customer who was trying to do [hard drug] business here. I have been here quite a long time, I have a lot of experience, and I can just tell'. 'Every time we suspect someone is selling hard drugs', Claire asserted, 'we tell them to leave. We tell them not to come back here.' 'We asked him kindly to get out' is how Sophie handled the drunk and presumably coked-up customer she talked about. And Maud affirmed: 'Sometimes it happens, a client comes inside, and then we have to throw him outside if they are acting weird. We don't want those kinds of people inside of the coffeeshop.'

The manner in which personnel expel suspects ranges from cool to hot, meaning from calm to aggressive.[13] When Guus rhetorically asked his customers if that was cocaine on the table, their response was 'This is a coffeeshop. This is legal'. Guus corrected them: 'I have to explain what it is. "You can use in a coffeeshop only hash [and marijuana]. You cannot use another drug." [Then] I asked him to leave.' Kamila told the customers who asked about how to get cocaine: '"Go to the police station and they will tell you very quickly!" They are ashamed and walk out.' After being asked the same question by patrons, Joseph asked his own question: '"Do you see it there [in the counter display]?" They say, "No". So I say: "Then why are you asking me? Everything I have is in the middle, so if you don't see it there I don't have that one. So why ask me?" I kick them out.'

A hotter response was described by Ruben. When he discovered open cocaine use at The Mighty, he 'blew up. I said, "Are you fucking sick in your head or something!? What the fuck are you thinking!?" They thought it was normal or something to use hard drugs in Amsterdam. I kicked them out. I just took his arm and helped him get the fuck out really quick.' 'Why did you react like that?' I asked. He answered: 'It's because the coffeeshop would be shut if they found hard drugs on the premises, and that is the number one rule.' Similarly, when customers asked Selma about getting cocaine, she 'flipped out' (her words) by yelling at and expelling the couple. She explained this reaction as due to being in a bad mood, noting that a few days earlier she had been asked the same by a customer, but that time responded, 'You're lucky I'm in a good mood. No, we don't. Get out of here'.

In addition to distancing, personnel described two other ways of discouraging street dealers, in particular, from being inside or even near their coffeeshops. These alternatives are comparatively uncommon, but still worth mentioning. One is to call the police or to threaten doing so.[14] This happens when dealers are unwilling to be shooed away while loitering outside. 'We will ring the police if they don't go' is how Mara put it. Maikel recalled: 'There have been some street dealers standing in front of my terrace. I ask them to walk away. Sometimes they are stubborn. I tell them it is my shop and I will call the police, then they walk away.'[15]

The other method of handling street dealers is to tolerate their presence.[16] James did so, albeit only for short stints, because he thought it is better than making a fuss: 'Pretty much they know not to [come inside]. If they come in and just want a paper I will do it, as long as they are respectful, because it is easier than going, "No, no", and causing a scene over what takes two seconds – they can just get a paper and go.' Gwen, on the other hand, tolerated their presence because she trusted them not to bring hard drugs into Like a Child:

> You kind of know who they are. They also know that they have to keep everything outside. Come inside with your stuff in your pockets and you are out of here, and they know that. Of course, you can never really know. To be honest, none of them actually stay for all that long, just a few minutes. The people that actually are allowed inside know the rules, and I think they do understand. I know they have stashes out there.[17]

Staying away

The previous section focuses on how personnel distance possessors from their coffeeshop, which is a matter of proterrence. So too, and even better, is preventing possessors from even coming near the establishment. Emma believed that street dealers 'know they shouldn't be here'. Sophie agreed: 'They just know this is not the place for them. If they come in here, they know that they are not welcome. Every dealer in the street knows that they cannot come in here.' And Luuk stated: 'We know them, and they know us, so they don't come. As long as they're not in front of the shop or near, that's OK. And they know, so they stay away from the shop, don't come in the shop, they're not in front of the shop, they're not near the shop.'

Those sentiments may seem optimistic, or naïve, but they are largely confirmed by the street dealers that I interviewed. When asked if they solicit or sell in coffeeshops, they normally gave answers like 'No, I don't' (Astrando), 'No, I try not to do that' (Sherida) and 'Never, honestly' (Damien).

There are a few reasons why possessors, especially street dealers, stay away from coffeeshops. One, it makes little sense to bring a punishable substance to a place subject to random police checks. Jack said it best: 'If you are up to dodgy shit, you wouldn't store anything in a place that could be raided by the [police] at any moment of the day or year. To me that makes sense.' Street dealers expressed the same opinion. Kenneth, for instance, steered clear of coffeeshops 'because if you happen to be in there when they get raided [you're in trouble]'. To be clear, this sort of motivation reflects deterrence (not proterrence), as the dealer's only concern is the action of police, not of personnel.

Additionally, street dealers worried that personnel would initiate police action by calling them. 'It gives you problems, man', said Amparo. 'The owner might kick you out and call the police immediately. So it is too high a risk. You will get problems.' This motivation is the product of proterrence in that personnel call the cops on street dealers to prevent their establishment from being punished for hard drugs.

Respect is another reason why possessors stay out of coffeeshops. This was mentioned by Soraida, who commented of making hard drug sales: 'No, never in a coffeeshop. I have respect for coffeeshops. It is the people's business. I have respect for the owner of the shop. I would not try to do my business in his shop. I do my business outside the coffeeshop.' Guus expressed the same sentiment regarding possessors: 'They know they do not belong here. I think that has to do with respect.'

In part, respect reflects common knowledge that coffeeshops are put at risk by bringing hard drugs inside. Selma believed that street dealers 'would really like to come here', but did not do it 'because of their respect. They really respect the fact that they cannot because [otherwise] they risk my job'. 'If the police come there, they will close it' is the reason Roy gave for not dealing drugs at coffeeshops.

Going a step further, another street dealer, Soerin, hints at a self-serving reason not to cause problems for personnel: 'The coffeeshop would not like that. He would blame you, and that is why I do not like going to coffeeshops to do that.' In a similar vein, Imra told me: 'It is better to have respect for the people. For respect, I don't go inside it [coffeeshops] because if the police come and they find something, you are the motherfucker, you bring shit to them.' This concern was echoed by a coffeeshop dealer, James, an occasional hard drug user. He never mixed cannabis and hard drugs while at coffeeshops because 'you know the police come in for checks, and if you lost him [the owner] his business because you had a bit of something in your pocket, he would be very unhappy with you. I would say [this street] is my centre of existence, so if I got one of them shut down for being a dickhead, it would reflect very badly on me.'

The words of Soerin, Imra and James show that, among other ways, coffeeshops prevent trouble by gaining respect.[18] From the perspective of personnel, the utility of being respected is that it stops possessors from bringing hard drugs to their establishment. And from the perspective of possessors, the utility of paying respect is avoiding the label, and concomitant bad treatment, of someone who puts a coffeeshop at risk or in trouble.

Yet even if possessors do not respect personnel or fear formal sanction, it may be rational for them to stay away from coffeeshops. After all, there is little reason to go there if you are going to be denied entry or expelled. Chamiel stopped trying to sell at coffeeshops because the personnel 'doesn't let me go inside'. 'No, never in a coffeeshop', Ashwin said of his business. 'Owners don't want anyone with hard rocks in their coffeeshop, so you would have a lot of problems.' On this point, Jens said of street dealers: 'They usually know not to come in. They know not to come in when I am working, because I know most of them now and know their faces. They know I would knock their fucking brains out.' Furthermore, possessors do not like to be watched, and coffeeshop personnel are well known for watching. 'We don't have a problem with them. I know them and I am very aware of them', said Anna. 'If they are sitting here I keep an eye on them. They don't like that.' Validating this perception, Enzio gave the following answer when asked if he sells at coffeeshops: 'Oh no, no, no. I don't sell things in a coffeeshop. In the coffeeshops there is a lot of watching, they listen, and people are coming and looking [like], "Who are you?"'

Notes

1. For information on hard drug use, trade and policy in Amsterdam and the Netherlands, see Buruma 2007; van der Gouwe, Ehrlich and Van Laar 2009; Grapendaal, Leuw and Nelen 1995; Jansen 1991; Korf 1995; Leuw 1991; Leuw and Marshall 1994; Monshouwer, van Laar and Vollebergh 2011; NMFA 2008; NMHWS 2003; Ooyen-Houben and Kleemans 2015; Reinarman 2016; van Solinge 1999; Trimbos Institute 2010; Zaitch 2002.

2. Wouters and Korf 2009. Also, living closer to more coffeeshops is unassociated with hard drug use, suggesting the former is not a gateway to the latter (Wouters et al. 2012).
3. See van Gemert and Verbraeck 1994; Grapendaal, Leuw and Nelen 1995; Leuw 1991; Leuw and Marshall 1994.
4. While living in Amsterdam, I interviewed 50 street dealers operating in the 1012. I will be brief about how I did so. Basically I walked around the red light district until a dealer solicited me by quietly whistling, whispering something like 'Cocaine, ecstasy', or giving me a coded head nod or look. I managed to recruit 18 street dealers that way. It was a time-consuming process, but luckily only two dealers said no and only three robbed me. To speed things along, I asked some of the initial street dealer respondents to ask their associates to do an interview as well, which helped me interview another 32 street dealers. For further information about this research, including the methods and findings, see Bernasco and Jacques 2015; Jacques and Bernasco 2013; Jacques et al. 2016.
5. See Verdurmen, Ketelaars and van Laar 2005.
6. To reduce verbiage I refer to 'hard drug possessors' as 'possessors' in some places. This category includes people who personnel suspect may possess hard drugs; those who are actually in possession of them; and those who are trying to be.
7. For information on appearance-based discriminatory control of drug suspects, especially with respect to race/ethnicity and class, see Alexander 2010; Jacques and Wright 2015; Mohamed and Fritsvold 2010; Provine 2007.
8. For information on managing individuals who are discredited, see Goffman 1963.
9. For information on the economics of illicit drug markets, including different approaches to researching it, see Caulkins and Reuter 2010; National Research Council 2010; Moeller 2017; Ritter 2006.
10. Seeing disorderly behaviour versus its remnants reflects the difference between social disorder and physical disorder respectively. For information on disorder, including its relationship to crime and control, see Kelling and Coles 1996; Sampson 2009, 2012a, 2012b; Sampson and Raudenbush 2004; St. Jean 2007; Wilson and Kelling 1982.
11. For information on drug dealers' use of avoidance to manage conflict, see Morselli et al. 2017; Jacques and Wright 2011, 2015. On the broad and specific ways that people manage conflict, see, respectively, Black 1998 and Emerson 2015.
12. One way that both control agents and offenders seek to reduce problems is by minimising provocations; see Clarke 2009; Jacques and Reynald 2012.
13. My use of 'cool' versus 'hot' here is different from, but perhaps causally related to, the use of those terms as synonymous with cognitive and emotional; see van Gelder 2013.
14. For information on calling police as a component of guardianship, see Reynald 2010.
15. Not every interviewee was in favour of this approach. Sophie, for example, saw its downside as raising the potential for retaliation: 'You just learn to live with it because if you call them every day, the next day they are out on the street again and then they remember your face and they know that you called the cops, so it's like [not the best way to handle this problem].'
16. For information on drug dealers' use of toleration to manage conflict, see Morselli et al. 2017; Jacques and Wright 2011, 2015. For information on mixed contacts between stigmatised persons and normals, see Goffman 1963.
17. It is possible for street dealers to visit coffeeshops without having hard drugs on their person due to their use of stash spots; see Bernasco and Jacques 2015; Jacques and Bernasco 2013. One street dealer, Coen, made a comment that validates Gwen's trust: 'No, [I] never [make sales] inside a coffeeshop. It is not the place for me to sell. It is the place where I relax, where I take my time for myself, take it easy for two seconds. That is my place of peace when I am not doing my job.'
18. For information on the importance of respect for preventing problems, see Anderson 1999. Similar in this regard is the importance of police legitimacy for generating obedience; see Tyler 2003, 2004.

6
Nuisance

Nuisance is a mercurial concept.[1] It includes everything from annoying noise and parking problems to disorderly offences such as loitering and littering to attracting violence, theft and vandalism.[2] If coffeeshops directly or indirectly cause these problems, they can be punished for violating the ban on nuisance.[3] Yet no personnel knew of a coffeeshop being closed or otherwise sanctioned for such an incident.[4] Nonetheless, personnel are in a daily struggle against boorish and threatening behaviour.[5] Lizzie said it best: 'You have to tell people all the time what to do, and especially what not to do.'

Nuisance ranges from minor to serious. At the lower end of the scale is impoliteness. Some bad manners are behavioural. 'The worst thing that happens in here', Finn exaggerated, 'which immediately means a red card [expulsion], is if a male person uses the female toilet. That is a capital crime in here.' Rudeness may be verbal, too. Jens told me: 'If you act up, you have to leave. We treat each other nice here. Say "Please" and "Thank you"'. Ruben's review of the house rules referred to both acts and words:

> Don't shout, don't put your feet with your shoes on the couch. Just treat the coffeeshop like it is my home. Everybody can have a [rolling] paper, but ask [don't just grab one]. When you are not buying anything and you just walk in for a paper, don't grab, just ask me. You want to go to the toilet when you are not a customer, no problem, but say 'Hello, can I go to the toilet?'

In addition to what should be said, another aspect of politeness is knowing what not to say. Gwen gave a couple of examples: 'Often [the problem at the coffeeshop] is just the boys [young customers] who are new, and they just want to show themselves [i.e. act tough]. Normally, they come in and they start bitching about the weed, saying it isn't good enough or [that] the person behind the dealer's bar doesn't treat them as they want to be.' Sophie described a verbal slight to which she responded in kind:

> This one time, I was in a very good mood and there were two Americans sitting at my bar. I started talking to him and he was, 'So, are you working in the red light [district] and are you standing in the window as well?' I was like, 'No', and I made a joke out of it. I was like, 'So what are you? You are from Texas are you? So, you are basically hillbillies?' He got mad, mad as hell, though five minutes ago he called me a whore. He was as mad as hell. He walked out.

Volume is a further facet of polite talk. When I was speaking with Willem about preferred types of customers, he pointed across the street and stated: 'A large crowd, like those guys there, they are the type of people I prefer not to come in.' He was referring to a 'stag party' or 'bachelor party' – an occasion in which a group of adult males get together to celebrate a member's upcoming marriage, often by acting like boys.[6] Typical of such groups in the 1012, the group in question was loud – and likely to be that way wherever they went, including coffeeshops.

At the serious end of the nuisance continuum is fighting between customers. Kamila laughed about an incident involving a couple of female customers: 'Someone was jealous and so they just started fighting here. They were shouting, "You were just looking at my boyfriend!" It was just so funny.' Wouter mentioned that at Live Long, the locals 'get in fights with each other a lot' over 'little bullshit'. A slightly more serious fight was described by Olivia:

> A psychotic guy felt like somebody was not listening to him. It was one of our neighbours, a guy who comes in quite often. We saw him deteriorate, just doing more and more drugs, just getting stranger in his head, just getting weird. I think he feels like he is attacked all the time, he was like [to my colleague], 'You don't respect me. You never listen to me'. There were some [customer] guys in the shop that were like, 'If he doesn't shut up now, we are going to kick him out', and my colleague was remaining quite calm. I think he [the psychotic guy] went on, and the other customers actually kicked him out. They hit him, and he did hit back.

Max talked about a conflict between black market traders who walked into Everybody. 'We had to laugh about it', he said, 'but it was for us, in the beginning, a little bit dangerous.' Here is the story:

> I was sitting upstairs. Two guys who looked like Moroccan guys, but they actually were from Algeria [we later found out], they wanted to buy cocaine from a Surinam guy on the streets. The guy, the Surinam guy, didn't have any cocaine, but just wanted to take their money. He said to them, 'Yeah, yeah, give me the money, and I have to go in here [to get the cocaine]'. He went into the shop, and locked himself into the toilet and thought, 'As long as I stay here in the toilet, after a while these guys will go away'. I was sitting upstairs, and we were focused on that [guy]. All of a sudden I see two Moroccan-looking guys in the shop looking around. As soon as I saw the Surinam guy was staying in the toilet a long time, I thought, 'What is happening?' Then a few [personnel] went to the guys to ask them 'What are you looking for?' He said, 'Yeah, we are waiting for the guy'. [Personnel told them,] 'No, you have to go out!' So they went outside, and then we heard that they were waiting for this guy in the toilet.
>
> I went knocking on the toilet door. 'Hey, get out, you have to go out of the shop!' But he didn't want to go. He was afraid to get out because the two guys were standing there like 'He took our money!' They wanted to grab him. [Once the Surinam guy left] one of the guys [who works at the coffeeshop] got in between them. 'I don't even know why you are helping him', I said. 'He wants to rob a few tourists, and they're not very smart because they want to buy drugs on the streets. But if they want to kick his ass, be my guest because he also went into our shop and thought it was safe or something. That will teach him a lesson.'

Customer fights are not common in coffeeshops, reportedly occurring at only 12 per cent of them in the previous year.[7] To give a point of comparison, they occur 10 times more often at bars in the 1012.[8] Perhaps there are relatively fewer fights in coffeeshops because personnel spend so much time controlling smaller problems,[9] or because cannabis intoxication inhibits aggression, especially compared to the effect of alcohol.[10] As Noah and Charlotte respectively commented, 'Smokers don't fight that much' and 'Weed calms you down, it doesn't make you aggressive'.

Sources of nuisance

Personnel think of three groups as being prone to cause nuisance. One is homeless individuals.[11] They are unwanted inside coffeeshops because they damage the atmosphere. Dean described how their appearance and smell affects the vibe:

> A lot of homeless people, they use the coffeeshop as a hangout place. You have different people. Some people who live on the street are looking very dirty. In the beginning [of being homeless], they look good. But after a half year, they have dirty clothes. In the first half year, they use the coffeeshops for hangouts and that kind of thing. [But after a while] the people who are standing on the streets, they smell of sweat. Then we have to tell them to go out and take a shower or something. They stink a lot.

The actions of homeless people damage the atmosphere, too. Maud recalled one incident: 'this guy who came in, he was looking around, and I saw he was a little bit lost. I thought there was something different about this guy. He was bothering my clients [by begging, I found out].' On other occasions, instead of asking for handouts, Emma commented that homeless individuals 'go by the ashtrays to see if there are any leftover joints'.

Drunk persons are another group cast as a common source of nuisance. In addition to being loud, as are many stag/bachelor parties, they say things that, to quote Jana, 'can be annoying. They make you think they have drunk a little too much'. Jens described an individual who 'wasn't a customer from the coffeeshop; he was someone who came in off the street, and was really off his face [drunk] and annoying'. Stefan recalled an encounter with 'a drunk asshole; he came in and was all mellow and sat down, and [then] started visibly annoying other groups of people'.

It is ironic that a cause of nuisance in coffeeshops is alcohol, as it cannot be sold or consumed on the premises as of 2007. 'In the beginning', Lola explained, 'you could start a coffeeshop also with an alcohol licence. After a few years, they changed to one or the other.' Each coffeeshop had to choose between the cannabis and alcohol trade. Remnants of this bygone era are still visible. Some coffeeshops have a counter with stools, like those common in bars. On the outside, coffeeshops have signage that includes a cocktail glass (visible at five coffeeshops) or writing on the windows or wall reading 'Café-Bar', 'Café', 'Bar' or 'Pool Café' (visible at seven coffeeshops).

No coffeeshop secretly sells alcohol, but customers try to consume it, covertly or openly. 'Before you realise', Joseph told me, 'you see their beer bottle, and it's not allowed to drink.' Some offences are due to ignorance of this rule. It is surprising to foreign customers, who assume that since you can smoke cannabis in coffeeshops you will also be able to drink alcohol there. But not all violations are due to ignorance. Signs specify the ban and personnel tell clients about it. Lizzie described a time that customers asked her about the rule, only to wind up ignoring her: '"Can I drink alcohol?" I say: "No, I don't serve any alcohol." "Oh, do you have beer?" So I say: "Well, beer is alcohol." "Oh, yeah. Can we bring our own?" "No, you cannot do that," I explain. Then I come over to the table, and there are three plastic cups and a bottle of Cognac on it. So I get very annoyed.'

Alcohol-related nuisance also includes passing out and vomiting. In a similar way to how people are warned not to mix grape (wine) with grain (beer), personnel think it is a bad idea for drunk people to 'start a fire' (smoke cannabis).[12] Lizzie gave an example of the effect:

> If you are really drunk and you smoke a joint, it can go badly. You can get very ill. One time I had a Japanese guy sitting where you are [at the counter]. He was like this [appearing nauseated]. I looked [away and then looked] again – there was a pool of puke. I told the guys [colleagues] to please help me pick him up because he passed out [and] carry him outside. The puke was running down his face, on his clothes and everything.

Dean narrated a similar incident:

> We had someone puke. A lot of people come in here drunk, and you have tourists, they think that they can smoke. A lot of people, they go and eat, they drink. Then they are a little bit drunk and they think, 'Oh yeah, come on, let's go to the coffeeshop and we will smoke a joint'. They smoke a joint after their drinks. If you drink and smoke together that is fine, but if you drink a lot and then you smoke, everybody can puke, for sure. Me, I am a regular smoker and a good smoker. If I drink a lot and then after a while I smoke, that happens to me, also.

Along with tourists, young people are characterised as drinking too much before smoking. In Mara's words: 'Young people drink, drink more, drink more, drink more. [Then say to themselves,] "I have to smoke, then I'm the big guy." They throw up!'

In fairness to alcohol, smoking on its own can make people sick.[13] People who smoke too much – in quantity or potency – are the third group identified as regular contributors to nuisance – albeit only that related to accidents and falling ill. Dean observed: 'Sometimes you can puke if you had a long flight. You come off the plane and smoke a big joint. Then you get too tired and puke.' More than any other nationality, personnel stereotyped Americans as smoking more than they can handle. Time and time again in coffeeshops, I heard them say to dealers 'Give me your best' or, in the form of a question, 'What is your best?' This is conspicuous consumption at its finest, or maybe foulest.[14] Victor talked about how this mindset affects the propensity to make themselves sick:

> They [Americans] always think they can handle the biggest, the baddest and the strongest stuff. Then 20 minutes later, they are blowing [vomiting] in the corner and I have to go over [to help] because they can't handle it. It just seems a little bit stupid, you know? Why don't they just slow down a little bit and then see how far you can go, instead of taking the strongest stuff and just falling down? It's not fun even. What is the fun of being sick on the floor?

Being high leads to accidental injury and property damage, too.[15] 'People do get hurt when they pass out', Linda commented, 'and bump their head against the table.' When I asked Luca about violence at the business, he answered: 'The only injuries are people so stoned that they fall off their stools!' In response to the same question, Victor replied: 'No [violence], except for people smoking too much and falling on the ground and smashing their own head. I have seen people fall through glass windows. They black out [meaning 'pass out']. They just walk and they black out. I have fucking seen people fall over chairs. They are like ghosts [in skin tone].' People being so high that they walk through a window is not hyperbole. Adam told me of one such instance: 'This American guy was really stoned; he thought it was the exit, but it was a big window. Just walked through it. He was actually all right, I think. He was just [like afterwards], "What did I do?"'

Managing nuisance

As with controlling minors and hard drug possessors, personnel look out for nuisance and work to distance it from their coffeeshop. If outside, sources of nuisance are asked to go further away. If trying to gain entry or make a purchase, they are denied. If already inside, they are expelled. Whether proterred to manage minors, hard drug possessors or nuisance, personnel use distancing techniques because their concern is stopping violations from occurring at their coffeeshop. Of much less concern is what happens beyond its borders.[16]

When I asked Elias if there are certain people refused entry, he gave homeless people as an example: 'Yes, junkies and some people are just too filthy to be inside; maybe they have slept on the street for a week. They are not going to sit on my seats.' Stijn gave a similar response: 'Junkies, people from the street, they cannot come in. They are not allowed to come in here.' Referring to 'bums or people that don't order anything', Emma stated: 'I tell them to leave, usually they leave. Usually they don't start to argue, but if they do, I just repeat myself again, and usually they go. I never have a problem with this.'

In response to being questioned about who is denied service, several personnel stated that drunk individuals are handled that way. 'If they come in and I see they are drunk', Hassan asserted, 'I put them out.' Stijn remarked: 'Sometimes people come drunk in the morning, like the English [tourists]. They come from the boat; they have been on the boat drinking all the time and they come in and they are agitated, they want to smoke, and then you don't want to serve them because they are drunk. You say, "No, go to your hotel, chill out and come back tonight".'

The main reason personnel distance minors and possessors is to protect the coffeeshop from punishment. However, this is less true of managing nuisance because single cases rarely, if ever, result in legal trouble. In these cases, therefore, personnel's motivation is to protect the establishment's atmosphere and customers. That is why Ruben distanced 'smelly ones and drunk ones, because we don't want to change the atmosphere in here. When somebody is really drunk they may start out being nice, but in five minutes they can change'. 'Sometimes', Anna stated, 'someone is very angry, but we don't let them in. We tell them they have to go out because they are drunk. We do not want to make problems here. We have our responsibilities to our customers. I don't want to only make money from them.'

In addition to distancing people from the coffeeshop, personnel prevent bad behaviour by limiting the amount of cannabis sold to people. Well, not all people, but only those acting improperly, or who appear on the fringe of doing so. Such clients are 'cut off', meaning they are allowed to stay in the coffeeshop, but not to buy any more cannabis. The goal is twofold: to protect the establishment and to protect customers from themselves. Lizzie put into words the way in which personnel act as stewards:

> You know people travel, they don't eat. They travel on the plane, don't eat breakfast, come with their suitcase to the coffeeshop, smoke so much, either puke or get so stoned, wander around the city and I say, 'Why do you do that? Why? Go check in first, then you know where your hotel is. You eat something, then you come to smoke'. That is why I think it is good that there are coffeeshops in Amsterdam, because we supply a lot of information. People come sometimes, they want to buy four space cakes. I say, 'Oh, are you going to have a party with your friends?' They say, 'No, it is all for me because I am going on the plane.' I say, 'Look, I am not going to sell you four space cakes. You can have two, maximum'. You have to be like [how you are] when you serve alcohol. At a certain point you have to say, 'Look, enjoy this last beer because after this, I am not serving you any more alcohol. You can have coffee, tea, juice, but that is it.' I tell them, 'I care and have responsibility for you. You are inside and from me you do not get another drop of alcohol, finished'.

A third, and certainly the nicest, way of managing nuisance is helping its source.[17] This is the response to intoxication-induced sickness. Lizzie talked about this as well, because it is how she reacted to the Japanese customer who vomited:

> I told the guys [working], 'Please help me pick him up because he passed out, carry him outside'. We picked him up like this [carrying him by his armpits]. We gave him a bucket of water to clean himself up. Then I asked the guy if he had a place to clean himself up. He said no, and that he was going on a train that afternoon. So [I] advised him to buy for €5 some clothes on the Waterloo secondhand market and to spend another €3 in having a shower at Central Station.

She went on to describe her general approach to helping:

> I always keep an eye on people. As soon as I see them change to a little bit grey, or the sweat drops come here [the forehead], I tell them to sit outside first of all because of the fresh air, and it does them a lot of good. I feed them sugar water. Many of them will throw up, but then it is already outside so I am happy. But people will sometimes get up, want to make it to the toilet, don't tell me they are ill, pass out here on the floor and then puke and lie in their own puke. The show must go on, so we grab a bucket of water and clean it up as fast as we can. That is the most disgusting part.

> We look after you when something happens. I had this one guy, he was walking down the street, the other guy passed out. He came back running in here: 'Call an ambulance!' He was screaming. [I said,] 'OK, sugar water'. Then he yelled at me: 'Don't make a fucking espresso! Call the ambulance!' I said, 'Look, first rule, relax, don't panic. We are already helping'. He was high, his friend was high, passed out. The guy doesn't know what is going on, and he starts to panic. I had [another time] one guy who went to walk out here, couldn't make it, fell on the steps and split his head open. So many stories like that. I sent him down the street there, where there is a medical post, with a towel.

Helpful behaviour is not unique to Lizzie and Whole Truth. Across coffeeshops, personnel lend a hand to customers who overdo it. For people who vomit, Mara explained: 'I put a chair outside and sit them in front of the door, and they get some fresh air.' While talking to Max, I mentioned what I had observed at Everybody, as it seemed odd to me:

> I've noticed twice, when I've been in this coffeeshop just by chance, someone would just be tripping their ass off [seemingly on hallucinogenic mushrooms]. So the way you guys handle that is you make them sit on a chair outside? Do you put a chair outside for them? Like how did this come up? Does this happen a lot? And where did you come up with that strategy, 'cause it's interesting to just put someone tripping outside your shop on a chair and tell them to hang out.

Max explained the rationale:

> You have to take responsibility for the people. I know we have a lot of tourists. What they do is they go to the museum, and they go to the Heineken Brewery, they don't eat well. Then they come to the shop, and they all want the strongest stuff. But your sugar level drops, and I don't want them to throw up in our shop. I have done that also many times – clean that up. I sold them the soft drugs, so that is my responsibility. But I take them outside so they don't throw up in my shop. They also get fresh air. They need the oxygen and then I give them sugar. Of course, it looks a little bit silly, for all the people who are passing by, that somebody is tripping out in front of my shop. But I am responsible for them. People pass out inside, they wet [piss] themselves, that also happens. People have passed

> out and then they let everything go, you know? I am responsible for that. I clean it up, no problem.

The representative of Dollar Room, Dean, described a similar response to sickness.[18] This came up after I asked him, 'When someone pukes, how do you guys respond?' He answered laughing:

> Smash them in the face! No, not really! It depends. It depends on what kind of customer it is. Most of the time, we are very kind. We help on our side. They need fresh air [so put them outside]. We give them sugar water. You mix hot water with a lot of sugar, or you mix it with cold water and let them drink it; that kind of thing. And we have to clean the place down where the bastard has puked.

Instead of distancing or helping sources of nuisance, personnel may warn them to shape up or ship out.[19] Jasper and his colleagues do so 'if somebody's shouting and being rude. We say [as a warning], "Go get your weed somewhere else, man", and next time he's very quiet'. Jens said emphatically: 'Don't act up or else I will put my foot in your ass and that will be the end!' He meant that figuratively, adding: 'I will tell you that you are being a dick! Like dude, "We don't do shit like that here, so pack it up and fuck off!"'

Warnings are not always sufficient, however. This becomes the case when a written or spoken warning fails to have its intended effect. After Lizzie's customers poured out Cognac, she told them: 'Look, you asked me. I explained to you, I explained to you twice [that alcohol is not allowed]. I want you to pick up and go now because now you are taking the piss. You come to ask me, I say no. I explain to you why so you can have more peace with the rule, and you take the piss. So now, you go.' Joseph had a similar response to people who drank alcohol, despite knowing it is not allowed: 'When you come, you can see my display and [the rule sign specifying] there is no alcohol. If you try to go contrary to that, I don't have the patience. I will tell you to go away.'

Personnel deem warnings as insufficient for unwanted persons, such as those who appear homeless, drunk or threatening.[20] Jack 'will sit down and chat to a drunk person who is being a bit lairy', for example, 'and then send them on their way'. When a homeless person walked into At Last and started talking to customers, Maud took action: '[I] went over to him. He said he just wanted weed. I just asked what he was doing, why he was bothering my clients. I told him if he wanted weed, I could give it to him, but if he did not have the money then I am sorry, I could do nothing for him.

I told him to please leave.' And when the 'drunk asshole' annoyed Stefan's customer, he 'asked him to leave and calm down a bit. We asked him to leave a second time and he left. I've never had to remove anyone forcibly'.

Hands-on expulsion

Distancing gets touchy.[21] Personnel universally see physical expulsion as a last resort. Yet it is one they are prepared to employ. To quote Victor: 'If somebody doesn't want to leave, if he doesn't want to listen and is not following the rules, then we make him leave. That is your job.' Physical expulsion ranges in severity from suggestive to forceful. The former is illustrated by how Ruben handled heavily intoxicated persons: 'Most of the time, the only thing that happens is like [I] grab somebody by the arm, turn them around and tell them where the door is. That's it. It's just putting someone on to the streets.' Gwen declared: 'If somebody is really annoying, then I actually take them from the table, and I will actually take their arm. Then I just get him out. That does not happen a lot. I think in the last year, it happened four or five times that I actually had to take somebody from the chair.' I asked, 'And are you actually like grabbing them?' She clarified: 'No, I always do it like this first [lightly placing her hand on my arm], with no force, but I will make sure that you understand what I am saying.'

Hands-on expulsion intensifies from suggestive to forceful when a troublemaker is asked to leave but refuses. Referring to the guy 'really off his face', Gwen explained that he 'wouldn't leave, so he got kicked out. He got shown the hole in the door, and landed on the pavement. He was launched out'. Sophie said of the 'hobo' collecting joints that 'we had to push him out'. Hassan described an encounter with a customer: 'He didn't keep to the house rules that I have here. He was taking off his shoes and walking around like that, talking to himself, that kind of shit; weird shit, crazy kind of weird shit. I think he was drunk and mentally ill, as well. He wasn't like 100 per cent, you know what I mean?' Initially personnel tried to talk sense into the guy, but things escalated:

> We said all these things like, 'You know that's not the way you should act here'. He made the business look bad, because we had customers here and they don't like that. He didn't want to listen. He [the employee] told the guy to leave. He [the nuisance] was like, 'No, I'm not going to leave'. He didn't want to go out. So he was like, 'Listen, I'm gonna tell you another time, you are going to leave if I have to drag you out of the business'. He was like, 'Yeah, if you touch

> me you will have [a] problem'. He didn't want to listen, that was the thing. He pulled him out, struggling. There was pushing.

I asked Hassan why it was important to remove the guy from the coffeeshop. He answered: 'Because you need some kind of order in the coffeeshop, and he was destroying it.'

There are notable, and I think explainable, differences in how personnel's responses to nuisance differed from those to minors and hard drug possessors. For one, personnel help customers who become sick, and warn people causing offence that their behaviour must change to remain inside. I did not hear or see these methods being used to deal with minors and possessors. The difference, I think, has to do with the risk posed by these respective groups. Coffeeshops are not punished for single cases of nuisance, not even serious incidents such as fighting, whereas they are sanctioned for the presence of minors or hard drugs. This makes helping and warning less appropriate for managing minors and possessors on the premises.

On the other hand, personnel physically expel people causing nuisance, which is rarer with minors and possessors. This is surprising, given that minors and possessors are a greater risk to coffeeshops. Perhaps hands-on distancing is more common with people who are drunk or mentally ill because these traits reduce their willingness to go away voluntarily. According to Luca, that effect is assumed: 'A lot of people come here drunk off their heads, and of course there is some shoving.' Another explanation pertains to respect and acknowledgement of one's wrongdoing. Minors and possessors may leave without a struggle because they realise they are in the wrong, but people who are drunk or mentally ill may see things differently.

As mentioned in Chapter 5, personnel involve the police if deemed necessary to handle a problem.[22] Lizzie, for example, said of fights between customers: 'If it is really a problem, we call them [police] and ask them to come.' Olivia told me what happened when the 'psychotic guy' got in a scuffle with customers at Elegy:

> The employee called them [police] because he knew the guy and he thought he was having some kind of paranoid fit, so I don't think the police even really arrested him. I think they just took him, gave him some valium and called his shrink or something. He is our neighbour, and his mum lives there, too. Sometimes she walks by and she is a really nice lady. She was just so embarrassed about what happened.

Jack reported a serious case of nuisance, including how and why personnel got the police involved:

We had about 15 very, very drunk Moroccan boys come in the shop. They were extremely loud and lairy and just not what we wanted and I sold them all some weed and then they all wanted to hang around. Then they started abusing my colleague behind the bar and generally abusing everyone else in the shop. They were standing there being abusive and it was getting to the point where they were looking to have a fight. I wanted them out and they weren't going. I was like it is about to kick off, and suddenly 12 of my regular customers stand up ready for a fight, and I am like I really don't want this to happen. Generally in my coffeeshop, I know that if it is ever going to happen I generally have someone at the back to help me. It was in that area [point of seriousness] where without police intervention, crimes would have occurred; there would have been a riot outside here.

The boss was thankfully here at the time, as well. I said to him, 'Look boss, can you go over the road and get the police because this is going to kick off real soon and I don't want to hit anyone?' They really riled me up and I was getting lairy and it was 'Get the police now because I will get in trouble if I hit someone'. They were there looking for a fight and I was about to give them one, so it was like, 'Boss can you go across the road?' – and the police were there. It was just a matter of saying [to them], 'Can you come over here, we have a little issue over the road?' and within 30 seconds there were six policemen here to take the drunk people away. They just arrested all of them. We pointed out these guys, they legged it and the police went after them and arrested them.

As much as the authorities do consider us criminal enterprises, the police do their best to work with us. As long as we can stay in line with them [with respect to the coffeeshop rules], we can count on them not treating us like gangsters, [for example] when I have a problem like that with 15 nutters about to start a riot in my coffeeshop. I can call on them for help in that respect and they will come running. They will come and help us. They don't mess around. If we ask for their help they come quick.

For coffeeshop personnel such as Jack, the good and bad news about the police is 'they are just right across the road'.

Notes

1. The Netherlands Ministry of Health, Welfare and Sport (2002: 30) specifies: 'Public nuisance occurs in many different forms … For this reason the concept of "nuisance" must be interpreted broadly.'

2. For information on nuisance with respect to coffeeshops, and Dutch drug policy more broadly, see Ooyen-Houben and Kleemans 2015.
3. NMHWS 2003.
4. Nuisance does appear to be used in a general way to close coffeeshops. This is why it is important to distinguish between nuisance incidents (for example, particular fights) and the general perception of a coffeeshop, or coffeeshops, as a nuisance.
5. This is the definition of nuisance adopted by Kelling and Coles (1996) and Wilson and Kelling (1982).
6. For information on stag/bachelor parties, see Briggs and Ellis 2017; Thurnell-Read 2012.
7. This pattern reflects the general inverse relationship between the seriousness and frequency of various forms of conduct, such as crimes of violence and property crime.
8. Jacques et al. 2016.
9. See Eck and Weisburd 2015; Newman 1972; Reynald 2015.
10. For information on the relationship between intoxication and aggression, see Boles and Miotto 2003; Felson et al. 2008; Meyerscough and Taylor 1985.
11. For information on homelessness and its relationship to crime and control, see Bourgois and Schonberg 2009; Cress and Snow 2000; Desmond 2016; Duneier 1999; Liebow 1993; Snow and Anderson 1993.
12. For information on the interaction between alcohol and cannabis consumption, see Lukas and Orozco 2001; Robbe 1998.
13. See Becker 2015.
14. This reflects Veblen's ([1899] 1994) notion of conspicuous consumption.
15. For information on the effect of cannabis on executive function and motor control, see Ramaekers et al. 2006.
16. This reflects the old approach of expelling offenders from city states and the like, as government officials and citizens prioritised what happened in their community over that of others. However, this dissipated with the coalescing of these smaller sovereign territories into nations (Spierenburg 2007).
17. Whereas the other techniques of reactive control are penal in style, helping is what Black (1976) refers to as therapeutic (see also Horwitz 1982; Tucker 1999).
18. Dean also recalled a time that he asked someone who puked for compensation, specifically enough to dry-clean his shirt. Asking for compensation is fairly rare, so far as I can tell. Here is his description of the incident: 'The guy comes in a little bit drunk [on the other hand] and the guy behind the bar tells him not to smoke. The guy here says, "OK, you can have something but don't smoke". But he [the customer] says he wants to, then he goes upstairs, smokes a little bit. Then the dealer goes upstairs and he sees him and says, "Go outside, I see in your face that you are not so good". The guy says, "Blah, blah, OK". After a few seconds he stands up and he pukes and a little bit over the dealer, pukes over the clothes of the dealer. The guy says, "Sorry for that". But the dealer says, "Yes, but I have to go to the cleaning company so you have to pay a little bit for the cleaning". For me that is totally good and if he pays the €20 then that is OK.' For information on drug dealers' use of negotiation to manage conflict, see Morselli et al. 2017; Jacques and Wright 2011, 2015; Taylor 2007.
19. For information on drug dealers' use of threats, both violent and nonviolent, to manage conflict, see Anderson 1999; Dickinson 2017; Jacques and Wright 2015; Jacques, Wright, and Allen 2014; Taylor 2007.
20. For a classic exchange on how the seriousness of an incident affects its handling, see Black 1979; Gottfredson and Hindelang 1979.
21. For information on drug dealers' use of physical force to manage conflict, see Anderson 1999; Goldstein 1985; Jacques and Allen 2015; Jacques, Wright and Allen 2014; Reuter 2009; Taylor 2007; Werb et al. 2011.
22. Evidence that the seriousness of the incident matters is seen, for example, in Hassan's explanation of why they did not call the police when the guy without shoes did not want to leave: 'Because it didn't go far. He wasn't using aggression or anything, no hitting or anything like that. He was just a drunk guy acting in a "Oh, I don't want to leave and this and that" kind of way. It was not necessary to get the cops involved.'

Conclusion

The utility of rules

Dutch coffeeshop policy is successful. It separates the markets for hard and soft drugs, without increasing the latter's consumption[1] and while reducing the cost – financial and moral – of imprisonment.[2] In addition to minimising harm, the policy has positive benefits. It allows coffeeshop owners and employees to earn income above board, plus generates revenue from taxes and tourism.[3] Yet the policy is not without problems.[4] As voiced by personnel, there are objections to holding coffeeshops responsible for the behaviour of non-personnel, for example, minors and street dealers.[5] Similar concerns are expressed over the requirement for coffeeshops to supply their *de facto* legal business through the black market. Nor are the rules entirely clear, as is evident in Chapters 2, 4 and 6, which discuss advertising, the 5 grams allowance and nuisance respectively. These problems are part and parcel of Dutch coffeeshop policy as currently practised. To put it differently, such problems are more or less inherent consequences of the government rules that currently regulate coffeeshops.

Another problem with the rules is that they may lead to conflict between personnel, customers and others who enter coffeeshops. People dislike being controlled. In response, they complain to the controllers, avoid them, seek formal redress or practise toleration.[6] They may also retaliate.[7] Overthrowing leaders. Shooting police. Yelling at parents. Breaking up with lovers. Writing bad reviews. These are just a few examples of vengeful actions that result from being controlled.[8]

Cases of rule-based conflict are found throughout this book. Coffeeshop personnel have a livelihood to protect, but put a target on their back by controlling others. They are well aware that enforcing rules causes problems, some of more concern than others. 'It is hard work', Ruben reflected discriminatorily, 'because what are you going to do if there are six black guys coming in [the coffeeshop,] opening their big mouths or whatever?' When I asked Jana whether she worried about anything, she answered:

> When it is time to go, they [troublesome customers] don't go – that's the only thing I worry about. I am not saying that this happens every day. But you do have, probably once a month, this annoying person, and maybe I feel a bit intimidated or something. That is the only thing I ever worry about.

Seemingly even small things, such as asking people to take off their hat or sunglasses, can be a catalyst for trouble. Gijs noted: 'There has been people coming in who have attitude. They don't like it if they have to [take] their caps off or something, even if we ask it nicely. Then there might have been some shouting like, "Fuck you this" or "Fuck you that", and then people leave.' He went on to describe how fear affects rule enforcement among his staff:

> I can't be afraid of how big you are. But I occasionally come in the shop and there are certain people working, and I can see that they didn't dare to ask [someone to take off his hat] because he is still wearing his hat. Then I just go up to him and say, 'Excuse me, we have a house rule'. Then it's, 'Oh, I'm sorry'. Then the people behind the bar think, 'Oh, I could have done that'.

Conflicts over rule enforcement may escalate from unkind words to violent threats. Selma described a hostile incident involving her colleague. She begins with the back story:

> I had this old neighbour from the sex shop; he was here a few weeks ago and we had a really nice chat. Then a Dutch man came in, he bought a joint and then they started talking with each other all about Ajax [the local football club]. He was really nice.

The man *was* nice, until he returned intoxicated and surprised not to see Selma. She explained what happened next: 'That Saturday night, who comes walking in really drunk? This Dutch guy because he had a good time here. But he was really drunk, and he looked at my colleague [Alex] like, "Who the fuck are you?"' Being drunk is bad enough inside a coffeeshop, but the customer also became, in her words, 'a bit aggressive'. Due to this disorder, Alex expelled the man. 'I think he [Alex] took his bag and put it by the door', Selma continued, 'and helped him towards it. I thought it was funny because my colleague was saying, "Yeah, I had to push him out of the coffeeshop, blah, blah", and he was like this [acting like he was pushing a wall].' The interaction ended with attempted intimidation: 'He [the drunk guy] said that he would be "coming back" or something like that, so that means he was threatening my colleague.'

Max described a scarier chain of events – 'a pretty big threat' – that also resulted from rule enforcement.

> We had a guy [customer] that we knew was no good. We had a feeling he was a coke dealer – not one who sells grams, but more like kilos. He was this big bodybuilder guy. One day I am there [at Everybody], and he is sitting there with another big guy with two really big American bulldogs. He was sitting there with big sunglasses on his face.

Max felt obliged to enforce the ban on shades, so he approached the customer and said, 'Sorry, but can you take your glasses off? We have this house rule.' Then the man went 'totally nuts'. Max explained that he started 'screaming at me and things like that. I was looking at him like, "No, I don't care". So he said, "You better call your boss [because they knew each other,] 'cause I am going to kick your ass".'

As directed, Max called his boss:

> He talked to the bodybuilder himself. 'You are threatening my manager. You cannot come in my shop any more. And I wouldn't do that [threatening] if I were you. It's not very smart. We grew up in the same neighbourhood, and you know I won't put up with this.' The guy simply responded: 'Yeah, but.' My boss continued: 'Why are you reacting in this way? You know I have a house rule. He only asked you to take off your glasses.'

The counter-threat and explanation successfully handled Max's troublemaker, as 'then he didn't go into the shop any more'.

For personnel, the worst-case scenario is for rule-based arguments to result in violent victimisation. For example, Jasper recounted that at The Hour, there was 'a guy [who] couldn't come in because his behaviour was not good and it was too busy. He went a little bit crazy [in response]. He started to try to hit the bouncers'. Though it is unlikely to cause bodily injury, spitting on someone is assault.[9] At Alike All Over, Jack told me:

> I had this Eastern European, crazy lunatic. He had been in the shop before. I remembered him being an odd one, and possibly having asked him to leave in the past. I was sat down eating my lunch and one of my colleagues, a young girl, was serving drinks. This guy kind of pushed in front of somebody she was serving and started demanding things. She said to him, 'Just wait a minute'. Then he started shouting again, and she said to him, 'I am not going to serve you if you are going to be rude'. The guy just jumped up and spat on her!

Jack also described how being high versus drunk affects people's response to being controlled. '[When] people are stoned, the chances of aggression are really slim. The fact is that levels of aggression are generally low among stoned people, with the chances of a disagreement reaching a level of physical confrontation being really slim.' Conversely, alcohol increases the likelihood of control leading to aggression: 'Whenever there has been any sort of [violent] incident, it is drunk people. It has always been somebody who has had far too much to drink. It has been one of my staff members escorting them out of the building, then there could be a bit of pushing and shoving.' Jack illustrates that process with a case he experienced:

> Generally, my hand on someone's shoulder is enough to let them know it is time to leave. Normally, I deal with it by sitting down with them at the table and saying, 'Look mate, I think you have had a little bit too much to drink. Tonight is not the night to be in a coffeeshop. Away you go'. Sometimes people take offence at that and take a swing at me. I kind of laugh at their drunkenness and escort them out of the shop.
>
> There was a geezer in here, probably about three months ago. It was such a funny conversation because I had my arm on his shoulder because I had taken him out of the shop. I said, 'Look mate, you are a little drunk, and I don't think smoking is going to do you any good tonight'. He was too drunk to manage a sentence really, but he was kind of taking offence at me escorting him out. So he had a really feeble effort at a head-butt at me, and kind of nearly fell over. 'Why did you just do that mate? I am being friendly here.' Then he took a swing at me. I said, 'Mate, that is really not necessary, on you go', and turned him round and walked him on his way. Then he sort of shrugged and walked off.

Persons who take offence at rule enforcement lash out in other violent ways. Linda recalled 'one incident with my manager. The guy wanted to go in and he [the manager] said, "No, sorry, you are too drunk, and alcohol and coffeeshops don't go together". Then he [the drunk guy] slapped him.' Unfortunately for that same manager, on a separate occasion he was poked in the neck for the same reason. Another employee of No Return, James, told me the story:

> The guy wanted to go into the coffeeshop and the manager refused him, like 'Sorry'. He was trying to talk to the guy. 'Hey you are drunk, blah, blah, I can't let you in.' Then the guy poked him in the neck with his fingers like this [fingers out and pressing against each other, really hard, in his neck]. I think he was searching for some [pressure] points. I think it was a combination of the booze and the refusal [that caused the aggression].

Rule-based retaliation shows that controlling others is risky. Then again, so is not exerting control. Many times a day, personnel have to ask themselves: Should I control a particular act by someone? If so, how? Every option has benefits and costs, though these vary by circumstance. Of course, those questions are not unique to coffeeshop personnel. We ask them of ourselves. We ask them of others. What, if anything, should be done to control something 'bad'? This question is asked by and of everyone: politicians, police, parents, lovers, teachers and more. If our guiding moral philosophy is hedonism,[10] specifically the type preached by Jeremy Bentham,[11] a 'good' approach is one with utility, meaning more benefit than cost; the 'best' approach is therefore that with the most utility.[12]

Does the Dutch coffeeshop policy have utility? The most honest answer I can give – indeed, that anyone can give – is 'maybe'. A complete and accurate assessment of the policy's benefits and costs is extremely difficult to generate. Perhaps it is impossible, if direct measurement and the variety of pleasures and pains are taken seriously.[13] Certainly, my data preclude such an analysis. Even more certainly, I would be remiss to compare the utility of Dutch coffeeshop policy to that of alternatives, such as a full-scale war on drugs or pure *laissez-faire* legalisation. There are too many factors to consider, such as effects on drug use, health, taxes, public expenditure, law enforcement, crime, nuisance and liberty.[14] And then there is the problem of different morals leading to different ways of weighing each variable.

In these closing pages, allow me to share my thoughts as an individual, not strictly in my role as a social scientist. In my teenage years

I believed legalisation and decriminalisation were better than prohibition for controlling cannabis. This belief stemmed from my personal policy: don't tell me what to do; let me be me. My first trip to Amsterdam, described in the Preface, reaffirmed my view that 'less is more' in the realm of social control.[15] Back in the States, first while in college and then graduate school, I gained understanding of what is wrong with prohibition: it is expensive; it puts many people behind bars; it breaks up family, friends and community cohesion; it exacerbates tension between police and citizens. Those are only a few of the problems.[16]

Yet my extended stay in Amsterdam taught me something about drug policy, and about social control more generally: in order to reduce bad things, people must be told both what to do and what not to do; their autonomy must be limited. People must be not only scared out of acting 'bad' (i.e. deterred), but also scared into stopping others from doing so (i.e. proterred). It is not a sunny view of human nature, but I believe it is valid. Frequently I abstain from being bad due to fear of what would otherwise result. Don't you do the same?[17] To argue in favour of fear need not – should not, I hope – have draconian results. Again, if Bentham's hedonism is our guide, the minimum amount of fear necessary to effect a 'good' outcome is optimal. This is because fear, like punishment, is a cost, and more cost equates to less utility.[18] To that point, fear is not only a bedfellow of prohibition and criminal punishment. Fear lies with rules and associated civil penalties, such as those controlling Dutch coffeeshops. Rules – formal and informal, *de jure* and *de facto* – guide decision-making and action.[19] In theory, rules are effective to the extent they are clear, known and associated with larger, more certain and faster acting benefits and costs.[20]

A problem, it could be said, with criminalisation is that it lacks regulation. Likewise I suspect that decriminalisation and legalisation are less effective when not paired with a set of rules that are properly crafted and enforced to achieve a set of goals. In Amsterdam, for instance, decriminalisation *per se* is not what separates the markets for hard and soft drugs. Rather what works is giving coffeeshops an incentive – namely, the potential to profit openly from cannabis sales – to keep hard drugs away from users.

Nor is legalisation necessarily better than decriminalisation for reducing drug-related problems such as violence.[21] It depends on the rules themselves. An example is that customer fights are 10 times less common in Amsterdam's (decriminalised) coffeeshops than in (legal) bars.[22] No doubt, the psychopharmacological effects of cannabis versus alcohol explain some of the difference.[23] What also matters, however, is that government rules motivate personnel of coffeeshops, more so than those of bars, to control problems.[24] I will provide evidence of this in my research on violence, theft and destruction in Amsterdam's coffeeshops.

Notes

1. See MacCoun 2011; Monshouwer, van Laar and Vollebergh 2011; Reinarman 2009.
2. For information on the moral dilemmas of punishment, see Bentham 1970 (1789).
3. See Grund and Breeksema 2013; MacCoun 2011. For information on the types of drug-involved pleasure, see Bunton and Coveney 2011; Holt and Treloar 2008; Jacques 2019.
4. Of course, almost every policy is imperfect. Problems are to be expected and certain things may backfire, though these are not always predictable in concrete form (see Eck 2010, 2017; Freilich and Newman 2018).
5. This objection should be weighed against its proterrent effect.
6. See Black 1998. Cf. Emerson 2015.
7. See Skinner 1971.
8. For information on retaliation, see Anderson 1999; Black 1998; Collins 2009; Cooney 2009; Emerson 2015; Jacobs and Wright 2006.
9. See AFP 2015. A street dealer, Shifran, described a rule-based conflict that led him to spit on a doorman: 'This guy [who worked at a coffeeshop], he told me because I worked on the street too much [that] I could not come in his coffeeshop. I tell him, "Listen, I work on the street, but I never do business in your place man, so don't fuck around with me." He was a bouncer and I knew the day that he was working. It is the old, bald guy; the old man. I go there with three friends of mine, and he was not working that day, so I go inside. So I was sitting there maybe two or three hours, we had a lot of joints and I think the shifts changed and the guy came to work. The guy talks to me: "You have to go outside now. You know that you cannot come inside, blah, blah." I tell him, "OK, I am going to finish my drink and then I will go outside." He grabbed my drink. He said, "No, you cannot finish your drink. You have to go outside now, and if you don't go outside I will put you outside." I looked that man in the face. "I take my drink. I told you I will finish and then I will go outside." The man took the drink and threw it in the sink. I spat in his face and I walked away, and the friends of mine came away with me. But as I am walking away he came to hit me. Yeah, he wanted to hit me, but the friends of mine were walking behind me and they grabbed him. Then the police came. Nothing happened. They broke it up. Nobody got arrested.'
10. Fairly so; not everyone will agree that hedonism should guide action.
11. Cf. Epicurus 2012.
12. Bentham 1970 (1789).
13. See Goldstein 1985; Nutt 2012; Jacques 2019.
14. For information on the complexity of drug policy and analysing it, see Houborg, Bjerge and Frank 2018. For examples, see Caulkins, Kilmer and Kleiman 2016; Caulkins and Reuter 2017; Kleiman 2009; MacCoun 2011; MacCoun and Reuter 1997, 2001; Nutt 2012; Pacula et al. 2014.
15. This belief also reflects the code of the suburb (Jacques and Wright 2015).
16. See, among many others, Alexander 2012; Goffman 2014; Kleiman 2009; MacCoun and Reuter 2001; Musto 1999; Nutt 2012; Phillips 2012; Provine 2007.
17. Some studies and meta-analyses indicate that fear is ineffective at preventing bad behaviour (Pratt et al. 2006). My guess is those findings are less indicative of reality than data problems (see National Research Council 2012). For information on drug prohibition's deterrent effect, or lack thereof, see Bushway and Reuter 2011; Caulkins and Reuter 2010, 2017; Levine 2013; MacCoun and Reuter 2011; Reinarman 2009; Reinarman, Cohen and Kaal 2004.
18. See Bentham 1970 (1789).
19. See Goffman 1963, 1969; Graeber 2018. For example, this is seen in the 'do's' and 'don'ts' associated with various forms of deviance or crime that prevent being discredited as an offender and punished as such (see Goffman 1963; Goffman, 2014; Jacobs 1996, 1999).

20. See Beccaria 1995 (1764); Bentham, 1970 (1789). I am sure other factors matter too (see, for example, ideas examined in any criminology or penology theory textbook, handbook, encyclopedia or reader).
21. See Goldstein 1985.
22. Jacques et al. 2016.
23. See Boles and Miotto 2003; Felson et al. 2008; Meyerscough and Taylor 1985.
24. See Jacques et al. 2016.

References

Advisory Committee on Drugs Policy. 2009. *New Emphasis in Dutch Drugs Policy*. The Hague, NL: Advisory Committee on Drugs Policy.

AFP. 2015. *Amsterdam Issues 'Spit-kits' against Slobber Assaults*. Retrieved 20 June 2018, from <https://www.expatica.com/nl/news/country-news/amsterdam-issues-spit-kits-against-slobber-assaults_512282.html>

Alexander, Michelle. 2010. *The New Jim Crow: Mass Incarceration in the Age of Colorblindness*. New York: The New Press.

Alpert, Geoffrey P., Roger G. Dunham and John M. MacDonald. 2004. 'Interactive Police–Citizen Encounters that Result in Force'. *Police Quarterly* 7:475–88.

Anderson, Elijah. 1999. *Code of the Street: Decency, Violence, and the Moral Life of the Inner City*. New York: W. W. Norton and Company.

Anderson, Elijah. 2011. *The Cosmopolitan Canopy: Race and Civility in Everyday Life*. New York: W. W. Norton and Company.

Arria, Amelia M., Kimberly M. Caldeira, Kathryn B. Vincent, Brittany A. Bugbee and Kevin E. O'Grady. 2014. 'False Identification Use Among College Students Increases the Risk for Alcohol Use Disorder: Results of a Longitudinal Study'. *Alcoholism: Clinical and Experimental Research* 38:834–43.

Barrett, Leonard E. 1997. *The Rastafarians*, 20th anniversary edition. Boston, MA: Beacon.

Bassanini, Andrea, Luca Nunziata and Danielle Venn. 2009. *Job Protection Legislation and Productivity Growth in OECD Countries* 24:349–402.

Bearman, Peter. 2005. *Doormen*. Chicago, IL: University of Chicago Press.

Beccaria, Cesare. 1995 (1764). *On Crimes and Punishments and Other Writings*, edited by Richard Bellamy and translated by Richard Davies. New York: Cambridge University Press.

Becker, Gavin de. 1998. *The Gift of Fear: And Other Survival Signals that Protect Us from Violence*. New York: Dell.

Becker, Howard S. 2007. *Telling About Society*. Chicago, IL: University of Chicago Press.

Becker, Howard S. 2015. *Becoming a Marihuana User*. Chicago, IL: University of Chicago Press.

Belackova, Vendula and Christian Alexander Vaccaro. 2013. '"A Friend with Weed is a Friend Indeed": Understanding the Relationship Between Friendship Identity and Market Relations Among Marijuana Users'. *Journal of Drug Issues* 43:289–313.

Belhassen, Yaniv, Carla Almeida Santos and Natan Uriely. 2007. 'Cannabis Usage in Tourism: A Sociological Perspective'. *Leisure Studies* 23:303–19.

Bentham, Jeremy. 1830. *The Rationale of Punishment*. London: Robert Heward.

Bentham, Jeremy. 1843. *The Works of Jeremy Bentham*, vol. 4, edited by John Bowring. Edinburgh, UK: William Tait.

Bentham, Jeremy. 1970 (1789). *The Principles of Morals and Legislation*. New York: Oxford University Press.

Bernasco, Wim and Scott Jacques. 2015. 'Where Do Dealers Solicit Customers and Sell Them Drugs? A Micro-Level Multiple Methods Study'. *Journal of Contemporary Criminal Justice* 31:376–408.

Biderman, Albert D. and Albert J. Reiss. 1967. 'On Exploring the "Dark Figure" of Crime'. *The Annals of the American Academy of Political and Social Science* 374:1–15.

Bieleman, B., R. Nijkamp and T. Bak. 2012. *Coffeeshops in Nederland 2011*. Groningen, NL: Intraval.

Bieleman, B., A. Beelen, R. Nijkamp and E. de Bie. 2008. *Coffeeshops in Nederland 2007*. Groningen, NL: Intraval.

Black, Donald. 1976. *The Behavior of Law*. New York: Academic Press.
Black, Donald. 1979. 'Common Sense in the Sociology of Law'. *American Sociological Review* 44:18–27.
Black, Donald. 1998. *Social Structure of Right and Wrong*, revised edition. San Diego, CA: Academic Press.
Black, Donald. 2011. *Moral Time*. New York: Oxford University Press.
Blumberg, Paul. 1989. *The Predatory Society: Deception in the American Marketplace*. New York: Oxford University Press.
Boles, Sharon M. and Karen Miotto. 2003. 'Substance Abuse and Violence: A Review of the Literature'. *Aggression and Violent Behavior* 8:155–74.
Bouchard, Martin, Eric Beauregard and Margaret Kalacska. 2013. 'Journey to Grow: Linking Process to Outcome in Target Site Selection for Cannabis Cultivation'. *Journal of Research in Crime and Delinquency* 50:33–52.
Bourgois, Philippe and Jeff Schonberg. 2009. *Righteous Dopefiend*. Berkeley and Los Angeles, CA: University of California Press.
Boyd, Brian. 2009. *On the Origin of Stories: Evolution, Cognition, and Fiction*. Cambridge, MA: Belknap Press of Harvard University Press.
Bozzo-Rey, Malik, Anne Brunon-Ernst and Michael Quinn. 2017. Editor's Introduction. *History of European Ideas* 43:1–10.
Braga, Anthony A. and David L. Weisburd. 2012. 'The Effects of Focused Deterrence Strategies on Crime: A Systematic Review and Meta-Analysis of the Empirical Evidence'. *Journal of Research in Crime and Delinquency* 49:323–58.
Braga, Anthony A. and David L. Weisburd. 2015. 'Focused Deterrence and the Prevention of Violent Gun Injuries: Practice, Theoretical Principles, and Scientific Evidence'. *Annual Review of Public Health* 36:55–68.
Braga, Anthony A., David L. Weisburd and Brandon Turchan. 2018. 'Focused Deterrence Strategies and Crime Control: An Updated Systematic Review and Meta-Analysis of the Empirical Evidence'. *Criminology and Public Policy* 17:205–50.
Briggs, Daniel. 2011. *Crack Cocaine Users: High Society and Low Life in South London*. London, UK: Routledge.
Briggs, Daniel and Anthony Ellis. 2017. 'The Last Night of Freedom: Consumerism, Deviance and the "Stag Party"'. *Deviant Behavior* 38:756–67.
Bright, David A. and Richel Sutherland. 2017. '"Just Doing a Favor for a Friend": The Social Supply of Ecstasy Through Friendship Networks'. *Journal of Drug Issues* 47:492–504.
Brown, Richard (ed.). 2013. *A History of Accounting and Accountants*. New York: Routledge.
Brownstein, Henry H., Timothy M. Mulcahy and Johannes Huessy. 2014. *The Methamphetamine Industry in America: Transnational Cartels and Local Entrepreneurs*. New Brunswick, NJ: Rutgers University Press.
Buerger, Michael E. 1992. 'Defensive Strategies of the Street-Level Drug Trade'. *Journal of Crime and Justice* 15:32–51.
Bunton, Robin and John Coveney. 2011. 'Drugs' Pleasures'. *Critical Public Health* 21:9–23.
Burnham, Thomas A., Judy K. Frels and Vijay Mahajan. 2003. 'Consumer Switching Costs: A Typology, Antecedents, and Consequences'. *Journal of the Academy of Marketing Science* 31:109–26.
Burns, Ronald G., Michael J. Lynch and Paul Stretesky. 2008. *Environmental Law, Crime, and Justice*. El Paso, TX: LFB Scholarly Publishing.
Buruma, Ybo. 2007. 'Dutch Tolerance: On Drugs, Prostitution, and Euthanasia'. In *Crime and Justice in the Netherlands*, edited by Michael Michael and Catrien Bijleveld, 73–114. Chicago, IL: University of Chicago Press.
Bushway, Shawn D. and Peter Reuter. 2011. 'Deterrence, Economics, and the Context of Drug Markets'. *Criminology and Public Policy* 10:183–94.
Caulkins, Jonathan P. 2017. 'Recognizing and Regulating Cannabis as a Temptation Good'. *International Journal of Drug Policy* 42:50–6.
Caulkins, Jonathan P. and Peter Reuter. 2010. 'How Drug Enforcement Affects Drug Prices'. *Crime and Justice* 39:213–71.
Caulkins, Jonathan P. and Peter Reuter. 2017. 'Dealing More Effectively and Humanely with Illegal Drugs'. *Crime and Justice* 46:95–158.
Caulkins, Jonathan P., Beau Kilmer and Mark A. R. Kleiman. 2016. *Marijuana Legalization: What Everyone Needs to Know*, second edition New York: Oxford University Press.
Chadillon-Farinacci, Veronique, Phillippe Apparicio and Carlo Morselli. 2015. 'Cannabis Cultivation in Quebec: Between Space-Time Hotspots and Coldspots'. *International Journal of Drug Policy* 26:311–22.

Childress, James F., Eric M. Meslin and Harold T. Shapiro (eds). 2005. *Belmont Revisited: Ethical Principles for Research with Human Subjects*. Washington, DC: Georgetown University Press.

Cialdini, Robert B. 2003. 'Crafting Normative Messages to Protect the Environment'. *Current Direction in Psychological Science* 12:105–9.

City of Amsterdam. 2011. *Key Figures Amsterdam 2010: Town Boroughs*. Retrieved 13 June 2011, from <http://www.os.amsterdam.nl/english/1443>

Clarke, Ronald. 1995. 'Situational Crime Prevention'. *Crime and Justice* 19:91–150.

Clarke, Ronald. 2009. 'Situational Crime Prevention: Theoretical Background and Current Practice'. In *Handbook on Crime and Deviance*, edited by Marvin D. Krohn, Alan J. Lizotte and Gina Penly, 259–76. New York: Springer.

Clarke, Ronald V. 2018. 'Regulating Crime: The Birth of the Idea, Its Nurture, and the Implications for Contemporary Criminology'. *The ANNALS of the American Academy of Political and Social Science* 679:20–35.

Clarke, Ronald and Marcus Felson. 1993. *Routine Activity and Rational Choice*. In *Advances in Criminological Theory*, vol. 5. New Brunswick, NJ: Transaction Press.

Clinard, Marshall B. and Peter C. Yeager. 2006. *Corporate Crime*. New Brunswick, NJ: Transaction Publishers.

Coffeeshop Guide Amsterdam. 2015. *Coffeeshop Guide Amsterdam, 2015/16*, second edition. Amsterdam, NL: Author.

Cohen, Lawrence E. and Marcus Felson. 1979. 'Social Change and Crime Rate Trends: A Routine Activity Approach'. *American Sociological Review* 44:588–608.

Coleman, Clive and Jenny Moynihan. 1996. *Understanding Crime Data: Haunted by the Dark Figure*. Philadelphia, PA: Open University Press.

Collins, Randall. 2009. *Violence: A Micro-sociological Theory*. Princeton, NJ: Princeton University Press.

Coomber, Ross. 2006. *Pusher Myths: Re-Situating the Drug Dealer*. London: Free Association Books.

Coomber, Ross and Lisa Maher. 2006. 'Street-Level Drug Market Activity in Sydney's Primary Heroin Markets: Organization, Adulteration Practices, Pricing, Marketing and Violence'. *Journal of Drug Issues* 36:719–53.

Cooney, Mark. 2009. *Is Killing Wrong? A Study in Pure Sociology*. Charlottesville, VA: University of Virginia Press.

Copes, Heith and J. Mitchell Miller (eds). 2015. *The Routledge Handbook of Qualitative Criminology*. New York: Routledge.

Copes, Heith, Scott Jacques, Andrew Hochstetler and Timothy Dickinson. 2015. 'Interviewing Offenders: The Active vs. Inmate Debate'. In *Routledge Handbook of Qualitative Criminology*, edited by Heith Copes and J. Mitchell Miller, chapter 11. London, UK: Routledge.

Cornish, Derek B. and Ronald V. Clarke (eds). 2017. *The Reasoning Criminal: Rational Choice Perspectives on Offending*. New York: Routledge.

Corsaro, Nicholas, Eleazer D. Hunt, Natalie Kroovand Hipple and Edmund F. McGarrell. 2012. 'The Impact of Drug Market Pulling Levers Policing on Neighborhood Violence'. *Criminology and Public Policy* 11:167–99.

Cress, Daniel M. and David A. Snow. 2000. 'The Outcomes of Homeless Mobilization: The Influence of Organization, Disruption, Political Mediation, and Framing'. *American Journal of Sociology* 105:1063–1104.

Cross, John C. 2000. 'Passing the Buck: Risk Avoidance and Risk Management in the Illegal/Informal Drug Trade'. *International Journal of Sociology and Social Policy* 20:68–94.

Crul, Maurice and Jeroen Doomernik. 2003. 'The Turkish and Moroccan Second Generation in the Netherlands: Divergent Trends between and Polarization within the Two Groups'. *International Migration Review* 37:1039–64.

Curtis, Ric and Travis Wendel. 2007. '"You're Always Training the Dog": Strategic Interventions to Reconfigure Drug Markets'. *Journal of Drug Issues* 37:867–91.

Cuskey, Walter, Arnold William Klein and William Krasner. 1972. *Drug-Trip Abroad: American Drug-Refugees in Amsterdam and London*. Philadelphia, PA: University of Pennsylvania Press.

Davenport, Steven and Jonathan Caulkins. 2016. 'Evolution of the United States Marijuana Market in the Decade of Liberalization before Full Legalization'. *Journal of Drug Issues* 46:411–27.

Dean, John P. and William Foote Whyte. 1958. 'How Do You Know If the Informant is Telling the Truth?' *Human Organization* 17:34–8.

Decker, Scott H. and Janet L. Lauristen. 2002. 'Leaving the Gang'. In *Gangs in America III*, edited by C. Ronald Huff. Thousand Oaks, CA: Sage.

Denning, Patt, Jeannie Little and Adina Glickman. 2003. *Over the Influence: The Harm Reduction Guide for Managing Drugs and Alcohol*. New York: Guilford.
Desmond, Matthew. 2016. *Evicted: Poverty and Profit in the American City*. New York: Broadway Books.
Dickinson, Timothy. 2017. 'Non-Violent Threats and Promises among Closed-Market Drug Dealers'. *International Journal of Drug Policy* 42:7–14.
Dickinson, Timothy and Richard Wright. 2015. 'Gossip, Decision-Making, and Deterrence in Drug Markets'. *British Journal of Criminology* 55:1263–81.
Du Bois, W. E. B. 1899. *The Philadelphia Negro: A Social Study*. Philadelphia, PA: University of Pennsylvania Press.
Duneier, Mitchell. 1999. *Sidewalk*. New York: Farrar, Straus, and Giroux.
Eck, John E. 2010. 'Super Controllers and Crime Prevention: A Routine Activity Explanation of Crime Prevention Success and Failure'. *Security Journal* 23:37–51.
Eck, John E. 2017. 'Regulation to Prevent Crime'. In *Handbook of Crime Prevention and Community Safety*, second edition, edited by Nick Tilley and Aiden Sidebottom. London, UK: Routledge.
Eck, John E. 2018. 'Regulation for High-Crime Places: Theory, Evidence, and Principles'. *The Annals of the American Academy of Political and Social Science* 679:106–20.
Eck, John E. and David L. Weisburd. 2015. 'Crime Places in Crime Theory'. *Crime and Place: Crime Prevention Studies* 4:1–33. Hebrew University of Jerusalem Legal Research Paper.
Eisner, Manuel. 2001. 'Modernization, Self-Control and Lethal Violence: The Long-Term Dynamics of European Homicide Rates in Theoretical Perspective'. *British Journal of Criminology* 41:618–38.
Eisner, Manuel. 2003. 'Long-Term Historical Trends in Violent Crime'. *Crime and Justice* 30:83–142.
Elias, Norbert. 1994. *The Civilizing Process: Sociogenetic and Psychogenetic Investigations*, revised edition New York: Blackwell.
Epicurus. 2012. *The Art of Happiness*. New York: Penguin.
Emerson, Robert M. 2015. *Everyday Troubles: The Micro-Politics of Interpersonal Conflict*. Chicago, IL: University of Chicago Press.
Emerson, Robert M., Rachel I. Fretz and Linda L. Shaw. 2011. *Writing Ethnographic Fieldnotes*, second edition. Chicago, IL: University of Chicago Press.
Emsley, Clive, Eric Johnson and Pieter Spierenburg (eds). 2004. *Social Control in Europe, Vol. 2: 1800–2000*. Columbus, OH: Ohio State University Press.
Engellandt, Axel and Regina T. Riphahn. 2005. 'Temporary Contracts and Employee Effort'. *Labour Economics* 12:281–99.
Felson, Marcus. 2006. *Crime and Nature*. Thousand Oaks, CA: Sage Publications.
Felson, Marcus. 2018. 'Policy Levels for Situational Crime Prevention'. *The ANNALS of the American Academy of Political and Social Science* 679:198–201.
Felson, Marcus and Mary Eckert. 2015. *Crime and Everyday Life*, fifth edition Thousand Oaks, CA: Sage Publications.
Felson, Richard, Jukka Savolainen, Mikko Aaltonen and Heta Moustgaard. 2008. 'Is the Association between Alcohol Use and Delinquency Causal or Spurious?' *Criminology* 46:785–808.
Fijnaut, Cyrille and Gary T. Marx (eds). 1995. *Undercover: Police Surveillance in Comparative Perspective*. New York: Springer.
Fisse, Brent and John Braithwaite. 1988. 'The Allocation of Responsibility for Corporate Crime: Individualism, Collectivism and Accountability'. *Sydney Law Review* 11:468–513.
Foucault, Michel. 1975. *Discipline and Punish: The Birth of the Prison*. New York: Vintage.
Foucault, Michel. 1980. *Power/Knowledge: Selected Interviews and Other Writings 1972–1977*. New York: Vintage.
Foucault, Michel. 1985. *The Use of Pleasure, Vol. 2 of The History of Sexuality*. New York: Vintage.
Freilich, Joshua D. and Graeme R. Newman. 2016. 'Transforming Piecemeal Social Engineering Into "Grand" Crime Prevention Policy: Toward a New Criminology of Social Control'. *Journal of Criminal Law and Criminology* 105:203–32.
Freilich, Joshua D. and Graeme R. Newman (eds). 2018. 'Regulating Crime: The New Criminology of Crime Control [Special issue]'. *The Annals of the American Academy of Political and Social Science*, 679.
Gebel, Michael. 2009. 'Fixed-Term Contracts at Labour Market Entry in West Germany: Implications for Job Search and First Job Quality'. *European Sociological Review* 25:661–75.
Geertz, Clifford. 1988. *Works and Lives: The Anthropologist as Author*. Stanford, CA: Stanford University Press.

Gehman, Andrew and Thomas Basboll. 2014. 'When Do Stories Work? Evidence and Illustration in the Social Sciences'. *Sociological Methods and Research* 43:547–70.
Geltner, G. 2008. *The Medieval Prison: A Social History*. Princeton, NJ: Princeton University Press.
Geltner, G. 2014. *Flogging Others: Corporal Punishment and Cultural Identity from Antiquity to the Present*. Amsterdam, NL: Amsterdam University Press.
Gibbs, Jack P. 1975. *Crime, Punishment, and Deterrence*. New York: Elsevier.
Giessen, Mark van der, Marianne M. J. Ooyen-Houben and Deborah E. G. Moolenaar. *International Journal of Drug Policy* 31:104–12.
Gill, Peter. 2002. 'Policing and Regulation: What is the Difference?' *Social & Legal Studies* 11:523–46.
Gleeson-White, Jane. 2013. *Double Entry: How the Merchants of Venice Created Modern Finance*. New York: W. W. Norton and Company.
Global Drug Survey. 2018. *Key Findings Report*. London, UK: Global Drug Survey.
Goffman, Alice. 2014. *On the Run: Fugitive Life in an American City*. Chicago, IL: University of Chicago Press.
Goffman, Erving. 1959. *The Presentation of Self in Everyday Life*. New York: Anchor Books.
Goffman, Erving. 1963. *Stigma: Notes on the Management of Spoiled Identity*. New York: Simon and Schuster.
Goffman, Erving. 1969. *Strategic Interaction*. Philadelphia, PA: University of Pennsylvania Press.
Goffman, Erving. 1979. *Gender Advertisements*. New York: Harper and Row.
Goldstein, Paul J. 1985. 'The Drugs/Violence Nexus: A Tripartite Conceptual Framework'. *Journal of Drug Issues* 15:493–506.
Gottfredson, Michael R. and Michael J. Hindelang. 1979. 'A Study of the Behavior of Law'. *American Sociological Review* 44:3–18.
Gottschall, Jonathan. 2012. *The Storytelling Animal: How Stories Make Us Human*. New York: Houghton Mifflin Harcourt.
Graeber, David. 2018. *The Utopia of Rules: On Technology, Stupidity, and the Secret Joys of Bureaucracy*. New York: Melville House.
Grapendaal, Martin, Ed Leuw and Hans Nelen. 1995. *A World of Opportunities: Lifestyle and Economic Behavior of Heroin Addicts in Amsterdam*. Albany, NY: State University of New York Press.
Grund, Jean-Paul and Joost Breeksema. 2013. *Coffee Shops and Compromise: Separated Illicit Drug Markets in the Netherlands*. New York: Open Society Foundations.
Gunter, Barrie, Anders Hansen and Maria Touri. 2010. *Alcohol Advertising and Young People's Drinking: Representing, Reception and Regulation*. New York: Palgrave.
Hall, Wayne and Louisa Degenhardt. 2009. 'Adverse Health Effects of Non-Medical Cannabis Use'. *The Lancet* 374:1383–91.
Harris, Anne-Marie G., Geraldine R. Henderson and Jerome D. Williams. 2005. 'Courting Customers: Assessing Consumer Racial Profiling and Other Marketplace Discrimination'. *Journal of Public Policy and Marketing* 24:163–71.
Harrison, Lana D., Patricia G. Erickson, Dirk J. Korf, Serge Brochu and Annemieke Benschop. 2007. 'How Much for a Dime Bag? An Exploration of Youth Drug Markets'. *Drug and Alcohol Dependence* 90:S27–S39.
Hawken, Angela, Jonathan Caulkins, Beau Kilmer and Mark Kleiman. 2013. 'Quasi-Legal Cannabis in Colorado and Washington: Local and National Implications'. *Addiction* 108:837–8.
Hazekamp, Arno. 2006. 'An Evaluation of the Quality of Medicinal Grade Cannabis in the Netherlands'. *Cannabinoids* 1:1–9.
High Times. 'Cannabis Cup'. Retrieved 8 May 2018, from <https://www.cannabiscup.com>
Hirschi, Travis. 1969. *Causes of Delinquency*. Berkeley and Los Angeles, CA: University of California Press.
Hobbes, Thomas. 1985 (1651). *Leviathan*. New York: Penguin Classics.
Hobbs, Dick, Philip Hadfield, Stuart Lister and Simon Winlow. 2003. *Bouncers: Violence and Governance in the Nighttime Economy*. New York: Oxford University Press.
Hollis-Peel, Danielle M. Reynald, Maud van Bavel, Henk Elffers and Brandon C. Welsh. 2011. 'Guardianship for Crime Prevention: A Critical Review of the Literature'. *Crime, Law and Social Change* 56:53–70.
Holt, Martin and Carla Treloar. 2008. 'Pleasures and Drugs'. *International Journal of Drug Policy* 19:349–52.
Horwitz, Allan V. 1982. *The Social Control of Mental Illness*. New York: Academic Press.
Houborg, Esben, Bagga Bjerge and Vibeke A. Frank. 2018. 'Comparing Drug Policies'. *International Journal of Drug Policy* 56:128–30.

Howard, John. 1792. *The State of the Prisons in England and Wales, with Preliminary Observations, and an Account of Some, Foreign Prisons and Hospitals*, fourth edition. London: J. Johnson, C. Dilly and T. Cadell.

Ichino, Andrea, and Regina T. Riphahn. 2005. 'The Effect of Employment Protection on Worker Effort: Absenteeism During and After Probation'. *Journal of the European Economic Association* 3:120–43.

Jacobs, Bruce A. 1993. 'Undercover Deception Clues: A Case of Restrictive Deterrence'. *Criminology* 341:281–99.

Jacobs, Bruce A. 1996. 'Crack Dealers and Restrictive Deterrence: Identifying Narcs'. *Criminology* 34:409–431.

Jacobs, Bruce A. 1999. *Dealing Crack: The Social World of Streetcorner Selling*. Boston, MA: Northeastern University Press.

Jacobs, Bruce A. 2000. *Robbing Drug Dealers: Violence Beyond the Law*. New York. Aldine de Gruyter.

Jacobs, Bruce A. 2010. 'Deterrence and Deterrability'. *Criminology* 48:417–41.

Jacobs, Bruce A and Richard Wright. 2006. *Street Justice: Retaliation in the Criminal Underworld*. New York: Cambridge University Press.

Jacques, Scott. 2017. '"A Run-In with the Cops is Really Few and Far Between": Negative Evidence and Ethnographic Understanding of Racial Discrimination by Police'. *Sociological Focus* 50:7–17.

Jacques, Scott. 2018. 'Which Source Possesses the Best Data on the Empirical Aspects of Criminal Events? A Theory of Opportunity and Necessary Conditions'. *Deviant Behavior*. DOI: <https://doi.org/10.1080/01639625.2018.1559635>

Jacques, Scott. 2019. '"Bentham, Not Epicurus". The Relevance of Pleasure to Studies of Drug-Involved Pain'. *Journal of Drug Issues* 49:118–38.

Jacques, Scott and Andrea Allen. 2014. 'Bentham's Sanction Typology and Restrictive Deterrence: A Study of Young, Suburban, Middle-Class Drug Dealers'. *Journal of Drug Issues* 44:212–30.

Jacques, Scott and Andrea Allen. 2015. 'Drug Market Violence: Virtual Anarchy, Police Pressure, Predation, and Retaliation'. *Criminal Justice Review* 40:187–99.

Jacques, Scott and Wim Bernasco. 2013. 'Drug Dealing: Amsterdam's Red Light District'. In *Cognition and Crime: Offender Decision Making and Script Analyses*, edited by Richard Wortley and Benoit Leclerc. London, UK: Routledge.

Jacques, Scott and Danielle Reynald. 2012. 'The Offenders' Perspective on Prevention: Guarding Against Victimization and Law Enforcement'. *Journal of Research in Crime and Delinquency* 49:269–94.

Jacques, Scott and Richard Wright. 2011. 'Informal Control and Illicit Drug Trade'. *Criminology* 49:729–65.

Jacques, Scott and Richard Wright. 2013. 'How Victimized Drug Traders Mobilize Police'. *Journal of Contemporary Ethnography* 42:545–75.

Jacques, Scott and Richard Wright. 2015. *Code of the Suburb: Inside the World of Young Middle-Class Drug Dealers*. Chicago, IL: University of Chicago Press.

Jacques, Scott, Andrea Allen and Richard Wright. 2014. 'Drug Dealers' Rational Choices on Which Customers to Rip-Off'. *International Journal of Drug Policy* 25:251–6.

Jacques, Scott, Richard Wright and Andrea Allen. 2014. 'Drug Dealers, Retaliation, and Deterrence'. *International Journal of Drug Policy* 25:656–62.

Jacques, Scott, Richard Rosenfeld, Richard Wright and Frank van Gemert. 2016. 'Effects of Prohibition and Decriminalization on Drug Market Conflict: Comparing Street Dealers, Coffeeshops, and Cafés in Amsterdam'. *Criminology and Public Policy* 15:843–75.

Jansen, A. C. M. 1991. *Cannabis in Amsterdam: A Geography of Hashish and Marihuana*. Muiderberg, NL: Dick Coutinho.

Johnson, Bruce D. and Mangai Natarajan. 1995. 'Strategies to Avoid Arrest: Crack Sellers' Responses to Intensified Policing'. *American Journal of Police* 14:49–69.

Johnston, Lloyd D., Patrick M. O'Malley and Yvonne Terry-McElrath. 2004. 'Methods, Locations, and Ease of Cigarette Access for American Youth, 1997–2002'. *American Journal of Preventative Health* 27:267–75.

Kahneman, Daniel, Jack L. Knetsch and Richard Thaler. 1986. 'Fairness as a Constraint on Profit Seeking: Entitlements in the Market'. *American Economic Review* 76:728–41.

Katz, Jack. 1988. *Seductions of Crime: Moral and Sensual Attractions in Doing Evil*. New York: Basic Books.

Katz, Jack. 1999. *How Emotions Work*. Chicago, IL: University of Chicago Press.

Katz, Jack. 2006. 'Ethical Escape Routes for Underground Ethnographers'. *American Ethnologist* 33:499–506.

Katz, Jack. 2007. 'Toward a Natural History of Ethical Censorship'. *Law and Society Review* 41:797–810.

Keizer, Kees, Siegwart Lindenberg and Linda Steg. 2008. 'The Spreading of Disorder'. *Science* 322:1681–5.

Kelling, George L. and Catherine M. Coles. 1996. *Fixing Broken Windows: Restoring Order and Reducing Crime in Our Communities*. New York: Simon and Schuster.

Kennedy, David M. 2006. 'Old Wine in New Bottles: Policing and the Lessons of Pulling Levers'. In *Police Innovation: Contrasting Perspectives*, edited by David Weisburd and Anthony A. Braga, 155–70. New York: Cambridge University Press.

Kennedy, David M. 2012. *Deterrence and Crime Prevention: Reconsidering the Prospect of Sanction*. New York: Routledge.

Kennedy, David M., Mark A. R. Kleiman and Anthony A. Braga. 2017. 'Beyond Deterrence: Strategies of Focus and Fairness'. In *Handbook of Crime Prevention and Community Safety*, edited by Nick Tilley and Aiden Sidebottom, 157–82. New York: Routledge.

Kleemans, Edward R. 2007. 'Organized Crime, Transit Crime, and Racketeering'. In *Crime and Justice in the Netherlands*, edited by Michael Tonry and Catrien Bijleveld. Chicago, IL: University of Chicago Press.

Kleiman, Mark A. R. 2009. *When Brute Force Fails: How to Have Less Crime and Less Punishment*. Princeton, NJ: Princeton University Press.

Kleiman, Mark A. R., Jonathan A. Caulkins and Angela Hawken. 2011. *Drugs and Drug Policy*. New York: Oxford University Press.

Knowles, Gordon J. 1999. 'Deception, Detection, and Evasion: A Trade Craft Analysis of Honolulu, Hawaii's Street Crack-Cocaine Traffickers'. *Journal of Criminal Justice* 27:443–55.

Korf, Dirk J. 1994. 'Drug Tourists and Drug Refugees'. In *Between Prohibition and Legalization: The Dutch Experiment in Drug Policy*, edited by Ed Leuw and I. Haen Marshall. New York: Kugler.

Korf, Dirk J. 1995. *Dutch Treat: Formal Control and Illicit Drug Use in the Netherlands*. Amsterdam, NL: Thesis Publishers Amsterdam.

Kort, Marcel de and Dirk J. Korf. 1992. 'The Development of Drug Trade and Drug Control in the Netherlands: A Historical Perspective'. *Crime, Law, and Social Change* 17:123–44.

Laub, John H. and Robert J. Sampson. 2003. *Shared Beginnings, Divergent Lives: Delinquent Boys to Age 70*. Cambridge, MA: Harvard University Press.

Laycock, Gloria. 2005. 'Deciding What to Do'. In *Handbook of Crime Prevention and Community Safety*, edited by Nick Tilley, 674–98. Portland, OR: Willan.

Leclerc, Benoit and Ernesto U. Savona (eds). 2017. *Crime Prevention in the 21st Century: Insightful Approaches for Crime Prevention Initiatives*. New York: Springer.

Lee, Helene. 2004. *The First Rasta: Leonard Howell and the Rise of Rastafarianism*. Chicago: Chicago Review Press.

Lee, Jennifer. 2000. 'The Salience of Race in Everyday Life: Black Customers' Shopping Experiences in Black and White Neighborhoods'. *Work and Occupations* 27:353–76.

Leuw, Ed and I. Haen Marshall (eds). 1994. *Between Prohibition and Legislation: The Dutch Experiment in Drug Policy*. New York: Kugler.

Leuw, Ed. 1991. 'Drugs and Drug Policy in the Netherlands'. *Crime and Justice* 14:229–76.

Levine, Harry G. 2003. 'Global Drug Prohibition: Its Uses and Crises'. *International Journal of Drug Policy* 14:145–53.

Levitt, Steven D. and Sudhir Alladi Venkatesh. 2000. 'An Economic Analysis of a Drug-Selling Gang's Finances'. *Quarterly Journal of Economics* 115:755–89.

Lewis, George H. and Jonathan F. Lewis. 1980. 'The Dog in the Night-time: Negative Evidence in Social Research'. *British Journal of Sociology* 31:544–58.

Liebow, Elliot. 1993. *Tell Them Who I Am: The Lives of Homeless Women*. New York: Penguin.

Lindegaard, Marie Rosenkrantz, Wim Bernasco and Scott Jacques. 2015. 'Consequence of Expected and Observed Victim Resistance for Offender Violence During Robbery Events'. *Journal of Research in Crime & Delinquency* 52:32–61.

Lindegaard, Marie Rosenkrantz, Wim Bernasco, Scott Jacques and Babet Zevenbergen. 2013. 'Posterior Gains and Immediate Pains: Offender Emotions Before, During, and After Robberies'. In *Affect and Cognition in Criminal Decision Making*, edited by Jean-Louis van Gelder, Hank Elffers, Daniel Nagin and Danielle Reynald, chapter 4. New York: Routledge.

Lindeman, Ellen, Simone Crok, Jeroen Slot, Lara ten Broeke, Lieselotte Bicknese, Harry Smeets, Karin Klein Wolt, Paolo van der Steenhoven, Manilde van der Oord, Dennis Beckers and Marcel Janssen. 2005. *The State of the City of Amsterdam III: Developments in Participation and Life Situation*. Amsterdam, NL: City of Amsterdam, Department of Research and Statistics.
Loughran, Thomas A., Ray Paternoster, Alex R. Piquero and Greg Pogarsky. 2011. 'On Ambiguity in Perceptions of Risk: Implications for Decision-Making and Deterrence'. *Criminology* 49:1029–61.
Lukas, Scott E. and Sara Orozco. 2001. 'Ethanol increases plasma Δ9-tetrahydrocannabinol (THC) levels and subjective effects after marihuana smoking in human volunteers'. *Drug and Alcohol Dependence* 64:143–9.
Lyman, Michael D. and Gary Potter. 2014. *Organized Crime*, sixth edition. New York: Pearson.
MacCoun, Robert J. 2011. 'What Can We Learn from the Dutch Cannabis Coffeeshop System?' *Addiction* 106:1899–1910.
MacCoun, Robert J. and Peter Reuter. 1997. 'Interpreting Dutch Cannabis Policy: Reasoning by Analogy in the Legalization Debate'. *Science* 278:47–52.
MacCoun, Robert J. and Peter Reuter. 2001. 'Evaluating Alternative Cannabis Regimes'. *British Journal of Psychiatry* 178:123–8.
MacCoun, Robert J. and Peter Reuter. 2001. *Drug War Heresies: Learning from Other Vices, Times, and Places*. New York: Cambridge University Press.
MacCoun, Robert J. and Peter Reuter. 2017. 'Assessing Drug Prohibition and Its Alternatives: A Guide for Agnostics'. *Annual Review of Law and Social Science* 7:61–78.
Mak, Geert. 2001. *Amsterdam: A Brief Life of the City*. New York: Vintage.
Malm, Aili, Martin Bouchard, Tom Decorte, Marieke Vlaemynck and Marije Wouters. 2017. 'More Structural Holes, More Risk? Network Structure and Risk Perception among Marijuana Growers'. *Social Networks* 51:127–34.
Marlatt, G. Alan. 1996. 'Harm Reduction: Come as You Are'. *Addictive Behaviors* 21:779–88.
Maruna, Shadd. 2001. *Making Good: How Ex-Convicts Reform and Rebuild Their Lives*. Washington, DC: American Psychological Association.
Marx, Gary T. 1989. *Undercover: Police Surveillance in America*. Berkeley and Los Angeles, CA: University of California Press.
Marx, Gary T. 2016. *Windows Into the Soul: Surveillance and Society in an Age of High Technology*. Chicago, IL: University of Chicago Press.
Mascini, Peter and Dick Houtman. 2011. 'Resisting Administrative Tolerance in the Netherlands: A Rightist Backlash?' *British Journal of Criminology* 51:690–706.
Mastrofski, Stephen D., Michael J. Reisig and John D. McCluskey. 2002. 'Police Disrespect Toward the Public: An Encounter-Based Analysis'. *Criminology* 40:519–52.
Meyerscough, Rodney and Stuart Taylor. 1985. 'The Effects of Marijuana on Human Physical Aggression'. *Journal of Personality and Social Psychology* 49:1541–6.
Miller, Jody and Wilson R. Palacios (eds). 2015. *Qualitative Research in Criminology*. New Brunswick, NJ: Transaction Publishers.
Ministry of Health, Welfare and Sport (MHWS). 2003. *Drug Policy in the Netherlands*. The Hague, NL: MHWS.
Moeller, Kim. 2017. 'Drug Market Criminology: Combining Economic and Criminological Research on Illicit Drug Markets'. *International Criminal Justice Review* 28:191–205.
Moeller, Kim and Sveinung Sandberg. 2015. 'Credit and Trust: Management of Network Ties in Illicit Drug Distribution'. *Journal of Research in Crime and Delinquency* 52:691–716.
Moeller, Kim and Sveinung Sandberg. 2017. 'Debts and Threats: Managing Identity to Repay Credits in Illicit Drug Distribution'. *Justice Quarterly* 34:272–96.
Moeller, Kim, Heith Copes and Andy Hochstetler. 2016. 'Advancing Restrictive Deterrence: A Qualitative Meta-Analysis'. *Journal of Criminal Justice* 46:82–93.
Mohamed, A. Rafik and Erik D. Fritsvold. 2010. *Dorm Room Dealers: Drugs and Privileges of Race and Class*. Boulder, CO: Lynne Rienner.
Monshouwer, Karin, Margriet van Laar and Wilma A. Vollebergh. 2011. 'Buying Cannabis in "Coffee Shops"'. *Drug and Alcohol Review* 30:148–56.
Moore, Theresa H. M., Stanley Zammit, Anne Lingford-Hughes, Thomas R. E. Barnes, Peter B. Jones, Margaret Burke and Glyn Lewis. 2007. 'Cannabis Use and Risk of Psychotic or Affective Mental Health Outcomes: A Systematic Review'. *The Lancet* 370:319–28.
Morrison, William Douglas. 1897. 'The Interpretation of Criminal Statistics'. *Journal of the Royal Statistical Society* 60:1–24.

Morselli, Carlo, David Decary-Hetu, Masarah Paquet-Clouston and Judith Aldridge. 2017. 'Conflict Management in Illicit Drug Cryptomarkets'. *International Criminal Justice Review*.

Musto, David F. 1999. *The American Disease: Origins of Narcotic Control*, third edition New York: Oxford University Press.

Nagin, Daniel S. 2013a. 'Deterrence in the 21st Century: A Review of the Evidence'. *Crime and Justice: An Annual Review of Research* 42:199–263.

Nagin, Daniel S. 2013b. 'Deterrence: A Review of the Evidence by a Criminologist for Economists'. *Annual Review of Economics* 5:83–106.

Naparstek, Belleruth. 1997. *Your Sixth Sense: Activating Your Psychic Potential*. New York: HarperCollins.

National Cancer Institute. 2008. *The Role of the Media in Promoting and Reducing Tobacco Use*. Bethesda, MD: US Department of Health and Human Services, National Institutes of Health.

National Research Council. 2003. *Protecting Participants and Facilitating Social and Behavioral Science Research*. Washington, DC: National Academies Press.

National Research Council. 2010. *Understanding the Demand for Illegal Drugs*. Committee on Understanding and Controlling the Demand for Illegal Drugs. Washington, DC: National Academies Press.

National Research Council. 2012. *Deterrence and the Death Penalty*. Washington, DC: National Academies Press.

Netherlands Ministry of Foreign Affairs (NMFA). 2008. *Q & A Drugs*. The Hague, NL: Ministry of Foreign Affairs.

Netherlands Ministry of Health, Welfare and Sport (NMHWS). 2002. *Progress Report on the Drug Policy of the Netherlands, 2001–2002*. The Hague, NL: NMHWS.

Netherlands Ministry of Health, Welfare and Sport (NMHWS). 2003. *Drug Policy in the Netherlands: Basic Principles and Enforcement in Practice*. The Hague, NL: NMHWS.

Newman, Oscar. 1972. *Defensible Space: Crime Prevention through Urban Design*. New York: Macmillan.

Niesink, Raymond J. M., Sander Rigter, Maarten W. Koeter and Tibor M. Brunt. 2015. 'Potency Trends of Δ^9-tetrahydrocannabinol, cannabidiol and cannabinol in cannabis in the Netherlands: 2005–15'. *Addiction* 110:1941–50.

Nordholt, Eric Schulte, Marijke Hartgers and Rita Gircour (eds). 2004. *The Dutch Virtual Census of 2001: Analysis and methodology*. Voorburg, NL: Statistics Netherlands.

Nutt, David J. 2012. *Drugs Without the Hot Air: Minimising the Harms of Legal and Illegal Drugs*. Cambridge, UK: UIT.

Nutt, David J., Leslie A. King and Lawrence D. Phillips. 2010. 'Drug Harms in the UK: A Multicriteria Decision Analysis'. *The Lancet* 376:1558–65.

Ooyen-Houben, Marianne van and Edward Kleemans. 2015. 'Drug Policy: The "Dutch Model"'. *Crime and Justice* 44:165–226.

Pacula, Rosalie Liccardo and Russell Lundberg. 2014. 'Why Changes in Price Matter When Thinking about Marijuana Policy: A Review of the Literature on the Elasticity of Demand'. *Public Health Reviews* 35:1–18.

Pacula, Rosalie, Beau Kilmer, Alexander C. Wagenaar, Frank J. Chaloupka and Jonathan P. Caulkins. 2014. 'Developing Public Health Regulations for Marijuana: Lessons From Alcohol and Tobacco'. *American Journal of Public Health* 104:1021–8.

Pakes, Francis. 2005. 'Penalization and Retreat: The Changing Face of Dutch Criminal Justice'. *Criminal Justice* 5:145–61.

Pardo, Bryce. 2014. 'Cannabis Policy Reforms in the Americas: A Comparative Analysis of Colorado, Washington, and Uruguay'. *International Journal of Drug Policy* 25:727–35.

Pennock, Pamela E. 2009. *Advertising Sin and Sickness: The Politics of Alcohol and Tobacco Marketing, 1950–1990*. Dekalb, IL: Northern Illinois University Press.

Petrone, Gerard S. 1997. *Tobacco Advertising: The Great Seduction*. New York: Schiffer.

Phillips, Susan A. 2012. *Operation Fly Trap: L.A. Gangs, Drugs, and the Law*. Chicago, IL: University of Chicago Press.

Pijlman, F. T. A., S. M. Rigter, J. Hoek, H. M. J. Goldschmidt and R. J. M. Niesink. 2005. 'Strong Increase in Total Delta-THC in Cannabis Preparations Sold in Dutch Coffee Shops'. *Addiction Biology* 10:171–80.

Pinker, Steven. 2011. *The Better Angels of Our Nature: Why Violence Has Declined*. New York: Viking.

Plattner, Stuart. 2003. 'Human Subjects Protection and Cultural Anthropology'. *Anthropological Quarterly* 76:287–97.

Provine, Doris Marie. 2007. *Unequal Under Law: Race in the War on Drugs*. Chicago, IL: University of Chicago Press.

Pogarsky, Greg and Alex R. Piquero. 2003. 'Can Punishment Encourage Offending? Investigating the "Resetting" Effect'. *Journal of Research in Crime and Delinquency*. 40:95–120.

Polsky, Ned. 1969. *Hustlers, Beats, and Others*. New York: Doubleday.

Pratt, Travis C., Francis T. Cullen, Kristie R. Blevins, Leah E. Daigle and Tamara D. Madensen. 2006. 'The Empirical Status of Deterrence Theory: A Meta-Analysis'. *Advances in Criminological Theory* 15:367–96.

Presser, Lois and Sveinung Sandberg (eds). 2015. *Narrative Criminology: Understanding Stories of Crime*. New York: New York University Press.

Provine, Doris Marie. 2007. *Unequal Under Law: Race in the War on Drugs*. Chicago, IL: University of Chicago Press.

Ramaekers, Johannes G., Gerhold Kauert, Peter van Ruitenbeek, Eef L. Theunissen, Erhard Schneider and Manfred R. Moeller. 2006. 'High-Potency Marijuana Impairs Executive Function and Inhibitory Motor Control'. *Neuropsychopharmacology* 31:2296–2303.

Ratcliffe, Jerry H. 2011. 'The Philadelphia Foot Patrol Experiment: A Randomized Controlled Trial of Police Patrol Effectiveness in Violent Crime Hotspots'. *Criminology* 49:795–831.

Reinarman, Craig. 2009. 'Cannabis Policies and User Practices: Market Separation, Price, Potency, and Accessibility in Amsterdam and San Francisco'. *International Journal of Drug Policy* 20:28–37.

Reinarman, Craig. 2010. 'Signs and Shapes of a Culture of Tolerance: Ethnographic Impressions from Amsterdam'. *Sustain: A Journal of Environmental and Sustainability Issues* 21:28–35.

Reinarman, Craig. 2016. 'Going Dutch: Drug Policy at the Crossroads'. *Criminology and Public Policy* 15:885–95.

Reinarman, Craig and Harry G. Levine (eds). 1997. *Crack in America: Demon Drugs and Social Justice*. Berkeley and Los Angeles, CA: University of California Press.

Reinarman, Craig, Peter D. A. Cohen and Hendrien L. Kaal. 2004. 'The Limited Relevance of Drug Policy: Cannabis in Amsterdam and in San Francisco'. *American Journal of Public Health* 94:836–42.

Reuter, Peter. 2009. 'Systemic Violence in Drug Markets'. *Crime, Law, and Social Change* 52:275–84.

Reuter, Peter. 2013. 'Why Has US Drug Policy Changed So Little over 30 Years?' *Crime and Justice* 42:75–140.

Reuter, Peter. 2017. 'Creating a Drug Law Enforcement Research Agenda'. *International Journal of Drug Policy* 41:160–1.

Reynald, Danielle M. 2010. 'Guardians on Guardianship: Factors Affecting the Willingness to Supervise, the Ability to Detect Potential Offenders, and the Willingness to Intervene'. *Journal of Research in Crime and Delinquency* 47:358–90.

Reynald, Danielle M. 2015. 'Environmental Design and Crime Events'. *Journal of Contemporary Criminal Justice* 31:71–89.

Reynolds, Matthew. 2016. *Translation: A Very Short Introduction*. New York: Oxford University Press.

Rhodes, Tim. 2009. 'Risk Environments and Drug Harms: A Social Science for Harm Reduction Approach'. *International Journal of Drug Policy* 20:193–201.

Ridgeway, Greg and Beau Kilmer. 2016. 'Bayesian Inference for the Distribution of Grams of Marijuana in a Joint'. *Drug and Alcohol Dependence* 165:175–80.

Rios, Victor. 2011. *Punished: Policing the Lives of Black and Latino Boys*. New York: New York University Press.

Ritter, Alison. 2006. 'Studying Illicit Drug Markets: Disciplinary Contributions'. *International Journal of Drug Policy* 17:453–63.

Robbe, Hindrick. 1998. 'Marijuana's Impairing Effects on Driving are Moderate When Taken Alone but Severe When Combined with Alcohol'. *Human Psychopharmacology-Clinical and Experimental* 13:S70–S78.

Roberts, Benjamin B. 2017. *Sex, Drugs, and Rock 'n' Roll in the Dutch Golden Age*. Amsterdam, NL: Amsterdam University Press.

Roodenburg, Herman and Pieter Spierenburg (eds). 2004. *Social Control in Europe, Vol. 1: 1500–1800*. Columbus, OH: Ohio State University Press.

Room, Robin. 2014. 'Legalizing a Market for Cannabis for Pleasure: Colorado, Washington, Uruguay and Beyond'. *Addiction* 109:345–51.

Ross, Jeffrey Ian (ed.). 2000. *Varieties of State Crime*. Monsey, NY: Criminal Justice Press.

S.N. 2017. 'Why Amsterdam's Coffeeshops are Closing'. *The Economist*. Retrieved 11 June 2018, from <https://www.economist.com/the-economist-explains/2017/01/10/why-amsterdams-coffeeshops-are-closing>

Sampson, Robert J. 2009. 'Disparity and Diversity in the Contemporary City: Social (Dis)Order Revisited'. *British Journal of Sociology* 60:1–31.

Sampson, Robert J. 2012a. 'When Things Aren't What They Seem: Context and Cognition in Appearance-Based Regulation'. *Harvard Law Review Forum* 125:97–107.

Sampson, Robert J. 2012b. *Great American City: Chicago and the Enduring Neighborhood Effect*. Chicago, IL: University of Chicago Press.

Sampson, Robert J. and John H. Laub. 1993. *Crime in the Making: Pathways and Turning Points through Life*. Cambridge, MA: Harvard University Press.

Sampson, Robert J. and Stephen W. Raudenbush. 2004. 'Seeing Disorder: Neighborhood Stigma and the Social Construction of Broken Windows'. *Social Psychology Quarterly* 67:319–42.

Sandberg, Sveinung. 2010. 'What Can "Lies" Tell Us About Life? Notes Toward a Framework of Narrative Criminology'. *Journal of Criminal Justice Education* 21:447–65.

Sandberg, Sveinung. 2012. 'The Importance of Culture for Cannabis Markets: Towards an Economic Sociology of Illegal Drug Markets'. *British Journal of Criminology* 52:1133–51.

Sandberg, Sveinung. 2013. 'Cannabis Culture: A Stable Subculture in a Changing World'. *Criminology and Criminal Justice* 13:63–79.

Sandberg, Sveinung, and Willy Pedersen. 2009. *Street Capital: Black Cannabis Dealers in a White Welfare State*. Bristol, UK: Policy Press.

Sandberg, Sveinung, and Sébastien Tutenges. 2018. 'Laughter in Stories of Crime and Tragedy: The Importance of Humor for Marginalized Populations'. *Social Problems*. Retrieved 12 December 2018, from <https://doi.org/10.1093/socpro/spy019>

Schofield, Philip. 2009. *Bentham: A Guide for the Perplexed*. London, UK: Continuum.

Scott, Marvin B. and Stanford M. Lyman. 1968. 'Accounts'. *American Sociological Review* 33:46–62.

Scott, Michael S. 2018. 'Effective Policing through Regulatory Control'. *The ANNALS of the American Academy of Political and Social Science* 679:86–104.

Schultz, P. Wesley and Jennifer J. Tabanico. 2009. 'Criminal Behavior: A Social Norms Perspective on Posting Public Warning Signs'. *Criminology* 47:1201–22.

Sevigny, Eric. 2013. 'Is Today's Marijuana More Potent Simply Because It's Fresher?' *Drug Testing and Analysis* 5:62–7.

Sevigny, Eric and Jonathan P. Caulkins. 2004. 'Kingpins or Mules: An Analysis of Drug Offenders Incarcerated in Federal and State Prisons'. *Criminology and Public Policy* 3:101–35.

Sevigny, Eric, Rosalie Liccardo Pacula and Paul Heaton. 2014. 'The Effects of Medical Marijuana Laws on Potency'. *International Journal of Drug Policy* 25:308–19.

Shaw, Clifford R. 1930. *The Jack-Roller: A Delinquent Boy's Own Story*. Chicago, IL: University of Chicago Press.

Sherman, Lawrence W., Patrick R. Gartin and Michael E. Buerger. 1989. 'Hot Spots of Predatory Crime: Routine Activities and the Criminology of Place'. *Criminology* 27:27–56.

Short, Martin B., P. Jeffrey Brantingham, Andrea L. Bertozzi and George E. Tita. 2010. 'Dissipation and Displacement of Hotspots in Reaction-Diffusion Models of Crime'. *Proceedings of the National Academy of Sciences* 107:3961–5.

Skinner, B. F. 1971. *Beyond Freedom and Dignity*. Indianapolis, IN: Hackett.

Shukla, Rashi K. 2016. *Methamphetamine: A Love Story*. Berkeley and Los Angeles, CA: University of California Press.

Simons-Morton, Bruce, William Pickett, Will Boyce, Tom F. M. ter Bogt and Wilma Vollebergh. 2010. 'Cross-National Comparison of Adolescent Drinking and Cannabis Use in the United States, Canada, and the Netherlands'. *International Journal of Drug Policy* 21:64–9.

Smokers Guide. 2015. Retrieved 10 March 2015, from <https://www.smokersguide.com/news/112/abraxas_coffeeshop_amsterdam_forced_to_close_its_d.html>

Snow, David A. and Leon Anderson. 1993. *Down on Their Luck: A Study of Homeless Street People*. Berkeley and Los Angeles, CA: University of California Press.

Spapens, Toine, Thaddeus Müller and Henk van de Bunt. 2015. 'The Dutch Drug Policy from a Regulatory Perspective'. *European Journal of Criminal Policy and Research* 21:191–205.

Spierenburg, Pieter. 1984. *The Spectacle of Suffering: Executions and the Evolution of Repression: From a Preindustrial Metropolis to the European Experience*. New York: Cambridge University Press.

Spierenburg, Pieter. 2007. *The Prison Experience: Disciplinary Institutions and Their Inmates in Early Modern Europe*. Amsterdam, NL: University of Amsterdam Press.
Spierenburg, Pieter. 2013. *Violence and Punishment: Civilizing the Body through Time*.Cambridge: Polity Press.
Spradley, James P. 1979. *The Ethnographic Interview*. New York: Harcourt Brace Jovanovich.
Spradley, James P. 1980. *Participant Observation*. New York: Harcourt.
Stafford, Mark and Mark Warr. 1993. 'A Reconceptualization of General and Specific Deterrence'. *Journal of Research in Crime and Delinquency* 30:123–35.
Steves, Rick. 2003. *Amsterdam Bruges and Brussels*. Everyville, CA: Avalon Travel Publishing.
St Jean, Peter K. B. 2007. *Pockets of Crime: Broken Windows, Collective Efficacy, and the Criminal Point of View*. Chicago, IL: University of Chicago Press.
Sutherland, Edwin. 1937. *The Professional Thief*. Chicago, IL: University of Chicago Press.
Sykes, Gresham M. and David Matza. 1957. 'Techniques of Neutralization'. *American Sociological Review* 22:664–70.
Sykes, Richard E. and John P. Clark. 1975. 'A Theory of Deference Exchange in Police–Citizen Encounters'. *American Journal of Sociology* 81:584–600.
Taylor, Angela P. 2007. *How Drug Dealers Settle Disputes: Violent and Nonviolent Outcomes*. Monsey, NY: Criminal Justice Press.
Thurnell-Read, Thomas. 2012. 'What Happens on Tour: The Premarital Stag Tour, Homosocial Bonding, and Male Friendship'. *Men and Masculinities* 15:249–70.
Toby, Jackson. 1957. 'Social Disorganization and Stake in Conformity: Complementary Factors in the Predatory Behavior of Hoodlums'. *Journal of Criminal Law, Criminology, and Police Science* 48:12–17.
Toonen, Marcel, Simon Ribot and Jac Thissen. 2006. 'Yield of Illicit Cannabis Cultivation in the Netherlands'. *Journal of Forensic Sciences* 51:1050–4.
Tonry, Michael and David P. Farrington (eds). 2005. *Crime and Punishment in Western Countries, 1980–1999*. Chicago, IL: University of Chicago Press.
Tonry, Michael and Catrien Bijleveld (eds). 2007. *Crime and Justice in the Netherlands*. Chicago, IL: University of Chicago Press.
Trimbos Institute. 2010. *Netherlands National Drug Monitor Annual Report 2009*. Utrecht, NL: Trimbos Institute.
Tucker, James. 1999. *The Therapeutic Corporation*. New York: Oxford University Press.
Tyler, Tom R. 2003. 'Procedural Justice, Legitimacy, and the Effective Rule of Law'. *Crime and Justice* 30:283–357.
Tyler, Tom R. 2004. 'Enhancing Police Legitimacy'. *The Annals of the American Academy of Political and Social Science* 593:84–99.
Uitermark, Justus. 2004. 'The Origins and Future of the Dutch Approach Towards Drugs'. *Journal of Drug Issues* 34:511–32.
Uriely, Natan and Yaniv Belhassen. 2005. 'Drugs and Risk-Taking in Tourism'. *Annals of Tourism Research* 33:339–59.
Van Maanen, John. 1988. *Tales of the Field: On Writing Ethnography*. Chicago, IL: University of Chicago Press.
van der Gouwe, D., E. Ehrlich and M. W. van Laar. 2009. *Drug Policies in the Netherlands*. Utrecht, NL: Trimbos Institute.
van Gelder, Jean-Louis. 2013. 'Beyond Rational Choice: The Hot/Cool Perspective of Criminal Decision Making'. *Psychology, Crime and Law*. 9:745–63.
van Gemert, Frank and Hans Verbraeck. 1994. 'Snacks, Sex, and Smack: The Ecology of Drug Trade in the Inner City of Amsterdam'. In *Between Prohibition and Legalization: The Dutch Experiment in Drug Policy*, edited by Ed Leuw and I. Haen Marshall. Amsterdam: Kugler.
van Hoof, Joris J., Jordy F. Gosselt and Menno D. T. de Jong. 2010. 'Shop Floor Compliance with Age Restrictions for Tobacco Sales: Remote Versus In-Store Age Verification'. *Journal of Adolescent Health* 46:197–9.
van Solinge, Tim Boekhout. 1999. 'Dutch Drug Policy in a European Context'. *Journal of Drug Issues* 29:511–28.
van Swaaningen, René. 2006. 'Criminology in the Netherlands'. *European Journal of Criminology* 3:463–501.
Veblen, Thorstein. 1994 (1899). *The Theory of the Leisure Class*. New York: Dover.
Verdurmen, J. E. E., A. P. M. Ketelaars and M. W. van Laar. 2005. *The Netherlands National Drug Monitor: Fact Sheet Drug Policy*. Utrecht, NL: Trimbos Institute.

Venkatesh, Sudhir. 2006. *Off the Books: The Underground Economy of the Urban Poor*. Cambridge, MA: Harvard University Press.

Venkatesh, Sudhir. 2008. *Gang Leader for a Day: A Rogue Sociologist Takes to the Streets*. New York: Penguin.

Volkow, Nora D., Ruben D. Baler, Wilson M. Compton and Susan R. B. Weiss. 2014. 'Adverse Health Effects of Marijuana Use'. *New England Journal of Medicine* 370:2219–27.

Waldorf, Dan, Craig Reinarman and Sheigla Murphy. 1991. *Cocaine Changes: The Experience of Using and Quitting*. Philadelphia, PA: Temple University Press.

Werb, Dan, Greg Rowell, Gordon Guyatt, Thomas Kerr, Julio Montaner and Evan Wood. 2011. 'Effect of Drug Law Enforcement on Drug Market Violence: A Systematic Review'. *International Journal of Drug Policy* 22:87–94.

Weiss, Robert S. 1994. *Learning From Strangers: The Art and Method of Qualitative Interview Studies*. New York: Free Press.

Whiting, Penny F., Robert F. Wolff, Sohan Deshpande, Marcello Di Nisio, Steven Duffy, Adrian V. Hernandez, J. Christiaan Keurentjes, Shona Lang, Kate Misso, Steve Ryder, Simone Schmidlkofer, Marie Westwood and Jos Kleijnen. 2015. 'Cannabinoids for Medical Use: A Systematic Review and Meta-Analysis'. *JAMA* 313:2456–73.

Whyte, William Foote. 1943. *Street Corner Society: The Social Structure of an Italian Slum*. Chicago, IL: University of Chicago Press.

Wilson, James Q. and George L. Kelling. 1982. 'The Police and Neighborhood Safety'. *The Atlantic* (March):29–38.

Winstock, Adam R., Kim Wolff and John Ramsey. 2001. 'Ecstasy Pill Testing: Harm Minimization Gone Too Far?' *Addiction* 96:1139–48.

Worden, Robert E. and Robin L. Shepard. 1996. 'Demeanor, Crime, and Police Behavior: A Reexamination of the Police Services Study Data'. *Criminology* 34:83–105.

World Health Organization. 2013. *WHO Report on the Global Tobacco Epidemic: Enforcing Bans on Tobacco Advertising and Promotion and Sponsorship*. Geneva, Switzerland: WHO.

Worrall, John L. 2012. 'The Police Sixth Sense: An Observation in Search of a Theory'. *American Journal of Criminal Justice* 38:306–22.

Wouters, Marije and Dirk J. Korf. 2009. 'Access to Licensed Cannabis Supply and the Separation of Markets Policy in the Netherlands'. *Journal of Drug Issues* 39:627–51.

Wouters, Marije, Annemieke Benschop and Dirk J. Korf. 2010. 'Local Politics and Retail Cannabis Markets: The Case of the Dutch Coffeeshops'. *International Journal of Drug Policy* 21:315–20.

Wouters, Marije, Annemieke Benschop, Margriet van Laar and Dijk J. Korf. 2012. 'Cannabis Use and Proximity to Coffee Shops in the Netherlands'. *European Journal of Criminology* 9:337–53.

Wright, Richard and Scott Decker. 1994. *Burglars on the Job: Streetlife and Residential Breakins*. Boston, MA: Northeastern University Press.

Wright, Richard and Scott Decker. 1997. *Armed Robbers in Action: Stickups and Street Culture*. Boston, MA: Northeastern University Press.

Zaitch, Damián. 2002. *Trafficking Cocaine: Colombian Drug Entrepreneurs in the Netherlands*. New York: Kluwer.

Zimmerman, Don H. and D. Lawrence Wieder. 1977. 'You Can't Help but Get Stoned: Notes on the Social Organization of Marijuana Smoking'. *Social Problems* 25:198–207.

Zimring, Franklin E. 2012. *The City that Became Safe: New York's Lessons for Urban Crime and Its Control*. New York: Oxford University Press.

Zimring, Franklin E. and Gordon J. Hawkins. 1992. *The Search for Rational Drug Control*. Cambridge, MA: Cambridge University Press.

Zinberg, Norman E. 1984. *Drug, Set, and Setting: The Basis for Controlled Intoxicant Use*. New Haven, CT: Yale University Press.

Index

Note: Page numbers in italics refer to illustrations.

CPSIA information can be obtained
at www.ICGtesting.com
Printed in the USA
LVHW071951260320
651319LV00006B/49